Hannah Arendt and the Politics of Friendship

Also Available from Bloomsbury

Action and Appearance: Ethics and the Politics of Writing in Hannah Arendt by Anna Yeatman
Hannah Arendt and the Law edited by Marco Goldoni and Christopher McCorkindale
Hannah Arendt and Theology by John Kiess

Hannah Arendt and the Politics of Friendship

Jon Nixon

Bloomsbury Academic
An imprint of Bloomsbury Publishing Plc

BLOOMSBURY
LONDON • NEW DELHI • NEW YORK • SYDNEY

Bloomsbury Academic
An imprint of Bloomsbury Publishing Plc

50 Bedford Square 1385 Broadway
London New York
WC1B 3DP NY 10018
UK USA

www.bloomsbury.com

BLOOMSBURY and the Diana logo are trademarks of Bloomsbury Publishing Plc

First published 2015

© Jon Nixon, 2015

Jon Nixon has asserted his right under the Copyright, Designs and Patents Act, 1988, to be identified as Author of this work.

All rights reserved. No part of this publication may be reproduced or transmitted in any form or by any means, electronic or mechanical, including photocopying, recording, or any information storage or retrieval system, without prior permission in writing from the publishers.

No responsibility for loss caused to any individual or organization acting on or refraining from action as a result of the material in this publication can be accepted by Bloomsbury or the author.

British Library Cataloguing-in-Publication Data
A catalogue record for this book is available from the British Library.

ISBN: HB: 978-1-4725-0641-2
PB: 978-1-4725-1317-5
ePDF: 978-1-4725-0754-9
ePub: 978-1-4725-0510-1

Library of Congress Cataloging-in-Publication Data
A catalog record for this book is available from the Library of Congress.

Typeset by RefineCatch Limited, Bungay, Suffolk

For Pauline

nulli cera domus
>Virgil, *The Aeneid*, Book VI

E l'un l'altro abbracciava
>Dante, *The Divine Comedy*, Canto VI

No man is an island, entire of itself
>Donne, *Meditation* XVII

Contents

Preface		viii
Acknowledgements		xiv
A Note to the Reader		xvi
Abbreviations		xvii
1	A Child of the Time	1
2	Friendship and Plurality	21
3	Friendship as Promise	41
4	Arendt and Heidegger: The Struggle for Recognition	61
5	Arendt and Jaspers: Becoming Worldly	85
6	Arendt and McCarthy: Becoming Ourselves	109
7	Arendt and Blücher: Flourishing Together	135
8	The Hermeneutics of Friendship	159
9	The Republic of Friendship	175
Epilogue: A Woman of the World		191
Appendix: Chronology of Arendt's Life and Works		197
Bibliography		201
Index		209

Preface

The notion of friendship is central to Hannah Arendt's conception of politics. This book explores that notion – and its relation to her political thinking – through her lifelong friendships with Heinrich Blücher, Martin Heidegger, Karl Jaspers and Mary McCarthy. It draws on the correspondence between Arendt and these four writers and thinkers in order to illuminate the emphasis in her own writing on plurality and promise and on what she termed 'worldliness'. What emerges from this correspondence is a deeply humanistic perspective on politics, which privileges deliberation and reciprocity as necessary constituents of participative democracy.

Her friendships and the correspondence they generated show her working through her political ideas and the ethical implications of these ideas in relation to complex interpersonal and professional issues. Each of the friendships is unique, but they all show her grappling in practice with the ethical implications of her own political thought. Her politics is always ethically purposeful and grounded in common discourse, which is precisely why – thirty-seven years after her death – she remains such an influential and significant presence.

Arendt's life was inextricably entwined with her work. This, of course, is true of many writers, thinkers and artists, but is particularly the case with Arendt given the particular circumstances under which she lived and worked. To understand her life we must, therefore, relate it to her work, and to understand the work we must relate it to her life. Friendships were a vital part of her lived experience, just as the notion of friendship is a crucial element within her constantly developing framework of ideas. This presents a methodological challenge that cannot be fully met by either an exclusively biographical account of Arendt's particular friendships or a purely analytical account of her concept of friendship. It can only be met by an approach that seeks to do justice both to the idea of friendship as a recurring theme throughout Arendt's work and to the experience of friendship as a necessary and sustaining element in her life.

That methodological assumption underpins the structure of this work. The book as a whole is organised thematically, although each of the central chapters (4–7 inclusive) loosely follows the chronological order of the particular friendship under discussion. In the main framing chapters (1–3 and 8–9) there is also a loose progression from Arendt's early to later work. The sequencing of chapters that follows from this structure necessarily involves a recapitulation of the major themes and a reiteration of the chronology. This is particularly apparent in the four central chapters, each of which loops back to the origins of the particular friendship and therefore to a relatively early point in Arendt's life. The timeline comprising the Appendix provides a basic roadmap by which to keep track of the chronology, but the reader may also find it useful to have an advance summary of both the thematic progression and the chronological sequencing within and across chapters.

A major premise upon which this book is based – and one that was shared by Arendt – is that authored works can only be understood fully in relation to the lives of their authors, and that the lives of their authors can only be understood with reference to the history of the period into which they were born. We begin – in Chapter 1 – between the wars with a child who by the time she was seven became the single child of a single mother. From the start Arendt was good at making friends, but equally good at antagonising those in authority through her unconventional behaviour and opinions. So, not surprisingly perhaps, she fell in love with her charismatic and utterly self-absorbed university tutor. History intervened in the form of Nazism with its particularly virulent anti-Semitic ideology. Making sense of that intervention was a lifetime's work, which involved migration, statelessness and – much later in life – the troubles and tribulations of the Eichmann trial.

Arendt's life was about making sense of things. Her big idea – by means of which she tried to make sense of the world into which she had been thrown – was 'plurality'. It sounds simple enough, but took her a lifetime to unravel and expound. Part of the difficulty – as explored in Chapter 2 – was that what she understood by plurality could only be inferred from what she had experienced as its absolute opposite: namely, totalitarianism. The only goods that could be salvaged from that experience were the goods that totalitarianism had sought to eradicate. Those goods included almost everything that Arendt most valued – among them the goods of friendship. This chapter focuses specifically on

Arendt's political writing published during the 1950s and early 1960s – particularly, but not exclusively, her 1951 *The Origins of Totalitarianism* and her 1963 *On Revolution*.

The big idea was – as Arendt well knew – not so much a solution to the problem of totalitarianism as a return to the age-old problem of how to live together in a world of contingency and incommensurable difference. How to overcome the blockages to plurality that plurality itself presents us with. That was the question that increasingly exercised Arendt. She addressed it in many ways, but came back again and again to the idea of promises as binding commitments to set against the uncertainty of human history. Promises may take the form of international treaties and alliances, governmental commitments and manifestos, and legally binding contracts. They may also – as suggested in Chapter 3 – provide us with some useful metaphors for thinking about the nature of friendship. This chapter explores, in particular, ideas developed by Arendt in her 1958 *The Human Condition* and her 1957 *Rahel Varnhagen: The Life of a Jewess*. It also distinguishes her notion of friendship from neo-Aristotelian notions of 'sovereign' or 'perfect' friendship.

So what is friendship *about*? What did Arendt's friendships mean to her? Her relationship with Heidegger did not begin with friendship. It began with what would now be termed sexual exploitation: a senior male academic taking advantage of an undergraduate student who was in awe of his charismatic presence and his academic reputation. But, having exited the sexual relationship, Arendt refused to consign Heidegger to the past and achieve closure on that period of her life. He was, it would seem, too big a presence in her life for her to simply let him go. So, she stuck with the relationship, but on her own terms and from a position of increasing authority as a public intellectual in her own right. She was determined to turn the relationship towards one in which she gained Heidegger's recognition and respect. Given Heidegger's deep self-absorption and lack of generosity, this was no easy task. But Arendt was dogged in her persistence. And – arguably – she eventually succeeded. By dint of sheer willpower she demanded Heidegger's recognition and thereby – as Chapter 4 argues – turned an exploitative relationship into a kind of friendship.

Her relationship with Jaspers was something very different. He, too, was older than her and an academic. But unlike Heidegger, he was repelled by the rise of Nazism, and highly vulnerable given that his wife was a Jew. He was first

Arendt's doctoral supervisor and then her academic mentor. But very quickly the mentorship relationship developed into friendship. One of the reasons for this shift was that early on in their relationship Arendt expressed her disagreement with Jaspers regarding a recently published book of his. This expression of disagreement remoulded the relationship. Arendt had – with courtesy – asserted her equality within their relationship. This in turn freed Jaspers from the role of mentor that he had previously adopted. From then on they spoke on equal terms. Their lifelong friendship became – as I seek to show in Chapter 5 – a deeply discursive exploration of the world of ideas and events to which they were both unreservedly committed.

Heidegger and Jaspers were both very much part of the old world of Europe: a world that was torn apart by the two great totalitarian regimes of Nazism and Stalinism but that had provided Arendt with a vast philosophical hinterland. On moving to the USA she took much of that world with her but had to readjust – and readjust quickly – to the very different tempo and outlook of the new world she had entered. In many ways McCarthy exemplified that world in her sometimes brash outspokenness, her will to succeed, her sometimes desperate search for erotic fulfilment. But she, like Arendt, had survived a deeply insecure childhood, which had in her case involved prolonged physical and mental abuse. She had also attended a Catholic school, against which she had rebelled but which had provided her with a deep respect for scholarship. Her friendship with Arendt was incomprehensible to some of those who were close to Arendt. But – as I argue in Chapter 6 – it was based on complex complementarities of personality and need. Each helped the other navigate the troubled waters into which each periodically – and wilfully – set sail.

Blücher was neither entirely of the old world nor fully committed to the new. Having fled to the USA with Arendt, he never lost his great love of the German language. He was by all accounts a supremely passionate and engaged conversationalist in both English and German, but he felt the loss of his beloved German language very keenly and always corresponded in German with Arendt. It was part of the world they shared. But – unlike Arendt – he rarely returned to Europe in spite of many opportunities to do so. He settled relatively easily into his adopted country, but was always ill at ease with its affluence and increasing consumerism. He was both lover and husband to Arendt, but he was also her fierce champion and steadfast friend. He was the still point to which she returned from her many and various travels. In a world in which each had experienced chronic insecurity and statelessness, home was where the other was. Theirs was a friendship that combined both *eros* and *philia* and that – as I illustrate in Chapter 7 – enabled each to flourish.

The final two chapters are concerned with what we might learn from these particular friendships about the notion of friendship and the part it plays in Arendt's view of the world. Arendt's final work – *The Life of the Mind* – explores the relation between thinking, willing and judging. Much of our thinking is solitary, but in some situations we can begin to think together. Friendship is one such situation. But friendship can only exist between individuals who exercise their free will and recognise the right of the other to do likewise. Friendship is a confirmation rather than a surrender of the self. It allows us to test and modify our judgements before they are exposed to the full glare of public scrutiny. The dialogue between friends is a halfway house between the private and the public in which – as I argue in Chapter 8 – we commit ourselves to the joint enterprise of seeking to understand the world.

In a world within which both the private and public realms are at risk from what Arendt termed mass society, friendship becomes dislodged from its two main frames of reference. Arendt's analysis regarding the erosion of the public realm is if anything more relevant now than when she was writing. A great deal of what was public has melted into the mystifying, late capitalist air of privatisation, where financial transactions criss-cross national boundaries and jurisdictions instantaneously and where the face-to-face of human interaction has been suborned by impersonal interchange. Chapter 9 highlights the continuing relevance of Arendt's critique of mass society and points to some of the ways in which friendship has been re-thought and re-worked in the recent past along Arendtian lines.

Friendship is important because it crosses so many boundaries. Arendt never claimed that friendship is in itself political. Friendship can be a refuge; it provides a space within which to think together and test one's judgements; a space within which to gather one's resources of will and affirm those same resources in one's friends. It is a space from which to move out as unique beings into the common space of the world. Arendt made no grandiose claims regarding friendship, but she knew from experience that friendship by its very presence denied totalitarianism its ultimate victory – and she became increasingly convinced that friendship was at risk from the encroachments of consumerism, privatisation and a mass culture of immediate gratification.

The power of friendship lies in its sheer ordinariness. Power, insisted Arendt, was located not in the individual person but in the space *between* people. Arendt was not interested in establishing a hierarchy of friendship, because she knew that the power of friendship lies in the fact that friendship is commonplace. By seeking to monopolise that power, notions of 'perfect' friendship or 'sovereign' friendship can only serve to restrict and ultimately diminish it. To speak of the politics of friendship is to speak of the power that is activated when human beings think together and act together.

Great thinkers meet us at every corner and at every crossroads. Occasionally they greet us, sometimes they slip by almost unnoticed, always they present us with that questioning glance: what do *you* make of it all? It is impossible for anyone who has read Arendt extensively and deeply not to imagine what she might have thought – what questions she might have asked – about, for example, the invasion of Iraq, the Arab Spring (and Fall), the state response to the release of classified data, the annexation of the Crimea, the economic policies pursued in response to the financial crisis of 2007 and its aftermath . . . This book is written in the spirit of correspondence with the incomparable Arendt – and in the hope that you, the readers of this book, will seek a similar correspondence with her ideas, her insights and, above all, her unique idiom. Her truthfulness.

Jon Nixon
Kendal, Cumbria
April 2014

Acknowledgements

I would like to thank the two anonymous referees who commented with care and insight on the original proposal for this book and the anonymous reviewer who read the final draft of the book with such attention to detail. Their comments – clearly based on a sophisticated knowledge of the field – were extremely helpful. Thanks also to Fred Inglis, Stewart Ranson and Jonathan Rée for their helpful comments on an early draft – and to Stewart for his unfailing and continuing encouragement. Claus Emmeche organised a seminar at the University of Copenhagen on 'friendship', which was attended by Adam Diderichson, Claus Emmeche, Brian McGuire, Di Ponti, Astrid Iris Ravnsdatter and myself. I am very grateful to Claus for initiating and organising the seminar and for all the participants for their generous and thoughtful comments on my paper, which fed directly into the book at a crucial stage in its drafting.

David Aldridge invited me to give a paper on 'Becoming thoughtful: Hannah Arendt and the problem of good and evil' at an Oxford meeting of the Philosophy of Education Society of Great Britain. That, too, was a very helpful seminar and I am grateful to all the participants for the stimulating discussion that followed the presentation of my paper. During the final phase of writing I was in dialogue with Maha Bali regarding her work on 'critical thinking', particularly within the Egyptian context. That ongoing dialogue helped clarify – and continues to help clarify – some of my own thinking about thinking. John Shenton also dug out from his treasure trove of audio tapes some highly relevant recordings that gave me fresh leads at an early stage in the project. My friend, Feng Su, sorted out my various computer glitches and fed me a variety of delicious Chinese dishes in the course of our various and ongoing conversations. Thanks, also, to Brigitte and Fritz Latzelsberger for their generous hospitality in Bonn and for the good talk – and to Anne Cornford whose friendship extends to the regular loan of her lovely home in York where one can think, write and read.

The librarians at the British Library on Euston Road, London, have as always been unfailingly helpful and patient. Like so many other scholars,

I owe them a debt of gratitude. I am also grateful to The Society of Authors, which generously contributed towards travel and accommodation expenses relating to this project. Similarly, I owe a great deal to those responsible for editing the correspondence upon which the central chapters of this book are based (Carol Brightman, Lotte Kohler, Ursula Ludz the and Hans Saner) and to those responsible for translating the German correspondence into English (Peter Constantine, Robert and Rita Kimber, and Andrew Shields). Thanks are due also to Caroline Wintersgill, senior commissioning editor at Bloomsbury Academic, for supporting my original proposal, and to Mark Richardson, editorial assistant, for his guidance and advice on relevant publishing procedures and for the unobtrusive but valuable support he has offered throughout.

Finally, I thank Pauline Nixon for her forbearance, insight and enduring friendship. Without her intelligence, sensibility and practicality this book would not have been written.

A Note to the Reader

The following conventions relating to the use of quotations have been employed throughout: (1) Writing in English Arendt typically wrote 'men' when she wanted to emphasise not the difference between the sexes but their common humanity. (In German she wrote *Menschen*, without gender specificity, not *Männer*.) I have retained her original usage throughout. (2) Emphases in quoted passages have been retained without exception and I have not imported any new emphases of my own into any of the quotations. I have not seen it necessary, therefore, to note this on each occasion an italicised emphasis occurs. Readers should assume that if such an emphasis occurs it was placed there in the original. (3) The letters between Arendt and Blücher – like those between Heidegger and Jaspers – were written almost entirely in German. Occasionally the correspondents inserted English words, which in any quoted passages are given in italics and are enclosed by <*and*>. This particular convention relates specifically to Chapter 7.

Abbreviations

Works frequently cited throughout the book have been identified by the following abbreviations. Full bibliographical details can be found in the bibliography. (All the following works are listed under Arendt, other than AB, AH, AJ and AM, which are listed under the relevant editor.)

AB *Within Four Walls: The Correspondence between Hannah Arendt and Heinrich Blücher 1936–1968* (edited by Lotte Kohler)
AH *Letters 1925–1975 Hannah Arendt and Martin Heidegger* (edited by Ursula Ludz)
AJ *Hannah Arendt Karl Jaspers Correspondence 1926–1969* (edited by Lotte Kohler and Hans Saner)
AM *Between Friends: The Correspondence of Hannah Arendt and Mary McCarthy 1949–1975* (edited by Carol Brightman)
BPF *Between Past and Future: Eight Exercises in Political Thought*
EJ *Eichmann in Jerusalem: A Report on the Banality of Evil*
EU *Essays on Understanding 1930–1954*
HC *The Human Condition*
JW *The Jewish Writings*
LM *The Life of the Mind* (2 volumes)
LSA *Love and Saint Augustine*
MDT *Men in Dark Times*
OR *On Revolution*
OT *The Origins of Totalitarianism*
OV *On Violence*
PHA *The Portable Hannah Arendt*
PP *The Promise of Politics*
RJ *Responsibility and Judgement*
RLC *Reflections on Literature and Culture*
RV *Rahel Varnhagen: The Life of a Jewess*

1

A Child of the Time

I have never in my life 'loved' any people or collective – neither the German people, nor the French, nor the American, nor the working class or anything of that sort. I indeed love 'only' my friends and the only kind of love I know of and believe in is the love of persons.

JW, 466–7

Between the wars

It was the period following the 'Great War'. Ireland had, in the words of its then foremost poet, seen the birth of 'a terrible beauty' in the Easter Rising of 1916; the people of Russia had witnessed the revolutions of 1917, the ensuing civil war, the death of the imperial Romanov family and the victory of the Red Army; and the geopolitical and economic map of Europe had been redrawn as a result of the Paris Peace Conference of 1919 and the ensuing Treaty of Versailles. John Maynard Keynes, the foremost economist of his generation, had pronounced his verdict on what he saw as the dire consequences of 'the peace'. 'The policy of reducing Germany to servitude for a generation, of degrading the lives of millions of human beings, and of depriving a whole nation of happiness should', he wrote, 'be abhorrent and detestable – abhorrent and detestable – even if it were possible, even if it enriched ourselves, even if it did not sow the decay of the whole civilized life of Europe' (Keynes, 2007, 127).

One way of thinking about the implications of all this is, as Tony Judt put it, that

> it took until the mid-1970s for even the core economies of prosperous Western Europe to get back to where they had been in 1914, after many decades of contraction and protection. In short, the industrial economies of the West

(with the exception of the United States) experienced a sixty-year decline, marked by two world wars and an unprecedented economic depression.

Judt with Snyder, 2012, 26–7

That, for Judt, constituted the background and context for the history of the last century. Europe had embarked upon what in retrospect can be seen as the years that led inexorably to World War II and to an economic decline that persisted well into the period of post-war reconstruction.

But at the time of the 1919 Paris Peace Conference no one in Europe could have known that they were living in the parenthesis between two 'wars to end all wars' – the years of *l'entre de guerres*. Nevertheless, some had strong intimations to that effect and the prevailing mood was far from cheerful. Three of the now classic texts of literary modernity were published in 1922: T. S. Eliot's *The Wasteland*, James Joyce's *Ulysses* and Virginia Woolf's *Jacob's Room*. These works marked the emergence of a new sensibility: elegiac in its evocation of the pre-World War I past, anxious regarding the economic, social and political uncertainties of the present, and apprehensive in its presentiment of fear and violence lurking in the future. That presentiment found expression in W. B. Yeats' chilling image of 'the second coming': the 'rough beast' of the anti-Christ 'slouch(ing) towards Bethlehem to be born' (Yeats, 1967, 211).

In Germany – which is where our story starts – reality was already aligning itself with Keynes' prophetic analysis. The Spartacus Group, formed as a radical leftist opposition to World War I, had been quashed. Rosa Luxemburg, who had opposed Germany's involvement in the war and was a leading figure in radical socialist democratic circles, had been brutally murdered in 1919 by members of the Freikorps – forerunners of the Nazis – and her body flung into Berlin's Landwehr Canal. She had, as it was later revealed, been knocked down with a rifle butt by Otto Runge and then shot in the head by Hermann Souchon. She was forty-seven years of age at the time. Her murder – and that of many of her comrades – ended all hope of a social democratic politics in and for Germany and ushered in the 'rough beast' of fascism (Hudis, 2011; Hudis and Anderson, 2004).

In Königsberg, then the regional capital of the German province of East Prussia, a widowed mother and an ardent admirer of Rosa Luxemburg took her young teenage daughter onto the streets in support of the general strike that erupted in the first week of 1919. She shouted to her daughter: 'You must pay attention, this is a historical moment!' The daughter would go on to write a serious appraisal of Luxemburg's life and work and to locate her as a crucial figure in the creation of what she termed 'spaces of freedom' (OR, 256). However, at the time this headstrong, intelligent and independent daughter – all of fourteen years of age – was about to define for herself her own 'historical moment'. She was about to *act* – to exercise her agency – and to do so in a way that was characteristically spontaneous, impetuous, risk-taking, infuriating and unconditionally generous. She was about to lay claim to friendship.

At the time she was living with her recently remarried mother in the house of her newly acquired stepfather and his two older daughters by a previous marriage. The remarriage offered some measure of financial and emotional stability, but assigned the young Hannah Arendt to a household that was conservative in its domestic routines and conformist in its social expectations. Its taken-for-granted homeliness no doubt intensified her feelings of estrangement and difference. A young Königsberger called Ernst Grumach, who was five years older than her, told her about his girlfriend Anne Mendelssohn who lived in a town to the west of Königsberg called Stolp. The young Arendt was forbidden to visit Anne because her father, who was a doctor, had been accused by one of his patients of improper behaviour – a charge which the doctor denied and attributed to the anti-Semitism of the accuser. Arendt, however, was not to be thwarted.

She left her house by her bedroom window at night and made her way to Stolp in time to awaken Anne by throwing a pebble against her window. We know nothing of the ensuing conversation, but the immediate effect on Arendt's family was predictably unsettling not least because it seemed to follow a pattern – Arendt was deemed to be headstrong, independent and sometimes highly temperamental. The long-term effect of Arendt's determination to act upon her impulse was, however, deeply settling – the friendship with Anne Mendelssohn was close and enduring, lasting until Arendt's death fifty-five years later. Moreover, the pattern of Arendt's adolescent behaviour never seriously breached her mother's intuitive and sympathetic understanding of her daughter's complex personality. Her mother was instinctively – but not uncritically – on her side.

This episode is in many ways emblematic of Arendt's life and thought: impulsive and quixotic, serious and single-minded, confrontational and uncompromising, generous and magnanimous. Always, she impelled herself into situations in such a way that the impulsion allowed no get-out: the consequences were irreversible. In spite of, or because of, being expelled from school at the age of fifteen – for leading a boycott of lessons taught by a teacher who had offended her – Arendt was fearsomely well read and capable from an early age of prolonged isolated study. Elizabeth Young-Bruehl (1982, 32) quotes Anne Mendelssohn as saying that the young Arendt had 'read everything' and comments that 'this "everything" covered philosophy, poetry, particularly Goethe, many, many romantic novels, German and French, and the modern novels considered inappropriate for the young by school authorities, including Thomas Mann's'.

We may not know what Arendt and Mendelssohn talked about, but we can be fairly sure that it was the urgent need for a particular kind of talk that prompted the young Arendt to transgress the cultural, familial and social mores of her tribe. It is difficult *not* to read back from the later essay she wrote on Socrates insights into what the meeting with Mendelssohn meant for Arendt: 'To have talked something through, to have talked about something, some citizen's *doxa*, seemed result enough. It is obvious that this kind of dialogue, which doesn't need a conclusion in order to be meaningful, is most appropriate for and most frequently shared by friends' (PP, 15–16).

'Goodbye to philosophy'

For Arendt, friendship had its origins in the need she felt for a particular kind of dialogue. Among the papers and lectures she was working on during the 1950s is an essay on Socrates in which she writes that this kind of dialogue 'doesn't need a conclusion to be meaningful'. It focuses on 'something the friends have in common' and in so doing constitutes 'a little world of its own which is shared in friendship'. Friends 'become equal partners in a common world'. This does not mean that they become the same or equal to each other, but 'that they together constitute a community'. In what she calls the 'truthful dialogue' that constitutes friendship, 'the friends can understand the truth inherent in the other's opinion'. They can understand the world from the other person's point of view. Moreover, she insists, it is this kind of understanding that yields 'the political kind of insight par excellence' (PP, 16–18).

From an early age Arendt sought this kind of understanding in and through philosophy. In 1964, shortly after her fifty-eighth birthday, she told the journalist Günter Gaus during a televised interview: 'I always knew I would study philosophy. Ever since I was fourteen years old . . . I read Kant . . . Jaspers' *Psychologie der Weltanschauungen* [*Psychology of World Views*] . . . I was fourteen. Then I read Kierkegaard, and that fit together' (EU, 8–9). Arendt does not say that she always knew she would *be* a philosopher, but that she always knew she would *study* philosophy. The distinction is important since at the very beginning of the interview she emphatically rejects Gaus' introductory remarks regarding 'her role in the inner circle of philosophers': 'I neither feel like a philosopher, nor do I believe that I have been accepted in the circle of philosophers, as you so kindly suppose. In my opinion I have said goodbye to philosophy once and for all. As you know, I studied philosophy, but that does not mean that I stayed with it' (EU, 1–2).

That is a very emphatic 'goodbye'. Yet, Arendt had studied philosophy, had, as we have seen, known from the age of fourteen that she would study philosophy, and, when she died eleven years after that interview took place, left behind an unfinished manuscript that was deeply philosophical in its content and its intellectual aspirations. So, one is left wondering why, given that she continued to engage with and draw inspiration from philosophy, she felt it necessary to bid such an emphatic farewell to it. It is highly unlikely that she was displaying false modesty – hardly her style – and, although her rejoinder is characteristically combative, she was too serious a thinker to be combative for the sake of it. To what, then, was she saying goodbye? And what did she think she was taking forward through her thought and writing, if not a living tradition of philosophical thought?

By 1964, when the interview was conducted, Arendt knew what she had left behind and why she had left it. In 1920, when on 14 October she had her fourteenth birthday, she could have had no such foreknowledge. But she did know what she wanted to carry forward: the kind of dialogue in which each can understand the inherent truth in the other's opinion. It was a kind of dialogue that she could have with herself, as if 'herself' were another. Indeed, only insofar as she was willing to have that inner dialogue could she be part of the world that was constantly speaking back to itself. 'I have to put up with myself', she wrote in that earlier essay, 'and nowhere does this I-with-myself show more clearly than in pure thought, which is always a dialogue between the two-in-one' (PP, 20). That was why she was reading, at the age of fourteen, Kant, Jaspers and Kierkegaard: not, as it turned out, in the hope of taking a role within 'the inner circle of philosophers', but with a view to joining an ongoing conversation about 'the truth inherent in the other's opinion'. It was truth as dialogue that she desired.

As we shall see, the *philosophical* turning point of Arendt's intellectual trajectory is its turn away from 'the inner circle of philosophers'. That turning away was partly a matter of circumstance, in that as a Jewish exile she necessarily crossed and re-crossed national, professional and academic boundaries. But it was also a matter of choice. Faced with what she saw as the necessary contingency of human life, do we turn inward to the world of self or outward to the world of others? Arendt was resolute in rejecting what she saw as the inward turn implicit in Heidegger's and Kierkegaard's reworking of the philosophical tradition and equally resolute in embracing a world of relationality, mutuality and reciprocity; a world characterised, that is, by forms of human interchange organised around values such as cooperation and conditional altruism. She saw the inward turn – associated in her mind with the work of Heidegger and Kierkegaard – as a manifestation of 'the withering away of everything *between* us'. It was a denial of the human world: 'the spread of the desert' as she called it (PP, 201). While the philosophers had recognised that we live and move in a desert world, they had assumed that the desert is in our selves. They had internalised it. In so doing they had in her view reduced philosophy to a kind of consolatory escapism.

Arendt was convinced that 'the withering away' must be confronted and resisted. The renewal of 'everything *between* us' – the flourishing of relationality, mutuality and reciprocity – was, for her, the prime end and purpose of politics. However, because we live in 'desert' conditions, we need what she called 'oases' within which to regroup and sustain ourselves. These oases are under constant threat from, for example, the all-engulfing 'sandstorms' of totalitarianism and the ceaseless drift of the desert into our private lives and public spaces. Both collectivism and isolationism encroach upon and erode the political grounds of our being: namely, 'everything *between* us'. '[I]t sometimes seems', as she put it, 'as though everything conspires mutually to generalize the conditions of the desert' (PP, 203). However, the oases can also be life-giving. 'Without the intactness of these oases', claims Arendt, 'we would not know how to breathe'. It is these oases that 'let us live in the desert without becoming reconciled to it' (PP, 202–3).

The life-giving oases include art, love and philosophy, but when and only when these are outward looking and magnanimous in their reaching out to the world: a world that, as Arendt conceived it, is neither a natural product nor the creation of God or of gods. Art, love and philosophy can, as Arendt knew, all too easily turn inward and become self-consuming. Friendship, for Arendt, was the most enduring and sustaining of the oases, with the resources necessary to withstand the deeply anti-political impulses that inform modernity: the despair of isolation and the anonymity of collectivism. Fragile and vulnerable, friendship is nevertheless an expression of the betwixt and between of the human world. As such it is emblematic of what Arendt understood by politics.

Politics, for Arendt, is concerned with the kinds of problems that will never have perfect solutions and that require people to think on their feet, to argue beyond the seeming end-point of disagreement, and to engage in critical discussion about the world as they see it and as they would like it to be. Politics so conceived requires us to converse freely and respectfully with each other as responsive citizens willing to negotiate all differences on the basis of complete equality. It depends on an open-hearted care for people not in the mass or in the abstract, but in the idiosyncrasy of their lives and the distinctiveness of their perceptions. That is why Arendt sees friendship as allied to politics: not as a substitute for politics, nor as a way of doing politics, but as a condition necessary for the survival of politics as she understood it. Friendship is what lies between the private world of familial, tribal and religious affiliation, and the political world of institutional and associative affiliation based not on family, tribe or religion but on equality.

Continuities across boundaries

In an address she gave on accepting the Lessing Prize of the Free City of Hamburg in 1959, Arendt spoke of Lessing's capacity for friendship not 'as a phenomenon of intimacy, in which the friends open their hearts to each other unmolested by the world and its demands', but as a relationship that 'makes political demands and preserves reference to the world' (MDT, 24–5). This idea of 'the political relevance of friendship' was, for her, part of what the modern world owes to the ancient Greeks: 'They held that only the constant interchange of talk united citizens in a *polis*. In discourse the political importance of friendship, and the humanness peculiar to it, were made manifest' (MDT, 24). She distinguishes friendship both from the 'intimately personal' and from the familial (what she termed 'fraternity'). Lessing, in her view, was exemplary in the practice of friendship because he 'wanted to be the friend of many men, but no man's brother' (MDT, 30). Friendship, for Arendt, was a distinct category that could not and should not be confused with the intimacy of erotic love or the bonds of kinship.

Arendt's own bonds of kinship were far from straightforward. She had neither brothers nor sisters, and, in October 1913, when she was only seven years old, her father died after having been admitted to Königsberg psychiatric hospital over two years earlier. A few months prior to that, her much loved grandfather, with whom she had enjoyed a Sunday morning ritual of story-telling walks in the park near his home, had also died. As an only child of a single parent she had an exceptionally strong relationship with her mother. When Arendt was thirteen, her mother married a local businessman and widower, Martin Beerwald, who had two teenage daughters, Clara and Eva, both of whom were older than Hannah. Arendt seems not to have established a close relationship with either her stepfather or her stepsisters, although during her university days she became closer to Clara who had severe mental health problems and finally committed suicide in April 1932.

Given the comparative paucity of 'given' relationships in her early life, it is hardly surprising that Arendt relied heavily on 'chosen' relationships. Of course, not all such relationships ripen into friendship. If Arendt was clear regarding the distinction between 'friendship', 'intimacy' and 'kinship', she was equally clear in distinguishing 'friendship' from relationships that were based solely on utility or pleasure. Friends could be and often were useful to one another and invariably found pleasure in one another's company, but neither utility nor pleasure constituted what Arendt saw as the *raison d'être* of friendship. Friendship was based on mutuality of respect and therefore on equality. People are unequal in countless ways, but within the context of their friendships they attain equality. In wanting the best for one another and wanting each to live up to the best in her or himself, friends ensure their mutual growth and flourishing. In that sense – the sense invariably employed by Arendt – friendship is virtuous.

That explains in part why, for Arendt, friendship involved lifelong commitment. If we respect what is good in the other and they respect what is good in us, and each wants that goodness in the other to grow and flourish, then there can be no equivalent in friendship to the 'one night stand' or 'the brief fling'. It was extremely difficult to be accepted into Arendt's circle of friends, but having been accepted it was virtually impossible to exit except by one's own determined volition. There are well-documented instances of Arendt's friends breaking off their friendship with her, sometimes quite publicly, but none of her initiating a break-up. Continuity was supremely important, even in the face of betrayal or behaviour that she found morally reprehensible; which is why, as we shall see, 'promise' and 'forgiveness' are ideas that she seeks to reclaim and, through that process of reclamation, locate at the centre of her understanding of 'the human condition'.

However, the longevity and variety of her friendships can also be explained by the precarious instability of her life. Prior to 1951, when she gained US citizenship, she had spent much of her adult life as a stateless person, initially in France (to which she migrated via Prague and Geneva in 1933) and then in the United States (to which she migrated in 1941). Her friendships tended to be formed within the artistic and intellectual cadre of the migrant communities within these localities. Given the importance Arendt placed on talk as a constitutive element of friendship, her widening circles of friendship necessarily required an expansion of her linguistic and cultural repertoire: from German (her mother tongue), to French (her language of first exile), to American English (her language of second exile). Because her friends were in the main located in minority and migrant groups within their adopted countries, she and they were often operating across these complex linguistic divides.

After having been arrested and interviewed by the Gestapo, Arendt fled Germany and settled in Paris with her first husband, Günther Stern, who had fled several months before. While in France she worked for organisations that helped Jewish refugees emigrate to Palestine and supplied legal aid to anti-fascists. She was part of a peer group that was largely German speaking, but cosmopolitan in outlook. Its members were acutely aware of the threat of fascism and its increasingly overt use of anti-Semitic propaganda and of violence directed towards Jews. The group – one of whose members, Heinrich Blücher, was to become Arendt's second husband – dispersed at the outbreak of World War II: some, like Arendt herself, were interned briefly in French camps; some fled to unoccupied territory; all began an urgent search for visas and exit routes; some never made it. The group was never re-formed in its entirety, but the bonds of friendship and loyalty that had been established were to have a lasting influence. For Arendt – and Heinrich Blücher – this group, together with earlier friendships formed in Germany, were to form the basis of the inner circle of friends that they would later refer to as their 'tribe'.

One member of the group who never made it out of France was Walter Benjamin, who committed suicide on 26 September 1940, at the Franco-Spanish border, at the age of forty-eight. He was attempting to emigrate to the United States via Spain. He had secured an emergency USA visa in Marseilles and obtained a Spanish transit visa. These would have allowed him to travel to Lisbon in Portugal and board a ship there for the United States. However, he also required a French exit visa. Travelling by foot over the mountains to a point on the border that was not usually guarded by French border police, he and the small group of refugees with whom he was travelling learnt that Spain had closed the border that same day and that the border officials did not honour visas issued in Marseilles. During the night Benjamin – no doubt suffering from physical exhaustion as a result of a serious cardiac condition – took his own life. The following day the border officials re-opened the border crossing thereby allowing his fellow refugees to proceed to Portugal. A few weeks later the embargo on visas was again lifted.

The significance of Benjamin's death for those who knew him is captured in Elaine Feinstein's (1984) fictionalised account of events following Benjamin's reported death on the Franco-Spanish border. In Feinstein's novel a young Jewish couple – Inge and Hans Wendler – escape from Vienna to Paris following the *Anschluss*. They are subsequently forced to flee Paris, and – with a small group that includes Hans' friend, Walter Benjamin – make their way to the Spanish border. It is not until the morning after Benjamin's suicide that news reaches his travelling companions that Benjamin has died under suspicious but as yet unexplained circumstances. In the novel Inge recalls over forty years later the impact of this news: 'Hans and I knew at once he had *chosen* to die ... It spelled out the bleakness of our own chances. The Europe to which we might be forcibly returned rang with the cries of the damned' (95–6). The novel records the terrible strains and tensions of being refugees in hostile France – and the desperate choices facing those who grasped the enormity of the Nazi threat and the irresistible logic of the Third Reich's programme of terror.

On the last occasion when Arendt had seen Benjamin he had entrusted to her and Blücher's care a collection of manuscripts to be delivered to the Frankfurt Institute for Social Research, which in 1935 had relocated to New York. On arrival in New York Arendt delivered the manuscript in person. However, it was not until 1945 that any of Benjamin's articles appeared in print in the Institute's journal, by which time Arendt had – along with Gershom Scholem, the German-born Israeli Jewish philosopher and historian and a friend of both Arendt and Benjamin – spent four years lobbying strenuously for their publication. In 1968 she edited an English volume of Benjamin's writings, *Illuminations*, and at the time of her death, in 1975, was still seeking to secure Benjamin's reputation. In the introduction she wrote for *Illuminations*, she likened Benjamin to a 'pearl diver' delving into the past to resurface with entirely new and original insights and saw the circumstances of his death as signifying the contingency of the human condition: 'One day earlier Benjamin would have got through without any trouble, one day later the people in Marseilles would have known that for the time being it was impossible to pass through Spain. Only on that particular day was the catastrophe possible' (MDT, 171).

Arendt and Blücher escaped France via Marseilles and Lisbon – thanks in part to Varian Fry, Albert O. Hirschman and others who, through the Emergency Rescue Committee, maintained an escape route through Marseilles as the Nazis swept across Europe (Adelman, 2013). They arrived in New York in May 1941. Arendt's mother followed in June. The situation in France had become increasingly dangerous and was becoming more so day by day. Earlier that year the Front National of the Resistance had been set up and had established a military wing with the express aim of hitting railway lines carrying men and material to the eastern front, punishing traitors and collaborators, sabotaging factories working for the Germans and executing soldiers of the occupying forces. A series of coordinated attacks by the Front National – in Rouen on 19 October, Nantes on 20 October and Bordeaux on 21 October – met with extreme and disproportionate retaliation by the Germans. The most notable of the mass reprisals took place in Chateaubriand where on 22 October twenty-seven 'hostages' were taken to a nearby quarry and 'executed' by firing squad. The youngest of the victims was still a schoolboy. On their way to the quarry and knowing their certain fate, the men sang the Marseillaise and kept singing as they were led before the firing squad in three separate batches. As Caroline Moorehead (2012) notes in her 'story of resistance, friendship, and survival': 'not one accepted a blindfold' (69). Arendt, Blücher and Arendt's mother were extremely fortunate to escape before the worst horrors of the occupation descended upon the French people.

In New York, Arendt became active in the German-Jewish community, writing a column for the German language Jewish newspaper *Aufbau* (1941–1945), working for the Commission for European Jewish Cultural Reconstruction (1944–1946) and visiting Europe on behalf of Jewish Cultural Reconstruction (1949–1950). She also accepted the senior editorial post at the New York headquarters of Schocken Books, an appointment which together with her freelance writing brought her into contact with an ever widening and increasingly cosmopolitan circle of academics, artists and intellectuals. Far from being sidelined by or excluded from this widening network, Arendt's former friends gained pre-eminence within it. Anne Mendelssohn, who took French citizenship and settled in France with her husband, remained one of Arendt's oldest and closest friends. It was to her friend from Königsberg that Arendt dedicated her first book, *Rahel Varnhagen: The Life of a Jewess*, with the inscription 'To Anne, since 1921' (RV).

In her frequent visits back to Europe, Arendt was punctilious in maintaining earlier relationships – such as those with Martin Heidegger and Karl Jaspers – and ensuring that their potential for friendship was sustained and as far as possible realised. That was far from easy given the deep mistrust that had been generated throughout Nazi-occupied Europe. She believed that the human world, unlike the world of inanimate objects, does not decay with time but gains in significance and vitality through time. New friendships and loyalties are enriching but can never supersede old friendships and loyalties; on the contrary, for Arendt, continuity increases the value of friendship and its potential for constant renewal. Time crystallises and distils. Many of the new relationships formed in New York developed into enduring friendships and had a significant influence on Arendt's life and thought. In time they, too, crystallised and distilled. Mary McCarthy was one such friend, but the New York circle also included, among many others, Waldemar Gurian and Randall Jarrell. These two friendships deepened Arendt's understanding of what it means to be a friend.

Gurian was, as Arendt wrote after his death in 1954, 'a man of many friends and a friend to all of them, men and women, priests and laymen, people in many countries and practically all walks of life. Friendship was what made him at home in this world and he felt at home wherever his friends were, regardless of country, language, or social background' (MDT, 251). He was a Russian Jew who had converted to Catholicism and had studied jurisprudence under Carl Schmidt, who later became a Nazi. Gurian's 'Jewishness' and his 'Russianness' were, for Arendt, defining features of his authority as an intellectual and his authenticity as a human being. The former committed him to becoming a historian of German anti-Semitism; the latter to becoming 'an outstanding expert in Bolshevism because nothing attracted him more deeply than the Russian spirit in all its ramifications' (MDT, 253). What she termed 'the crime of oblivion' was completely alien to him; 'faithfulness to his friends' was the dominant note to which his life was tuned (MDT, 254)

Jarrell, whom she met through her work at Schocken Books, was a poet and literary critic (see Burt, 2002). He met the world 'head-on', as she put it, through his 'marvellous wit' and 'the precision of his laughter'. She found his laughter 'so exactly right'. Although different in temperament and background, Gurian and Jarrell had both preserved what Arendt saw as a kind of innocence. She viewed that preservation of innocence as an exercise in moral courage. Jarrell, as she put it, 'had nothing to protect him against the world but his splendid laughter, and the immense naked courage behind it' (MDT, 266–7), while Gurian 'needed all the courage he could muster to keep his original innocence alive and intact. He was a very courageous man' (MDT, 259). To keep faith with one's origins, while acknowledging the need for new beginnings, requires both innocence and courage: the courage to gather the past into the future. Friendship, for Arendt, is one of the spaces within which that gathering can be enacted and constantly renewed.

Eichmann and evil

If Arendt had a genius for gaining friends, she also had a talent for winning enemies. Nowhere was that talent on better display than in her coverage of the trial of the former Gestapo officer Adolf Eichmann. On 9 April 1961 Arendt checked into the Hotel Maria on King George V Street in West Jerusalem to cover the trial for *The New Yorker*. The trial was a highly significant supplement to the Nuremberg War Tribunal of 1945, since it brought to justice a man alleged to have organised the murder of 6 million Jews. In so doing, it also established the enormity of the Holocaust and the immense scale of the Nazi regime's project of anti-Semitic genocide. Arendt – a Jewish public intellectual and by this time one of the most prominent political thinkers of her time – was, on the face of it, an inspired editorial choice by William Shawn, the then editor of *The New Yorker*. (Margarethe von Trotta's 2013 film *Hannah Arendt* focuses primarily on this period of Arendt's life. See Lilla, 2013.)

In order to grasp the significance of Arendt's appointment to this journalistic assignment, we need to bear in mind the following biographical facts: Arendt fled Germany in 1933 after having been held and questioned by the police; in France, from 1934, she began work with Agriculture et Artisanat, an organisation that helped train young émigrés to Palestine, and later became director of another Jewish organisation, Youth Aliyah, with a similar mission; in 1941 she escaped Vichy France, after being held with her mother as an 'enemy alien' in an internment camp, and arrived in New York; from 1944 she directed research work for the Commission on European Jewish Cultural Reconstruction and in 1949 became executive director of Jewish Cultural Reconstruction; in 1951 she published *The Origins of Totalitarianism*, the tripartite structure of which is informed by an analysis of anti-Semitism as providing the basis of both imperialism and totalitarianism. Although she had become increasingly critical of the Zionist Movement's focus on events in Palestine rather than Europe, her reputation as a leading spokesperson for the Jewish diaspora was by the late 1950s internationally acknowledged.

Arendt's account of the trial was published as a five-part article entitled 'A reporter at large: Eichmann in Jerusalem' in *The New Yorker* during the spring of 1963. (Revised, it was published in book form in the same year as *Eichmann in Jerusalem: A Report on the Banality of Evil*.) It immediately provoked bitter controversy among intellectuals in the United States and Europe and among her wide circle of friends. Within the UK, Isaiah Berlin was one of her most influential critics, who used his pre-eminence within the Oxford academic establishment to undermine her reputation and denigrate her work: a use – or abuse – of influence which as Caute (2013) has shown was not uncharacteristic of this Russian-born icon of liberalism.

Three issues were crucial in the often acrimonious debate that ensued: Arendt's obvious antipathy towards the chief prosecutor, Gideon Hausner, whom she saw as a showman concerned less with establishing the specific case against Eichmann than with documenting every wrong that had been suffered by the Jews; her insistence on the collusion of the Jewish leadership – the Jewish Councils – in the deportation of the Jews to the concentration camps and death camps of Eastern Europe; and her characterisation of 'evil' as 'banal' and of Eichmann as the personification of 'the banality of evil'. These three elements combined to produce an explosive reaction. The community that had contributed so much to Arendt's sense of public identity and moral authority was riven by outrage, incomprehension and disappointment by what it saw as her betrayal.

Four decades and a new millennium later, Seyla Benhabib (2000, 65), a writer sympathetic to Arendt, still found it necessary to point to what she saw as 'an astonishing lack of perspective, balance of judgement, and judicious expression' in Arendt's report on the trial. Arendt's attitude towards Attorney General Hausner was perhaps the least controversial issue, but it was bound to annoy the government of the Israeli state and all its friends. Some also perceived an element of intellectual snobbery in Arendt's attitude. Indeed, Leora Bilsky seems to hint at a kind of inverted anti-Semitism: 'She was a German from a family that was very educated, middle-class, and Hausner represented to her the "Ostjuden" – the Jews from the East – who talked with great pathos and sentimentality ... and she could not stand it; she wanted calmness and objectivity ... It was a personal disliking there' (quoted in Rée, 2003).

This impression of Arendt being, at the very least, 'off-side' was reinforced by her discussion of the second crucial issue in the debate: the role of the Jewish Councils in the deportation of the Jews. Any suggestion that the Jewish leadership had been willing to collaborate with the Nazi authorities was anathema to those who saw the trial as a means of placing on record the enormity of the crimes perpetrated by the Nazi regime, not only against the Jewish people but against humanity. From this perspective the Jews were unequivocally the representatives of suffering humanity, just as Eichmann was the archetype of undeniable evil. So, when – and here we come to the third crucial issue – Arendt presented that evil as 'banal' and characterised Eichmann as the personification of that 'banality' she crossed an invisible line that led to what Amos Elon has described as her 'excommunication' (EJ, vii–xxiii). 'It seemed', comments Benhabib (2000, 68), 'as if Arendt was accusing her own people and their leaders of being complicitous in the Holocaust while exculpating Eichmann and other Germans through naming their deeds "banal".'

Susan Neiman (2002, 302), in her powerful study of evil in modern thought, has argued that Arendt's reference to banality was ironic: '[C]alling evil banal is a piece of moral rhetoric, a way of defusing the power that makes forbidden fruit attractive ... The ironic tone she took toward Eichmann was entirely calculated ... To call evil banal is to call it boring. And if it is boring, its appeal will be limited.' What Arendt was struggling with was not only the sense that Eichmann was 'normal' according to his own distorted world view, but that his 'normality' carried with it no awareness whatsoever of the criminal – and amoral – nature of his acts. Tony Judt, speaking more recently, argues that '[Arendt] gets one thing absolutely right'. In using the phrase 'the banality of evil', he argues, 'Arendt is writing in terms that reflect a Weberian grasp of the modern world: a universe of states governed by administrative bureaucracies themselves subdivided into very small units where decisions and choices are exercised by, so to speak, individual non-initiative'. Inaction thereby becomes action and 'the absence of active choice substitutes for choice itself' (Judt with Snyder, 2012, 34).

What nobody could fully acknowledge at the time was that it was the norms by which Eichmann had operated, and which he had so thoroughly and unquestioningly internalised, that were monstrous. Half a dozen psychiatrists had certified him as 'normal'. Yet, the prosecution preferred to conclude from occasional lies that he was a liar. In so doing, they had missed, according to Arendt, the moral and legal challenge of the whole case: 'Their case rested on the assumption that the defendant, like all "normal persons", must have been aware of the criminal nature of his acts, and Eichmann was indeed normal insofar as he was "no exception within the Nazi regime'" (EJ, 25–6). Ironically, the prosecution had, according to Arendt's analysis, failed to grasp the moral and political significance of Eichmann's 'abnormality': namely, the unshakeable belief he had in his own 'normality'.

Ironic or not, Arendt's reportage of the trial caused a firestorm. 'She suffered enormously', claims Neiman in a later interview: 'She lost ... many and deep friendships. She was the subject of one of the most violent smear campaigns in the history of twentieth-century intellectual life. And it was enormously painful for her' (quoted in Rée, 2003). Moreover, the break-up of some of these friendships was a public – and highly publicised – affair; none more so than her break with Gershom Scholem whose tireless work on behalf of Walter Benjamin and his legacy had complemented her own. Scholem found *Eichmann in Jerusalem* shocking and unacceptable. In a letter dated 23 June 1963 he dismissed the phrase 'the banality of evil' as no more than a 'catchword' or 'slogan'. He charged Arendt with irresponsibility, with misreading the role of the Jewish agencies under Nazi occupation and with lacking a 'love of the Jewish people' – *Ahabath Israel*. In her reply to Scholem, she said (as quoted at the head of this chapter) that she had never in her life 'loved' what she called 'any people or collective', but only her friends: '[T]he "only" kind of love I know of and believe in is the love of persons' (JW, 466–7). But as far as Scholem was concerned, the charge of *Ahabath Israel* disqualified Arendt from any worthwhile insights into either the Holocaust or the Zionist vision. From his standpoint Arendt was henceforth an irrelevance. A handful of letters followed, but the friendship had ended (Arendt and Scholem, 2010).

Equally upsetting for Arendt was the reaction of Kurt Blumenfeld. He was one of her earliest and most influential mentors in Berlin and, in the ensuing years, had become one of her oldest and dearest friends with whom she had sustained a lively correspondence (Arendt and Blumenfeld, 1995). Although Blumenfeld was more than twenty years older than Arendt, they enjoyed one another's company and shared a similar sense of humour. There were many issues on which he and Arendt disagreed – relating, in particular, to his deep commitment to Zionism – but these did not adversely affect the intellectual respect and admiration each had for the other. He had been in close contact with Arendt during her stay in Jerusalem covering the trial, and she returned to Israel in early May 1963 to visit him when he was hospitalised with the illness from which he died later that month. Although he had not read Arendt's articles as they appeared in *The New Yorker*, he had been given reports of these from other sources and was outraged. Arendt felt she had been completely misrepresented and tried to explain to Blumenfeld that her critics were in her view seriously misreading her work. Blumenfeld remained unappeased; Arendt was devastated. As Arendt's biographer, Elisabeth Young-Bruehl, comments: '[T]his end to a friendship of so many years was dreadful. She was very shaken after the visit' (Young-Bruehl, 1982, 353).

What her critics and many of her advocates missed at the time was Arendt's contribution to what Leora Bilsky (2010) has termed the 'legacy of jurisdiction' bequeathed by the Eichmann trial. Although Arendt recognised the jurisdiction of the Israeli court, she had serious misgivings regarding the justification offered by the court in support of its jurisdiction. The issue, for her, was the nature of the crimes committed by Eichmann. She argued that these crimes were primarily 'crimes against humanity' and only secondarily 'crimes against the Jewish people'. 'It was', she maintained, 'when the Nazi regime declared that the German people not only were unwilling to have any Jews in Germany but wished to make the entire Jewish people disappear from the face of the earth that the new crime, the crime against humanity – in the sense of a crime "against the human status," or against the very nature of mankind appeared'. A 'crime against humanity', she argued, 'is an attack upon human diversity as such, that is, upon a characteristic of the "human status" without which the very words "mankind" or "humanity" would be devoid of meaning'.

It was not the choice of victims, but the nature of the crime itself, that for Arendt was the crucial point. Had this point been acknowledged, she argued, it would have become clear that 'the supreme crime' with which the court in Jerusalem was confronted 'was a crime against humanity, perpetrated upon the body of the Jewish people, and that only the choice of victims, not the nature of the crime, could be derived from the long history of Jew-hatred and anti-Semitism' (EJ, 268–9). Bilsky provides a crisp summary of Arendt's position: 'An attempt to annihilate one group should be understood as an attack on the condition of human plurality' (Bilsky, 2010, 206). Since, for Arendt, plurality is the defining feature of humanity, any attempt to annihilate an integral element of that plurality is not only a crime against the body of the people comprising that element but a crime against humanity itself. Far from belittling the crime,

Arendt was – by focusing on the nature of the crime itself rather than the choice of victims – highlighting its enormity. It was, in her view, a crime that should and must be addressed not only by the Jewish people, but collectively by the whole of humanity.

Arendt's friendships constituted the one sure line of continuity throughout her early life. As she fled across Europe – and from Europe to the United States – her circle of friends broadened and individual friendships deepened. Some of her Jewish friends failed to make it out of Europe or escaped by a different route and were reunited years later. All were deeply affected by the experience of living through the Nazi years and experiencing the full force of anti-Semitism. The break-up of some of her lifelong friendships that followed her reporting of the Eichmann trial was a bitter blow from which she never fully recovered. But the continuity of friendship was also a theme that threaded its way through Arendt's work, knitting together the evolving patchwork of ideas into a complex pattern of political theory. The following two chapters relate the theme of friendship to two of those ideas: plurality and promise. The former, as we shall see in Chapter 2, was her defiant rejoinder to what she saw as the unique phenomenon of totalitarianism; the latter, as discussed in Chapter 3, was her response to the uncertainty inherent in the plurality she embraced. The notion of friendship was unthinkable without an acknowledgement of the plurality of the world and unsustainable without the promise of binding commitments within the world.

2

Friendship and Plurality

It may be well to recall that for Thomas Aquinas, for example, the perfecta beatitudo consisted entirely in a vision, the vision of God, and that for this vision the presence of no friends was required . . . Jefferson, on the contrary, could think of a possible improvement on the best and happiest moments of his life only by enlarging the circle of his friends so that he could sit 'in Congress' with the utmost illustrious of his 'Colleagues'.

OR, 122–3

Total domination

Having fled Germany for France in 1933 and France for the United States in 1941, Arendt was in effect a 'stateless person' between 1933 and 1951 when she finally gained US citizenship. In the year that she became a US citizen, the first edition of *The Origins of Totalitarianism* was published. This established the intellectual foundations of her political thought and confirmed her reputation as a major political thinker and public intellectual. She had also by this time set up home with Heinrich Blücher, her second husband, and re-established her association with Martin Heidegger and Karl Jaspers, who had been two of the most formative influences on her early life and career. At the age of forty-five Arendt had crossed and re-crossed national, linguistic and disciplinary boundaries, and finally achieved some measure of personal security and public recognition. In the course of those crossings and re-crossings she had also gathered friendships that, in different ways and to varying degrees, would sustain her for the remaining twenty-four years of her life.

The Origins of Totalitarianism is Arendt's attempt to comprehend what was incomprehensible in terms of the political categories of thought that were available to her. The unprecedented nature of totalitarian domination had exploded those categories. What was unprecedented in totalitarianism, she argued in response to one critical review of her book, was not its ideological content, 'but the *event* of totalitarian domination itself'. It was 'the deeds of its considered policy' – the fact of it having happened – that made it unthinkable. It scandalised 'the standards of our judgement' by rendering them not only inadequate but wholly redundant. The lexicon of criminality – 'murder' and 'murderer' – was stretched beyond its limits by the crimes of totalitarianism and the perpetrators of those crimes (EU, 405). The problems Arendt faced in drafting *The Origins of Totalitarianism* were both methodological – how to think the unthinkable – and stylistic: how to write about totalitarian domination in such a way that the moral abhorrence it generates is seen as integral to our understanding of it. '[T]he question of style', as she put it, 'is bound up with the problem of understanding' (EU, 404).

In writing about totalitarianism, Arendt was no longer able to write within what she called 'the tradition of *sine ira et studio*': the tradition of reportage – without hate or zeal; with neither bitterness nor partiality – that since the *Annals* of Tacitus had been hugely influential in shaping the scholarly discipline of history and, more recently, the work of professional journalists located in war zones. For Arendt, who had been steeped in this tradition through her classical education, this was no easy sacrifice. The tradition was one, as she put it, 'of whose greatness I was fully aware'; and her distancing of herself from that tradition was undertaken only because she saw it as 'a methodological necessity closely connected with my particular subject matter'. It was because that subject matter was morally abhorrent that it demanded – as a condition of its 'objective' description – moral outrage: 'To describe the concentration camps *sine ira* is not to be "objective", but to condone them; and such condoning cannot be changed by a condemnation which the author may feel duty bound to add but which remains unrelated to the description itself' (EU, 404). The condemnation, argued Arendt, is integral to the author's position and perspective which inform and shape both the descriptive method and the style of description.

There was another respect in which Arendt found it necessary to break with the tradition of historical writing that she had inherited. How was she to write the history of a historical phenomenon that she judged to be entirely without precedent? How does one trace the origins of that which is – in this case outrageously and monstrously – new? She could not trace the history of totalitarianism, because it 'did not exist before it had come into being'; she could, as she saw it, only 'talk of "elements" which eventually crystallise into totalitarianism' (EU, 405). Those 'elements' may have left a historic trace, but their 'crystallisation' in history was a new and unprecedented phenomenon. Totalitarianism broke into history, exploding the categories that traditionally inform our understanding of history. Her method was to identify those 'elements' and locate them historically while acknowledging the phenomenon of totalitarianism as unaccountable and inexplicable in historical terms.

The particular 'elements' that concerned her were anti-Semitism and imperialism: the 'element of Jew-hatred and the element of expansion insofar as these elements were still clearly visible and played a decisive role in the totalitarian phenomenon itself' (EU, 405). As she herself acknowledged, in her response to her critical reviewer, 'the book ... does not really deal with the "origins" of totalitarianism – as its title unfortunately claims – but gives a historical account of the elements which crystallised in totalitarianism' (EU, 405). Having earlier broken with philosophy as a discrete discipline, she was now distancing herself from the idea of history as chronological record. Her achievement, as she saw it, was not to have written 'a history of totalitarianism but an analysis in terms of history' (EU, 403). Arendt was aware that she was doing a different kind of history – or doing history in a different kind of way. She was respectfully – but knowingly – subverting the tradition 'of whose greatness [she] was fully aware'. This strong sense she had of herself as both custodian and critic of those traditions within which – and against which – she positioned herself was to become one of the defining features of her intellectual identity and of her public presence as writer and thinker.

Reading *The Origins of Totalitarianism* from an early twenty-first century perspective, one has to remember that Arendt finished writing the book in 1949, a little over four years after the defeat of Hitler and four years before the death of Stalin. As she explained in her preface to the 1966 edition of the book, this was in her view 'the first possible moment to articulate and to elaborate the questions with which [her] generation had been forced to live for the better part of its adult life: *What happened? Why did it happen? How could it have happened?*' (OT, xxiv). The book was written in the thick of it – between the end of World War II and the commencement of the long Cold War – and

Arendt's *modus operandi* reflects her location *in medias res*. She was writing, as always, from within the middle – and the inevitable muddle – of history.

One of the consequences of writing history close-up is that one cannot know the extent or significance of one's own ignorance. This, of course, is always a problem in the production of any historical account, but it is particularly acute when the provenance of documentary sources is unsure and the extent of the documentary record untested and untried. Timothy Snyder (2011), in his study of Europe between Hitler and Stalin, has shown how the opening of the archives after the end of the Cold War has provided new perspectives on the crimes of totalitarianism. Referring specifically to the area covered by today's Ukraine, Belarus, Poland, western Russia and the eastern Baltic coast – what Snyder terms 'the bloodlands' – he writes: 'It is not that American and British forces saw none of the places where the Soviets killed, leaving the crimes of Stalinism to be documented after the end of the Cold War and the opening of the archives. It is that they never saw the places the *Germans* killed, meaning that understanding of Hitler's crimes has taken just as long' (xiv). The reason 'they never saw the places the *Germans* killed' is that those places fell within what were to become the new territorial boundaries of the USSR. Yet, according to Snyder, it was 'those places' that were the prime killing fields of totalitarianism: 'The photographs and films of German concentration camps were the closest that most westerners ever came to perceiving the mass killing. Horrible though these images were, they were only hints at the history of the bloodlands. They are not the whole story; sadly, they are not even an introduction.'

The Origins of Totalitarianism cannot, in retrospect, be criticised for failing to tell 'the whole story'. The facts to which we now have access were not available to Arendt at the time of writing. The lasting importance of Arendt's book rests not on the originality of its contribution to the historical record, but on what Tony Judt (2008, 75) has called 'the quality of its central intuition'; namely, 'the psychological and moral features of what she called totalitarianism'. Arendt showed that totalitarianism works only insofar as it colonises human mentality and consciousness. It requires assent and acquiescence: 'Totalitarianism has discovered a means of dominating and terrorizing human beings from within' (OT, 325). Its defining purpose, as she saw it, is to eradicate *totally* any trace of human freedom. She grasped this crucial aspect of both Nazism and Stalinism, and her subsequent work – highly varied and wide-ranging though it is – can be seen as a working through of the implications of this 'central intuition'.

Arendt was not the first to see the unholy alliance between Nazism and Stalinism. Karl Popper had arguably got there before her in his 1945 *Open Society and its Enemies*, but Popper had generalised the historic conjuncture of these two regimes in terms of an ideological confrontation between fascism and Marxism. Arendt, on the other hand, focused on the specificity of Nazism and Stalinism, and saw in that specificity one of the distinguishing features of totalitarianism: its mechanistic and de-humanising obsession with the bureaucratic technicalities of control. She also saw that it was through those mechanisms of total domination that both Nazism and Stalinism reduced the heterogeneity and plurality of humankind to a homogeneous mass. It was, she argued, this eradication of plurality that made possible – as 'considered policy' – the organisation of genocide and mass starvation; and, she further argued, it is only through the reassertion of that plurality that humanity can safeguard itself against totalitarian domination in the future.

Massification and atomisation

Central to Arendt's intellectual project, embarked upon in *The Origins of Totalitarianism* and carried forward in her subsequent work, was the reclamation of politics from what she saw as the anti-politics of totalitarianism and its apolitical legacy as manifest in many aspects of modernity. In the conclusion to her study of Arendt's political thought, Margaret Canovan (1992, 280–1) remarks that Arendt 'augmented' the world by the one word 'plurality' – and, indeed, the notion of 'plurality' was central to Arendt's project. As she asserted in the opening pages of her 1958 *The Human Condition*: 'While all aspects of the human condition are somehow related to politics, this plurality is specifically *the* condition – not only the condition *sine qua non*, but the *conditio per quam* – of all political life' (HC, 7). 'Human plurality', she maintained, is 'the basic condition of both action and speech' and 'has the twofold character of equality and distinction' (HC, 175). Both the equality of human worth and the distinctiveness of each human being are central to her notion of plurality:

> If men were not equal, they could neither understand each other and those who came before them nor plan for the future and foresee the needs of those who will come after. If men were not distinct, each human being distinguished from any other who is, was, or will ever be, they would need neither speech nor action to make themselves understood.
>
> HC, 175–6

Arendt defined power as the vital link between plurality and politics: '[P]ower springs up between men when they act together and vanishes the moment they disperse' (HC, 200). Power is latent in human plurality and is actualised through collective action. All power is, therefore, by definition *collective* power, and the notion of '*coercive* power' becomes a contradiction in terms. Arguably, as Jonathan Schell (2004, 226) points out, Arendt's definition 'leave[s] dictatorship dangling, linguistically speaking, in midair, without any political properties of its own'. If dictators and tyrants, such as Hitler and Stalin, were not 'powerful', what were they? 'What word was appropriate for the sway they exercised in that period?' Arendt was adamant that the appropriate word for the 'sway they exercised' was not 'power' but 'force' – and force, she insisted, is diametrically opposed to power and, therefore, entirely outside the realm of politics. Her insistence upon this clear and unambiguous set of distinctions was a strategic element in her attempt to reclaim politics from those forces that the totalitarian regimes of Nazism and Stalinism had operationalised to such deadly effect.

That effect, argued Arendt, was manifest in the interrelated processes of 'massification' and 'atomisation' that characterised those totalitarian regimes, but whose origins ran deeper and seeped into the fabric of modernity as understood in the context of post-World War II society. Totalitarianism had sought to reduce human plurality to an undifferentiated mass of atomised individuals incapable of either independent thought or collective action. It had sought, that is, to eradicate from the human species all traces of its humanity. What Arendt had experienced – and survived – was not a war between opposing powers, but a war between the power of human plurality and the force of totalitarian inhumanity committed to the total annihilation of that plurality. This was not a war that, having been endured, could be signed off by the return to an earlier settlement or the institution of a formal treaty. A politics based on 'the twofold character of equality and distinction' inherent in human plurality – the only kind of politics that Arendt recognised – would need to be reclaimed from the troubled aftermath of World War II. The world had changed – changed utterly – but the human beings who made that world were the same human beings who had almost destroyed it. The task, as Arendt saw it, was to restore the human condition – and, in so doing, to create the conditions necessary for collective, that is, *political*, action.

The immensity of that task cannot be overestimated. Arendt was tackling it through her regular writing for *Aufbau*, her work on behalf of Jewish Cultural Reconstruction, her work for Schocken Books and her writing and teaching (she took her first full-time teaching post – as visiting professor – at the University of California, Berkeley, in 1955). She also pursued that task through her commitment to her widening circle of friends, which now included some of her earlier acquaintances in Europe from whom she had been separated by the war but with whom she became reunited on her increasingly regular trips to Europe under the auspices of Jewish Cultural Reconstruction. It was on one such trip, undertaken in 1949, that she was reunited with Jaspers and met with Heidegger after an absence of almost twenty years.

Arendt's analysis of totalitarianism led her to the belief that underlying the mechanisms of total domination – the purges, the slave labour camps and death camps, the mass exterminations and genocide, and the use of enforced famine – was an attempt to reduce society to what she called 'mass atomisation'. She noted how, in Soviet society, 'the purges are conducted in such a way as to threaten with the same fate the defendant and all his ordinary relations, from mere acquaintances up to his closest friends and relatives' (OT, 323). The result, she argued, is an all-pervasive 'guilt by association' so that 'as soon as a man is accused, his former friends are transformed immediately into his bitterest enemies' (OT, 323). There can be no loyalty other than the 'total, unrestricted, unconditional, and unalterable loyalty of the individual member' to the party or movement. 'Such loyalty', she maintained, 'can be expected only from the completely isolated human being who, without any other social ties to family, friends, comrades, or even mere acquaintances, derives his sense of having a place in the world only from his belonging to a movement, his membership in the party' (OT, 323–4).

The desire for total domination that is implicit in totalitarianism can never be fully satisfied. Its logic is premised on the inexhaustibility of domination and has no endpoint beyond that of total domination. Totalitarianism is therefore 'a movement that is constantly kept in motion' (OT, 326). It cannot – and will not – provide stability or continuity in respect of a goal that lies beyond itself: '[T]he practical goal of the movement is to organise as many people as possible within its framework and to set and keep them in motion; a political goal that would constitute the end of the movement simply does not exist' (OT, 326). Nothing in a totalitarian state can be loved for its own sake other than the totalitarianism itself. Totalitarianism is in that sense totally introverted: it cannot conceive of anything – beyond its own totalising influence – as having any integrity. It demands the integration and assimilation of everything. The continuity of relationship, mutuality of commitment and recognition of plurality that were, for Arendt, fundamental to friendship are negated by totalitarianism. Totalitarianism necessitates the eradication of precisely those elements of social relationship – plurality, mutuality, and continuity – that constitute friendship.

Friendship might, then, be seen as a defensive bulwark against the possibility of totalitarianism. However, it might also be seen – more positively and less defensively – as a proactive engagement with human plurality. Conceived as a voluntary and mutual relationship – within which each friend recognises and respects the equality and distinctiveness of the other – friendship becomes a microcosm of a pluralistic world based on the equal worth of each unique individual. Friendship is worldly and, as such, participates in both the realm of the private and that of the public. In this respect, argued Arendt, friendship differs radically from romantic love: '[L]ove, in distinction from friendship, is killed, or rather extinguished, the moment it is displayed in public' (HC, 51). Friendship is worldly, whereas love is unworldly; love achieves equality through oneness, whereas friendship achieves it through plurality; friendship is pro-political, whereas love is apolitical or even antipolitical: '[L]ove, by its very nature, is unworldly, and it is for this reason rather than its rarity that it is not only apolitical but antipolitical, perhaps the most powerful of all antipolitical human forces' (HC, 242). These are the distinctions that order, arrange and elucidate Arendt's thinking on the complex relation between friendship as a distinct mode of human relationship and plurality as a constituent element of the human condition.

It is important to remember what Arendt was arguing against in *The Origins of Totalitarianism*. As we have already noted, she was arguing *against* the assumption that totalitarian domination could be interpreted according to the existing categories of dictatorial or tyrannical rule. She was also arguing *against* those who interpreted Nazism and Stalinism exclusively in terms of the ideologies of fascism and Marxism. Nazism and Stalinism were facts. They had occurred as events in history. Their facticity – their appearance in history as phenomena – was what had to be understood regardless of the unprecedented difficulty of this hermeneutical task. She was arguing, too, by implication, *against* those who would deny that facticity – the Holocaust deniers, the Stalinist fellow-travellers and those who simply did not want to know. Finally, she was arguing – albeit more tentatively – *against* the increasingly influential idea informing the post-war *avant-garde* that political action was 'to do something, heroic or criminal, which was unpredictable and undetermined by anybody else' (OT, 331). Arendt opposed the hedonistic, anarchistic, individualistic and violent tendencies implicit in this emergent politics. As the 1950s rolled into the 1960s and the tide of popularist revolt rose, Arendt continued to affirm and clarify the core values of democratic pluralism. What had to be reclaimed was the idea of human plurality, and from that idea a new politics of collective action had to be constructed.

Dead ends and cul-de-sacs

The Origins of Totalitarianism acknowledged not only the human capacity for inflicting unspeakable cruelty on its own species, but also its capacity for destroying what Arendt saw as the defining characteristic of our species – namely, its 'twofold character of equality and distinction' (HC, 175). Humanity had discovered in totalitarianism its own negative potential: the potential, that is, not for human growth and flourishing, but for dehumanisation. Totalitarianism was the realisation of this implosive potential. These were not random deeds – or the consequences of what is now euphemistically termed 'collateral damage' – but the outcomes of a 'considered policy': human consciousness conceived such a policy and human agency enacted it. Against the Renaissance and Enlightenment norms of human reason and human sovereignty, totalitarianism sought to redefine humanity according to the norms of Nazism and Stalinism. These regimes had – through 'the deeds of their considered policies' – shown that this radical redefinition of what constitutes humanity was not only conceivable but also enactable. It had entered history.

Having entered, it could not be easily dismissed. In the penultimate paragraph of the 1973 third edition of *The Origins of Totalitarianism*, Arendt insisted upon 'the fact that the crisis of our time and its central experience have brought forth an entirely new form of government which as a potentially and ever-present danger is only too likely to stay with us from now on' (OT, 478). Arendt threaded the twin strands of Nazism and Stalinism into her highly original analysis of totalitarianism, but she was not alone in highlighting the moral and political significance of what she saw as an entirely new force that had broken into – and fractured – human history: as early as 1940, Arthur Koestler had exposed the terror of the Stalinist purges in his novel *Darkness at Noon*; Albert Camus' 1947 allegory, *La Peste*, had also shown the precariousness of human existence in the face of Nazi occupation; and George Orwell, in 1949, had given expression to the vulnerability of human beings in the face of totalitarianism in his futuristic *Nineteen Eighty-Four*. In declaring totalitarianism to be the dead end of history – and the cul-de-sac of humanity – Arendt was expressing a sense of blockage that was shared by many at the time, while also showing solidarity with a European social democratic left as exemplified in the work of such diverse writers and intellectuals as Camus, Koestler and Orwell (see Scammell, 2010; Taylor, 2003; Zaretsky, 2010).

The rise of McCarthyism – with its virulent anti-communism and its relentless accusations of disloyalty, subversion and treason – intensified this feeling of internal and external constraint. Senator Joseph McCarthy had what Sheldon S. Wolin (2010) has described as 'a short-lived career that began and ended in obscurity' (37). However, in the short period during which this 'bizarre, crude, an unscrupulous' character had influence, he managed to generate within the United States a bitter and aggressive 'culture war'. McCarthyism was, as Wolin puts it, 'totalizing and unapologetic for its absolutism' (224). Its targets were not confined to politicians but included academics, writers, actors, film directors and executives: the makers of culture who comprised the predominantly liberal intelligentsia. The McCarthy 'crusade' provided ironic confirmation in the early 1950s of the insidious spread and continuing influence of totalitarianism: the fear and suspicion it engendered – and the threat of 'guilt by association' it employed as a deliberately intimidating investigatory tactic – was a reminder that no single regime had a monopoly on the impulse towards totalitarian domination. In its crude and unscrupulous mode of opposition to the totalitarianism of Soviet communism, McCarthyism had raised the spectre of what Wolin has termed 'inverted totalitarianism'.

Arendt and Blücher were both vulnerable in this situation, but Blücher was particularly at risk given his communist past and his denial of that past on the official immigration papers by which he had gained entry to the United States in 1941. Arendt had until recently been stateless, and – notwithstanding her newly acquired citizenship and her increasingly international profile – she was a potential target for incrimination through her marriage to Blücher. It is worth bearing in mind that innocence was no protection against the accusation of being a 'subversive' or an 'anti-American'. As Arthur Miller knew to his cost – and gave metaphorical expression to in *The Crucible* as first staged in January 1953 – McCarthyism was in large part a hysterical witch-hunt. Friendships, loyalties and professional associations were under immense strain during this period as the United States battened down the hatches and opted for polarisation as opposed to plurality.

The risks implicit in that global polarisation were incalculable. In an extended piece of writing produced in the late 1950s – and used as the basis of a course she delivered at the University of Chicago in 1963 – Arendt wrote: 'When the first atomic bomb fell on Hiroshima, preparing the way for an unexpectedly quick end to World War II, a wave of horror passed over the world' (PP, 153). That 'horror', she wrote, quickly became mixed with and was soon overshadowed by 'outrage': outrage at the fact that this new weapon of mass destruction had in effect been tested on the densely populated cities Hiroshima and Nagasaki, 'whereas it could just as well, and with no less political effect, have been exploded by way of demonstration in the desert or on some uninhabited island' (PP, 158). The aim was not – as traditionally the case in war – to subdue the enemy, but to gain 'a victory whose aim is the total political or even physical destruction of the enemy' (PP, 158). The fear of a third world war between the United States and the USSR was widespread at the time, as was the belief that any such war 'can hardly end in anything but the annihilation of the loser' (PP, 159). All wars were now, potentially, 'total wars' – and all 'total wars' were wars of annihilation in which politics itself was the prime object.

During this troubled period Arendt travelled back to Europe for three extended visits – in 1949, 1952 and 1956. On the first of these visits, as already noted, she met with Heidegger and was reunited with Jaspers. Within the United States she began and consolidated one of the most important relationships and written correspondences of her life with a very different McCarthy: Mary McCarthy, who, as we shall see, was to remain her lifelong friend. Arendt also embarked upon what she saw as a sequel – or complement – to *The Origins of Totalitarianism*: a book provisionally entitled *Totalitarian Elements of Marxism*. This book – for which all the writing she produced between 1952 and 1956 was originally designed – would have located anti-communist propaganda within a reasoned analysis of Marxist thought and placed that intellectual trajectory within the wider arc of the Western tradition of Enlightenment and post-Enlightenment thinking. The relation between the old world of Europe from which she had escaped and the new world of the United States to which she had escaped – and the deep relationships formed within and across that geopolitical nexus – held promise of a possible, although uncharted, way forward.

In 1956, while Arendt was in Europe, the geopolitical nexus fell apart and with it the imagined symmetry of her projected book, which was already well underway. What we now retrospectively describe as 'the Suez crisis' erupted with potentially catastrophic global consequences, while at the same time the people of Hungary performed the unthinkable: a revolution mounted by an almost forgotten national entity within an equally forgotten Eastern European 'bloc' of the supposedly all-powerful USSR. The architectonics of Arendt's projected book collapsed as the old categories disintegrated and the people of Hungary reasserted themselves as a polity to be reckoned with. In Hungary the tanks won – for a time – but would not be the final statement. Plurality had, albeit briefly, reasserted itself – with power and against force – through the polity: not an amalgam of atomised individuals, nor an undifferentiated mob, but a people with complex histories, diverse trajectories and a desire for freedom.

The fact that the Hungarian Revolution took almost everyone – including Arendt – by surprise is significant in that it highlights the extent to which the Cold War had become a world view as well as a geopolitical reality. Having been absorbed into the USSR, the diverse nations of Eastern Europe – stretching from the Baltic to the Adriatic – were perceived, as Anne Applebaum (2012) puts it, 'solely through the prism of the Cold War' (xxxvi). They had become an undifferentiated 'bloc'. 'Until it actually happened,' she argues, 'few analysts – even fiercely anti-Soviet analysts – had believed that revolution was possible within the Soviet bloc' (489). Arendt, too, argues Applebaum, is implicated in what she sees as a fundamental misinterpretation of history: 'Like the CIA, the KGB, Krushchev and Dulles, Arendt had come to believe that totalitarian regimes, once they worked their way into the soul of a nation, were very nearly invincible. They were all wrong' (489). According to this analysis, even Arendt – notwithstanding her insistence that 'politics is based on the fact of human plurality' (PP, 93) – failed to recognise the complex and multi-layered plurality of the national regions comprising Eastern Europe and the political potential implicit in that plurality. Hungary was a wake-up call not only for post-Stalinist USSR, but for those in the United States and Europe – including many liberal and leftist intellectuals – whose thinking was being shaped by the dichotomies and polarities of the increasingly dominant Cold War ideology.

Tony Judt, in conversation with Timothy Snyder, makes a similar point, but his argument inflects towards a more sympathetic appraisal of Arendt's position. Like many others, argues Judt, Arendt felt that 'the foundation for a modern, democratic politics must be our historical awareness of the consequences of *not* forging and preserving a modern, democratic polity'. The need to understand 'the possible risks of getting it wrong' seemed at the time to be the overriding task – 'rather than devoting ourselves over-enthusiastically to the business of getting it right'. In retrospect – and, indeed, from some contemporary perspectives – this could be seen as 'the liberalism of fear' or, as Judt rephrased it, 'the republicanism of fear'. The terms of the debate were couched in terms of negative freedom (*freedom from* Soviet oppression), rather than positive freedom (*freedom to* build 'the foundation for a modern, democratic politics'). In that limited sense, the mood of the times was undoubtedly deterministic – and Arendt's writing had, without doubt, contributed to that mood (Judt with Snyder, 2012, 38).

Nevertheless, at this crucial juncture Arendt did apply herself to 'the business of getting it right' and in so doing radically reconfigured both her intellectual project and its outcomes. Between 1958 and 1962 she was to publish three books: *The Human Condition*, *Between Past and Future* and *On Revolution*. Each of these – together with numerous lectures she delivered during this period – grew out of the ideas she had been developing in her now abandoned *Totalitarian Elements of Marxism*. It was the last of these three books, *On Revolution*, that elaborated and reframed many of the central insights that had informed *The Origins of Totalitarianism* and that pushed her intellectual project from an analysis of origins to a formulation of beginnings. The notion of 'natality' would from now on be central to her political outlook.

The diaspora of friendship

In *On Revolution* Arendt seeks to distinguish 'the political' as a discrete category and then apply that category to two 'revolutionary' events: the French Revolution and the American Revolution. Like her earlier *The Origins of Totalitarianism*, this work offers political analysis and historical interpretation within a broad philosophical context of ideas and conceptual distinctions. Underpinning both works is her assumption of a conceptual link between plurality as intrinsic to the human condition, and power as the potential for political action implicit in that plurality. Although Arendt provided no detailed or extended discussion of friendship, her references to it would suggest that she locates it within this conceptual frame: if the human world is one of irreducible plurality, and friendship an expression of that plurality, then the question of how the notion of 'friendship' relates to that of 'the political' becomes unavoidable. *On Revolution* provides us with some albeit tentative answers to that question.

In this work, Arendt had in her sights two traditions of political thought: the liberal democratic tradition with its emphasis on political freedom as realised through the exercise of individual liberty, and the Marxist tradition with its emphasis on political freedom as realised through the struggle for a classless society. Her argument with both these traditions was that neither of them had fully grasped what is revolutionary about revolution – namely, that people acting as free and equal citizens address their common concerns through collective action. Revolution constitutes a radically new beginning, the consequences of which cannot be prefigured. The liberal democratic and Marxist traditions both assumed that the meaning of political action, and of the revolutionary form such action can take, is to be found beyond 'the political'

– in, for example, the private happiness of the liberal democratic state or the classless society of the communist state. The public space of political action was usurped by one or other system of socioeconomic management, each offering its own version of what Arendt saw as an antipolitical utopia. Politics thereby became the preserve of either a governing elite of democratically elected representatives or a bureaucratic elite of party apparatchiks.

Arendt's argument with Marxism, although nuanced and appreciative of elements within the Marxist tradition, was readily accommodated within the anti-communist orthodoxy of the times. Her argument against the liberal democratic tradition was less easily accommodated and less readily understood. Indeed, it is perhaps only in recent years – in the increasingly protracted aftermath of the economic crisis of 2008 – that we can appreciate Arendt's forebodings regarding liberalism's impulse towards individualism, consumerism and privatisation. At the time Arendt was writing, it was not immediately apparent that the price of the liberal democratic utopia would be an exponential rise in social and economic inequality, the emergence of unaccountable and largely unregulated oligarchies, and an economic crisis of global proportions. 'The American dream', as Arendt herself put it, was 'the dream of a "promised land" where milk and honey flow' and where the increasing affluence brought about through the development of modern technology 'had the effect of confirming for the dreamers that they really had come to live in the best of all possible worlds' (OR, 131).

Whereas *The Origins of Totalitarianism* had focused on the immediate past and its import for the present state of political affairs in the mid-twentieth century, *On Revolution* approached the challenges facing the late twentieth century by focusing on events that had occurred in the second half of the eighteenth century. Arendt chose a distant mirror through which to view contemporary events. The eighteenth-century American and French Revolutions allowed Arendt to develop her argument through a set of contrasting analyses. Conceptual distinctions were central to Arendt's mode of thinking and argumentation: in this case, the French Revolution was juxtaposed against the American Revolution in order to advance her argument regarding the nature of – and conditions necessary for – political action. The French Revolution had in her view failed because it had sacrificed the ideal of political engagement to the expedience of mob violence; sacrificed, that is, the political potential of a free and equal citizenry to the antipolitical violence of an undifferentiated mob. It had failed – with tragic consequences – to *politicise* that mob and instead had simply unleashed its legacy of misery and oppression: '[T]he men of the Revolution', as she put it, 'set out to emancipate the people not *qua* prospective citizens but *qua malheureux*' (OR, 102).

Central to the American Revolution, on the other hand, was what Arendt called 'public happiness', which was premised upon the notion of 'public freedom' – 'not an inner realm into which men might escape at will from the pressures of the world', but the 'public space or market-place which antiquity had known as the area where freedom appears and becomes visible to all' (OR, 115). She maintained that 'the central idea of revolution ... is the foundation of freedom, that is, the foundation of a body politic which guarantees the space where freedom can appear' (OR, 116). That freedom 'appears' not when individuals will it, but when citizens enact it – and, crucially, when that enactment creates the conditions necessary for the sustainability of freedom: hence the importance, for Arendt, of 'a constitution to lay down the boundaries of the new political realm and to define the rules within it ... so that [the] "revolutionary" spirit could survive the actual end of the revolution' (OR, 117). The founding act of 'constitution' created a political space within which citizens could meet – as citizens – on equal terms. It was their freedom to do so – their 'right of access to the public realm' – that made possible such a thing as 'public happiness': 'men knew they could not be altogether "happy" if their happiness was located and enjoyed only in private life' (OR, 118).

This notion of 'public happiness' lies at the heart of friendship as conceived and practised by Arendt. In the quotation that heads this chapter, Arendt plays with the idea of contrasting versions of 'eternal bliss'. For Aquinas, she suggests, this would have been 'the vision of God [in which] the presence of no friends was required', whereas for Thomas Jefferson the only 'possible improvement on the best and happiest moments of his life' would have been the enlargement of 'the circle of his friends' (OR, 122–3). Both '*public* happiness and *political* freedom' are 'revolutionary notions' – and complementary notions – because each is 'part and parcel of the very structure of the political body of the republic' (OR, 129). Through its expression of 'public happiness' friendship finds its own place within that structure and in doing so contributes to the sustainability of 'political freedom'.

It is within that place – the place of friendship – that friends are able to explore the truth of their opinions by 'talking things over' and through the 'give and take' of conviviality. Arendt sets against the Platonic *opposition* of truth and opinion the Socratic idea of the *complementarity* of truth and opinion: truthfulness as the exploration of opinions relating to matters of common concern. It is the commonality of that concern that both unites and distinguishes friends and that defines the *telos* – the purposiveness – of the friendship. Viewed in this light friendship might be seen as a microcosm of the polity – not seeking to replace or juxtapose itself against the polity, but sustaining and modelling it. So, for example, in *The Origin of Totalitarianism* Arendt insisted that the polity must hold open its own plurality if democracy is to survive. She feared the potential for 'elective despotism' within representative democracy and warned against the democratic procedures of majority decision-making degenerating into 'the "elective despotism" of majority rule' (OR, 156). Majority decisions should in their processes and consequences seek as far as possible to accommodate minority opinion. The process of 'talking things over' and of 'give and take' – of seeking win-win outcomes over win-lose outcomes – is, as she saw it, indispensable to both the sustainability of the democratic state and the continuity of the state of friendship.

This common ground of plurality, within which equality and differentiation are held in balance, enables us to appreciate some of the distinctions that define Arendt's notion of 'friendship'. It enables us, for example, to distinguish between relationships of friendship and relationships that privilege unity over difference. Arendt draws this distinction with reference to the relationship between lovers, the purpose of whose erotic desire is a mutually self-sacrificial union one with the other. It also allows us to distinguish between friendship and relationships that, in Arendt's view, rightly and properly presuppose an element of necessary inequality. She locates relationships between young people and adults – particularly those between pupils and teachers or students and teachers – within this category. Finally, it allows us to distinguish friendship from relationships that recognise both the equality and differences within the relationship, but do not occupy a significant area of common concern. Such relationships might include social acquaintances and work colleagues, and might span the spectrum from likeable to disagreeable. Friendship, from Arendt's perspective, is significantly different from these other kinds of relationships, each of which may be significant in its own right.

In practice these conceptual categories are fluid and permeable. Arendt in her own life was well aware of the drifts and shifts inherent in human relationships: Martin Heidegger was Arendt's teacher, then her lover and teacher, and finally someone with whom Arendt sought friendship; Karl Jaspers was her teacher who became her lifelong mentor and friend; Heinrich Blücher was both friend and husband; while Arendt and Mary McCarthy, whose early acquaintanceship was decidedly frosty, became enduring friends. It is hardly surprising that, as a migrant Jew, Arendt – who had been brought up without a father or natural siblings, who had fled what was then Germany to the seemingly safe haven of France, and who then fled France to reside as a stateless person in the United States – would need the security of friendship and value the continuity of it. 'The experience of Diaspora, of life in exile, is', as Natan Sznaider (2011, 140) writes, 'the clearest example modernity offers of a sustained community life that does not need a territorial container in order to preserve its history'.

What is more surprising is Arendt's trust in the transformative potential of friendship – its capacity for constant self-renewal and for ensuring that human relationships, in all their diversity, endure, develop and interconnect. Friendship, as understood and practised by Arendt, tended not towards closure but towards greater openness and inclusivity. Her working model of friendship – based on the common sense and commonplace assumption that over time friendships become richer in their historical layering and their breadth of shared experience – owed much to the premium she placed on the idea of plurality as implicit in the human condition.

If Arendt spoke back to totalitarianism by affirming the boundless plurality of the world, how was she to address the problems inherent in that boundlessness? The plurality that makes possible friendships between free agents also renders those friendships vulnerable to the uncertainty, unpredictability and contingency that human freedom necessarily brings with it. Plurality gives us freedom, but it takes away security; it gives us agency, but takes away any surety regarding the outcomes of our actions. So, how can friendships between free agents be safeguarded from the chronic insecurity and indeterminacy that plurality pulls in its wake? That question dogged Arendt throughout her life. It is, of course, the classic philosophical and theological problem of free will. Constantly reframing and redefining that problem as her own thinking developed, she was intent upon revealing its ethical and political implications. The idea that promising is a power that may be set against the unpredictability of the world was central to that task. Friendships do not usually involve promising. But – as the following chapter seeks to show – they share with promises the power to establish some provisional security within the ceaseless flux of human unpredictability.

3

Friendship as Promise

The remedy for unpredictability, for the chaotic uncertainty of the future, is contained in the faculty to make and keep promises ... [B]inding oneself through promises, serves to set up in the ocean of uncertainty, which the future is by definition, islands of security without which not even continuity, let alone durability of any kind, would be possible in the relationships between men.

HC, 237

New beginnings

In New York, Arendt and Blücher gathered around them a widening circle of writers, artists and activists, many of whom like them were fugitives from the war. Bound together both by circumstance and in many cases by their Jewish origins, they came together to share and make sense of news that was beginning to filter out of Europe regarding the German concentration and extermination camps. The Brooklyn-born writer and literary critic Alfred Kazin has provided a vivid account of his first meeting with Arendt at one such gathering. The meeting took place in 1946 – five years after Arendt's arrival in the United States, and five years prior to her gaining American citizenship – at a dinner party given by Elliot Cohen, the founding editor of *Commentary,* for Rabbi Leo Baeck:

> She was a handsome, vivacious forty-year-old woman who was to charm me and others, by no means unerotically, because her interest in her new country, and for literature in English, became as much part of her as her accent and her passion for discussing Plato, Kant, Nietzsche, Kafka, even Duns Scotus, as if they all lived with her and her strenuous husband Heinrich Blücher in the shabby rooming house on West 95th Street.
>
> Kazin, 1982, 3

This was a highly cosmopolitan milieu: literate and intellectual, politically engaged and endlessly talkative.

The move to America proved to be a turning point in Arendt's life and thought. It is important to remind ourselves, therefore, of the instability of Arendt's life up to this point. In 1941 she had escaped from France to Lisbon, and from Lisbon had set sail with Heinrich Blücher, whom she had married a year earlier, to the United States. They had arrived in May of that year and, after a brief stay in Massachusetts, settled in New York. As news of the German concentration and extermination camps for Jews began to filter out, Arendt started work on what was to become *The Origins of Totalitarianism*. She also directed research for the Commission on European Jewish Cultural Reconstruction, which involved visits back to Europe during which she was reunited with Jaspers and his wife, Gertrud, and – more complicatedly – with Heidegger and his wife, Elfriede. In 1950 she became senior editor at Schocken Books. A year later she gained American citizenship and *The Origins of Totalitarianism* was published to wide acclaim. By this time she was in her mid-forties and had lived most of her life in state of transition.

Unlike many migrants before and since, Arendt did not hold out the hope of returning permanently to her homeland. Indeed, there was no homeland to which she could return. Hamburg, where she had been born, had endured ferocious Allied bombing raids during the war resulting in the devastation of much of the inhabited city as well as the harbour areas. In 1949 the city had been wrapped into the Federal Republic of Germany. Königsberg, where she had grown up, had also been heavily damaged by Allied bombing during the war. Captured and annexed by the Soviet Union and its German population expelled, it had been repopulated with Russians and others from the Soviet Union. In 1946 it had been renamed Kaliningrad in honour of the Soviet leader Mikhail Kalinin. The reshaping of Europe had occasioned not only devastation and destruction, but also the global dispersal of whole communities: at the end of World War II, in an act of population transfer that would now be termed 'ethnic cleansing', some 12 million ethnic Germans fled or were driven out of east and central Europe with Churchill's approval and British participation. Stateless exiles such as Arendt had no option other than to go forward. If the idea of 'home' was to mean anything other than the experience of irreparable loss, then it would have to be remade and rethought.

In Arendt's case it had to be remade without any reccurse to family. Her father and much loved grandfather had died when she was only a child, and in 1948 her mother, Martha Beerwald, died. Martha had been unstinting in her support of her wayward and sometimes difficult daughter. She had shared with her the difficulties and privations of exile. She was in her own right a strong woman, but increasingly felt the need to remain close to Hannah. Given what mother and daughter had endured together, this need for proximity was perfectly understandable. However, it was not an easy situation for Arendt as she struggled to forge a career for herself in New York and began to settle into a new marriage with a man whose background and outlook were very different from those of her mother. Martha Arendt became increasingly estranged from her daughter towards the end of her life and Hannah's feelings towards her mother became increasingly ambivalent. Such ambivalence is likely to complicate and intensify the sense of profound change that the death of a parent – particularly a single parent – provokes. Arendt was now on her own with only her second marriage and her friends to provide stability and reliability.

The experience of exile left Arendt with a sense of profound uncertainty: a conviction that human action was irreversible and its consequences unpredictable. If there was no going back – and if going forward was both uncertain and unpredictable – then there was nothing much between blockage and stasis on the one hand and the affirmation of possibility on the other. Arendt had survived for over a decade as a stateless person in a country that, notwithstanding the deep insularity of McCarthyism, had offered her hospitality. In granting her citizenship, America had provided her with a vantage point from which to view the past and survey the future. For the rest of her life she regularly returned to and maintained strong links with Europe, but increasingly Europe was now identified as a point of departure and America as a point of arrival. With the publication of *The Origins of Totalitarianism* in 1951 she had achieved a kind of settlement with Europe – Europe as both a geopolitical entity and as an Enlightenment ideal. While continuing to respect and draw on the European tradition of Enlightenment thought, she turned increasingly to the American tradition of emancipatory thought for her key reference points.

Nowhere is this turning point more apparent than in the content and argument of her 1963 *On Revolution*. Her central thesis is that revolution involves not just liberation from the old order but the constitution of a new order within which citizens can exercise collective agency: '[T]he end of rebellion is liberation, while the end of revolution is the foundation of freedom ... [T]here is nothing more futile than rebellion and liberation unless they are followed by the constitution of the newly won freedom' (OR, 133). Freedom is not merely freedom from obstruction, but the freedom to take positive action with others. In developing this thesis she contrasts two great eighteenth-century political upheavals: the American and French Revolutions. The latter, she argues, stalled at the point of rebellion and liberation, while the former followed through to 'the constitution of the newly won freedom'. Moreover, the American Revolution provides us with a rare example of a revolution that results not in 'a constitution imposed by a government upon a people' but a 'constitution by which a people constitutes its own government' (OR, 136). Although there are significant continuities between *On Revolution* and *On the Origins of Totalitarianism*, there is also a perspectival shift that reflects Arendt's experience as an American citizen in the twelve years between the publication of these two works.

Arendt still looked to Europe – for ideas and, in the case of the Hungarian Revolution, for inspirational practice – but from a rather different point of view. She was part of a generation of Jewish intellectuals who were never fully assimilated, but who were central to how America was identified – and identified itself – as a global hub of cultural and intellectual influence. Arendt remained betwixt and between – betwixt the old world and the new world, between the past and the future – and that positioning became a central part of her increasingly important role as a public intellectual and public educator. But just as she never sentimentalised Europe, she never sentimentalised her point of arrival: her new world of America. She lived at the epicentre of Western power and influence through what Eric Hobsbawm (1995) called 'the golden years' from the dropping of the atom bombs on Hiroshima and Nagasaki to the 'crisis decades' following the stock market crash of early 1973 and the oil crisis that followed later that year. If – as Hobsbawm maintains – the early 1970s constituted a watershed in the post-World War II history of what he termed 'the short twentieth century', then Arendt lived, in the main, on the 'golden' side of that watershed.

The major published works that were to flow directly and indirectly from her abandoned *Totalitarian Elements of Marxism* – namely, *The Human*

Condition ([1958] 1998), *Between Past and Future* ([1961] 1977) and *On Revolution* ([1963] 2006a) – were all informed by the particular circumstances of 'the golden years': circumstances shaped by both the nightmare reality of the Cold War and the American dream of ever increasing prosperity. Both the dream and the reality were consequences of an exponential increase in technological capability. From the Cuban missile crisis of 1962, through the USSR Luna 9 and Luna 13 unmanned Moon landings of 1966, to the first successful US Apollo 11 manned mission to the Moon in 1969, technology drove the geopolitics of the post-World War II era. Arendt – from her new vantage point – grasped the implications of this new phase of technological innovation. She saw that, far from making the world a safer place, it added a wholly new dimension to the unpredictability and uncertainty that she saw as intrinsic to the human condition.

In *The Human Condition* she characterised this new dimension as both dehumanising and demoralising – and, in so doing, foreshadowed later critiques of industrialised and standardised forms of mass production and consumption. Her argument was driven by historical analysis. Whereas, during the early stages of the Industrial Revolution, technological innovations such as the steam engine harnessed natural processes to human ends and 'did not differ in principle from the old use of water and wind power', later technological developments such as the use of electricity required that 'we no longer used material as nature yields it to us' (HC, 148). Instead, 'we changed and denaturalized nature for our own worldly ends, so that the human world or artifice on one hand and nature on the other remained two distinctly separate entities' (HC, 148). What she termed 'automation' – 'the process of the conveyor belt and the assembly line' (HC, 149) – was the culmination of this separation of the human from the natural. It introduced into the human world the possibility of mass production and the corresponding need for mass consumption, while the technological advances that drove it put both the human and the natural worlds at incalculable risk.

The unpredictability and uncertainty of the human condition remained an abiding preoccupation which Arendt carried forward from the old world of pre-World War II Europe to the new world of post-war America. The new world was as complicatedly unpredictable as the old world: the clash of American dream and Cold War reality held unforeseen – and unforeseeable – consequences.

As her and Blücher's circle of friends expanded – with an inner circle of friends that were part of her own European, mainly Jewish, community, but now including a wider circle of friends from New York and beyond – the stability and reliability of friendship became increasingly important. She made no grand claims for friendship, but the friendships she formed held out the promise of continuity and stability in a world of discontinuity and instability. As such, they played into her thinking about the nature of power and politics and her understanding of the human condition.

'Isolated islands'

Arendt was forging a language – a rationale and a conceptual apparatus – for analysing what we now perhaps take for granted: the chronic instability of a world that is possessed of the knowledge and resources necessary for global self-destruction. Irreversibility and unpredictability had, she maintained, always been constitutive elements of the human condition. The outcomes of our individual acts of human agency are the consequence not only of those individual acts, but of countless other acts of human agency which interconnect and collide in unpredictable ways and with unforeseeable outcomes. Every action, in other words, enters a dynamic process which proceeds according to its own irreversible and inscrutable logic. 'We can', as Arendt put it, 'at best isolate the agent who set the whole process into motion', but 'we never can point unequivocally to him as the author of its eventual outcome' (HC, 185). The insight that Arendt now added to this analysis was that, in developing advanced technologies that 'changed and denaturalized nature', we had introduced into the field of human action an entirely new element of incalculability and uncertainty: an element that having once entered the world gained permanency within it. 'Modern natural science and technology . . . have', as she put it, 'carried irreversibility and human unpredictability into the natural realm, where no remedy can be found to undo what has been done' (HC, 238).

Although human agents cannot 'undo what has been done', they can exercise their agency in such a way as to interrupt the seemingly inevitable consequential logic of 'what has been done'. Arendt saw the act of forgiveness in precisely these terms – as an interruption to the irreversibility of human affairs.

Forgiveness is usually seen as a moral act, but for Arendt it is also a political act in that it activates the power implicit in plurality. It empowers people to start again, to make a new beginning, to move forward. It is, as she put it, 'the only reaction which does not merely re-act but acts anew and unexpectedly' (HC, 241). There were, for Arendt, many unresolved issues relating to forgiveness: the conditions necessary for forgiveness, the category of the 'unforgiveable', the relation between friendship and the possibility of forgiveness. These issues surface throughout her life and work and, as we shall see in the central chapters of this book, have a particular bearing on her lifelong friendships. However, Arendt was adamant that forgiveness provides the possibility of empowerment at the level of the interpersonal and therefore introduces power into the field of human affairs at that level. Power may be embedded in systems and structures, but it is activated by free agents acting in relation to one another. With regard to forgiveness, this acting-in-relation-to breaks the vicious circle of automatic action-and-reaction: 'In this respect forgiveness is the exact opposite of vengeance' (HC, 240).

If the act of forgiveness interrupts the irreversibility of human affairs, then the act of promising pits itself against the unpredictability of the human condition: 'The remedy for unpredictability, for the chaotic uncertainty of the future, is contained in the faculty to make and keep promises' (HC, 237). While forgiveness is between persons, promises have a wider remit. Forgiveness operates at the level of interpersonal injustice. The making and keeping of promises, on the other hand, is a wider category embracing a broad field of mutual obligation: inter-state treaty and alliances; within-state social contracts; marital and pre-marital arrangements; and binding relations between individuals. At all these levels the act of promising provides a bulwark against the unpredictability of plural agents exercising their freedom to act. If human plurality generates boundless unpredictability in human affairs, it also generates – through its capacity for mutuality and reciprocity – the possibility of making and keeping promises and thereby setting boundaries to that unpredictability.

This idea of promises as a stabilising power in human affairs has a long history. 'We may', suggests Arendt, 'trace it back to the Roman legal system, the inviolability of agreements and treaties (*pacta sunt servanda*); or we may see its discoverer in Abraham, the man from Ur, whose whole story, as the Bible tells it, shows such a passionate drive toward making covenants' (HC, 243). However, Arendt's analysis of totalitarian regimes and modes of thinking made her wary of promises that seek 'to cover the whole ground of the future'. Promises, in her view, need to be 'isolated islands of certainty in an ocean of uncertainty'. Insofar as they seek to colonise 'the whole ground of the future' they become self-defeating in that they eradicate freedom and impose homogeneity and stasis on the heterogeneous flux of human plurality: 'The moment promises lose their character as isolated islands of certainty in an ocean of uncertainty, that is, when this faculty is misused to cover the whole ground of the future and to map out a path secured in all directions, they lose their binding power and the whole enterprise becomes self-defeating' (HC, 244). Messianic and utopian promises – whether premised on religious or secular values – erode the political.

From this perspective the covenant between Yahweh and Abraham was deficient in that it imposed upon the future a preordained destiny: a destiny determined by the radical inequality between, on the one hand, the maker and keeper of the promise (Yahweh) and, on the other hand, the beneficiaries of the promise (Abraham, Isaac and their descendants). It sought, that is, 'to cover the whole ground of the future and to map out a path secured in all directions' (HC, 244). Its basis in inequality and its closure in respect of the future are at odds with what Arendt most valued in the act of promising. Promising, for her, was not a defensive recoil from the unpredictability of the future – not a way, that is, of transcending, denying or erasing the unpredictable – but an acknowledgement of the *fact* of that unpredictability: a way of moving forward together into the unbounded uncertainty that constitutes the human condition. It presupposes equality and freedom and finds form and expression through the many different ways in which 'the many [are] bound together'.

It is the specificity of promises – their boundedness – that ensures the possibility of their fulfilment: to promise everything is to promise nothing; to promise something is to be bound by a specific commitment. Implicit in the substance of any promise are the terms of its fulfilment. The specificity of what is being promised – the substance of the promise – is fundamental to the making and keeping of promises. Promises, then, are defined by what it is they promise: by their content. But they are also defined by the nature of the relationships within which they are undertaken. While maintaining that a fundamental characteristic of all promises is that they can 'only be achieved by the many bound together', Arendt highlights the significance of the terms upon which 'the many [are] bound together' (HC, 245). She distinguishes between promises on the basis not only of what is being promised but of how the promise is being undertaken: the quality of relationship within which the promise is embodied.

When these conditions are fulfilled, argued Arendt, promise activates power: '[B]inding and promising, combining and covenanting are the means by which power is kept in existence' (OR, 166). The making and keeping of promises thereby becomes a key element in what Arendt called 'the syntax of power': '[P]ower is the only human attribute which applies solely to the worldly in-between space by which men are mutually related, combine in the act of foundation by virtue of the making and the keeping of promises, which, in the realm of politics, may well be the highest human faculty' (OR, 167). Commenting on her notion of power, J. M. Bernstein (2012, 64) argues that 'mutual promising is the analogue in Arendt's political theory of the Aristotelian doctrine of friendship'. It is in the specificity and equality of that mutuality – as expressed, in exemplary fashion, through friendship – that the power of promising emerges: 'It is speaking as promising, speaking as the positioning of oneself in social space in the mode of answerability, and hence responsibility, that finally gives substance to Arendt's notion of power – power as nothing other than the social bond formed by speaking in a promissory mode' (p. 64). A 'specific promise', as Bernstein puts it, '*institutes* or *creates* a social bond ... a promise is, in miniature, a beginning and a founding: it begins a new history in our relation by creating a bond between us that stretches out into the future' (p. 67).

Considered in this light, a friendship provides the promise of certainty and continuity in a world of uncertainty and discontinuity, but always within the bounds and constraints of that particular friendship. The promise implicit in friendship loses its 'binding power' when it seeks 'to cover the whole ground of the future' and thereby control the boundless uncertainty and discontinuity within which it is located. Friends may offer a respite from a world of uncertainty and discontinuity, but they cannot rescue one another from it. They are inextricably bound to its plurality. Through our friendships we learn to relate to one another as free and equal agents and, crucially, to carry what we have learnt from those friendships – by way of the exercise of freedom and the recognition of equal worth – back into the world. The promise that friendship provides is not the promise of an escape from the world, but the promise of a gathering of the resources necessary to enter the world as free and equal agents. Friendships sustain us: their intrinsic promise is one of mutual sustainability within the wider world.

That is why Arendt placed a value premium on enduring friendships. Old friends understand one another not only as friends, but also as persons with complex histories that include all the multi-layered unpredictability and discontinuity of the human condition. In Arendt's case that unpredictability and discontinuity involved exile and resettlings, divorce and remarriage, and the necessity of writing for – and to – the moment. The longer and more enduring a friendship is, the greater the possibility of that friendship comprehending and sustaining the broad sweep of the personal narratives of each of the friends. 'It is not only', argues Seyla Benhabib (2003, 126) in her analysis of Arendt's account of human action, 'that we are the subject matter of the stories of others but also that we discover who we are and come to know ourselves through the words and deeds we engage in, in the company of others'. New friends may enjoy the excitement of relating their life stories, but for old friends the knowledge is there already: tacit and implicit in each new meeting, lodged in the memory of the friendship.

As Arendt settled into her life as a US citizen and public intellectual, she gathered around her an ever-widening circle of friends from different walks of life. Her old friendships were special, but not exclusive. She never sought to distinguish friendships on any other basis than their promise of mutual sustainability in a world of uncertainty and discontinuity. She was at one with the Aristotelian and post-Aristotelian canon of writings on friendship in emphasising its ethical and political relevance in any attempt to lead a good life, build the good society and strengthen the polity. However, she was at odds with much of that canon in her implicit rejection of its exclusionary categories, its schematic ordering of friendships and its idealisation of 'sovereign' friendship. If we are to understand what, according to Arendt, friendship holds in promise, then we need to distinguish her notion of friendship from some of the strands of thought comprising the tradition within which – and against which – she wrote.

'Truthful dialogue'

Friendship is the major subject of two of the ten books comprising Aristotle's *Nicomachean Ethics* – so called because they are believed to be based on notes from his lectures at the Lyceum, which were edited by or dedicated to his son Nicomachus. These two books – Book 8 and Book 9 – are placed immediately prior to the final book and provide the conceptual bridge between the earlier books that focus primarily on the virtues and the final book that focuses on pleasure and the life of happiness. (Contemporary usage fails to capture the full ethical weight that Aristotle attaches to 'pleasure' and 'happiness', which in the *Nicomachean Ethics* and elsewhere in the Aristotelian canon carry the sense of 'human fulfilment' or 'flourishing'.) The notion of friendship is therefore pivotal to the ethical framework elaborated by Aristotle and – in its emphasis on the civic bases of the good life – provides vital linkage to his political thought. Friendship, insists Aristotle, is a necessity: it is 'most necessary for living' (Aristotle, 1976, 258). Through friendship we actualise the virtue of justice – 'friendliness is considered to be justice in the fullest sense' (Aristotle, 1976, 259) – and through justice we achieve the conditions necessary for civic and political order. Friendship is a necessity because without it we are unable to engage fully as citizens in the life and work of the polity.

This emphasis on the centrality of virtue in the formation of friendship reverberates through the classical literature on friendship. Cicero, writing in the first century BCE, concludes the final section of his epistolary essay, 'On friendship', with the affirmation: 'I repeat what I said before. It is virtue, virtue, which both creates and preserves friendship' (Cicero, 2012, 43). Plutarch, who spanned the first and second centuries CE and whose view of the world informed and inspired the European Renaissance world view, argues – in his essay on 'How to distinguish a flatterer from a friend' – that a friend is like a musician: '[I]n retuning his instrument for the mode of goodness and benefit, he loosens here and tightens there, and consequently, although he may often be likeable, he *always* does good' (Plutarch, 1992, 74). What Suzanne Stern-Gillet (1995, 109), in her study of Aristotle's philosophy of friendship, calls 'the moral community' comprises both the citizenry and friendship: 'At its widest the moral community coincides with the polis (city-state), and at its narrowest it consists of the circle of primary friends'.

This general insight into the relation between goodness and friendship is part of the classical legacy that Arendt inherited and that infuses her own thinking about friendship. For Arendt the promise inherent in friendship is that of truthfulness, which constitutes a necessary condition for what Arendt understands by politics: 'The political element in friendship is that in the truthful dialogue each of the friends can understand the truth inherent in the other's opinion' (PP, 19–20). Truthfulness, which for Aristotle was the virtuous mean between the excess of boastfulness and the deficiency of understatement, is for Arendt a state of mutual understanding that exists between friends and that forms the moral bases of the polity. Politics is, as it were, ethically grounded in 'the truthful dialogue' that constitutes friendship.

There is, however, another albeit related strand of Aristotelian thought that is less amenable to Arendt's way of thinking. Book 8 of Aristotle's *Nicomachean Ethics* focuses on the distinction between three kinds of friendship: friendship based on utility, friendship based on pleasure and friendship based on goodness. This schema is hierarchical with reference to the values Aristotle ascribes to each of the kinds of friendship: friendship based on goodness provides the apex of a triangular formation, the baseline of which comprises utility and pleasure. The terminology used to define this category of friendship invariably highlights its superiority: 'perfect friendship', 'sovereign friendship', 'primary friendship'. Although this superior form of friendship may be useful and is certainly pleasurable, it is distinguished from the other categories by inclusion of virtue as its prime constituent: 'Only the friendship of those who are good, and similar in their goodness, is perfect' (AE, 263). At the apex of the triangle is the kind of friendship that is different not just in degree but in kind from ordinary friendships.

This strand of Aristotelian thought led – possibly erroneously – to an idealisation of friendship that is alien to how Arendt thought about and lived her friendships. Notwithstanding the premium she placed on categorical distinctions, these were not distinct categories of thought that she applied to her understanding of friendship and its ethical and political implications. One of the best-known idealisations of friendship is that contained in Michel de Montaigne's essay 'On friendship', which is in effect a eulogy to his friend Étienne de La Boétie who died in 1563 just before his thirtieth birthday. This friendship, we are told, was incomparable, unique: 'a friendship so complete and perfect that its like has seldom been read of, and nothing comparable is to be seen among the men of our day' (Montaigne, 1958, 92). It was a friendship destined to happen and made in heaven: 'There is ... some inexplicable power of destiny that brought about our union ... I believe that this was brought about by some decree of Heaven' (97). It involved a submission of one's will to that of the other such that the friendship became all-consuming:

> it was some mysterious quintessence of all this mixture which possessed itself of my will, and led it to plunge and lose itself in his; which possessed itself of his whole will, and led it, with a similar hunger and like impulse, to plunge and lose itself in mine. I may truly say *lose*, for it is left us with nothing that was our own, nothing that was either his or mine.
>
> Montaigne, 1958, 97–8

To the modern ear, Montaigne's metaphors evoke a sense of charged romantic eroticism. Yet he clearly, and without any hint of defensiveness, distinguishes his friendship with Etienne from what he calls 'that alternative permitted by the Greeks' – by which, presumably, he means what we would now term homosexuality. He is, he insists, providing us with an account of a 'complete and perfect friendship' that is intimate but not sexual. The promise of friendship, for Montaigne, can only be fulfilled through a 'complete and perfect friendship' that is unique and incomparable and that finds its fulfilment in 'some mysterious quintessence' in which the will of the other is compelled 'to plunge and lose itself in mine'. It is in an attempt to highlight the uniqueness and exclusivity of this kind of friendship – and distinguish it from 'commonplace and everyday friendships' – that he quotes a statement traditionally attributed to Aristotle: 'Oh my friends, there is no friend!' (99). There is, he seems to be saying, no 'complete and perfect friendship' among all my 'commonplace and everyday friendships'.

Montaigne sharpens the Aristotelian distinctions between kinds of friendship to the point at which, as Lorraine Smith Pangle (2003) in her study of Aristotle's philosophy of friendship states, 'it becomes puzzling why [Aristotle] continues to call the lesser forms friendships at all': 'Why does he waffle on this point and pull back from saying unambiguously that only a union of virtuous men who love one another for their characters is friendship at all?' (45). Her response to this question is that although only one of Aristotle's three categories of friendship has as its primary object pleasure, all three categories are infused with pleasure: 'Both friendships of pleasure and those of virtue truly aim at pleasure and truly achieve it, although the perfect friendship does this in a more stable and reliable way and brings other benefits in addition' (55). Aristotle requires a broad and inclusive categorisation of friendship in order to prioritise pleasure; but within that broad and inclusive categorisation he requires a hierarchical ordering of friendships in order to prioritise stability and reliability. All friendships provide pleasure, but the best friendships hold out the additional promise of stability and reliability within which virtue may be nurtured and sustained.

Given her emphasis on the unpredictability and uncertainty of human affairs, Arendt placed great importance on the stability and reliability of friendship. It is unsurprising therefore that she placed a premium on her older and more enduring friendships, the stability and reliability of which had been tried and tested by time and exile. In that sense, her thinking is all of a piece with Aristotle's ordering of friendship as interpreted by Pangle. However, the exclusivity that Montaigne read into Aristotle's notion of 'perfect friendship' – and the loss of 'my will' in the 'mysterious quintessence' of such friendship – is totally alien to Arendt's notion of friendship: friends do not lose themselves in friendship, but gain an affirmation of their distinct identities through friendship. Nor do they cut themselves off from the world through their friendship. Friends share some measure of intimacy, but carry the plurality of that world into their friendships in such a way as to both enrich those friendships and enhance one another. This emphasis on individual autonomy within friendship – and the openness of friendship to the world – is central to Arendt's notion of what constitutes friendship.

As Jacques Derrida (1997, 215–16) – in his unravelling of the exclamatory statement 'Oh my friends, there is no friend!' – suggests: *'there is never a sole friend*. Not that there would be none, but that there never is one. And one is already more than one, with or without my consent . . . This multiplicity makes the taking into account of the political inevitable'. Plurality for Derrida – as for Arendt – is the defining feature of friendship, which is why 'there is no friend' (in the singular), only 'my friends' (in the plural) who relate to one another within the context of what Derrida calls 'the desire for multiplication' (215). It is because of this desire that friendship inevitably takes into account the political: the power implicit in plurality. Friendship promises protection from the unpredictability and uncertainty of human affairs and the resources of stability and continuity necessary to engage with that unpredictability and uncertainty. It promises a sense of self-worth and of mutual recognition. Friendship is not an escape from but a re-engagement with the plurality and – as Arendt would term it – the worldliness of the human condition.

The fragility of friendship

Montaigne's idea of 'perfect friendship' – whereby, as Sarah Bakewell (2010, 108) puts it, La Boetie 'changed from being Montaigne's real-life, flawed companion to being an ideal entity under Montaigne's control' – has political implications in that it addresses issues relating to the power that is generated between persons: the power, that is, of plurality. The idea of friendship as consisting of two free and equal individuals who protect and border each other – while also reaching beyond the protective boundaries of their particular friendship – speaks back to the idealising assumptions underpinning the notion of 'perfect friendship'. The friendship between free and equal individuals is necessarily a relation between real-life and flawed companions. For friends to idealise the entity of the other is to seek control of that entity and thereby deny the freedom and equality upon which the friendship is based.

Such friendship also speaks back to the patriarchal assumptions underpinning the notion of 'perfect friendship': if women share friendships on the basis of freedom, then they are affirming both their freedom as women and their gender equality. In a patriarchal order, such friendships between women are subversive – between men and women such friendships threaten the very bases of that order. In the case of Arendt we also have to throw into this complex mix her own 'Jewishness': her sense of herself as being socially located within a category that predetermined her identity as 'Jewish'. Against that predetermined identity she demanded her own self-determination: a self-determination that did not deny its origins, but required of those origins the capacity for new beginnings. Friendship, for Arendt, constitutes one such beginning in that it forms from two independent substances a relationship based on mutuality: 'The paradigm for a mutually predicated relationship of independent "substance" is *friendship*'. Central to that paradigmatic formulation, as understood by Arendt, is that neither of the friends loses her or his 'substantial independence and identity' (LM, 98).

Arendt's preoccupation with the complex interplay of origins and beginnings in the constitution of 'substantial independence and identity' is a thread running through all her work. It is clearly discernible in her early *Rahel Varnhagen: The Life of a Jewess*. This strangely autobiographical biography explores the life of Varnhagen – born in Berlin in 1771 as the daughter of a Jewish merchant – with reference to her Jewish origins. It was the origins that necessitated what Arendt presents as Varnhagen's tragic struggle to overcome her 'pariah' status as a Jewish woman while avoiding the fate of the 'parvenu' who is never fully accepted within the society to which she is a newcomer. How to enter fully into a world of established interests and hierarchies? The tragic irony upon which the biographical narrative turns is that Varnhagen can only ever insert herself into history by acknowledging that she will forever be an outsider. Through that acknowledgement comes an acceptance of the inescapability of her origins. So, at the end of a life dedicated to conversing and corresponding in German and French with many of the literary luminaries of her time, she reverts – Arendt tells us – to writing 'whole paragraphs in her letters to her brother in Hebrew characters, just as she had done in her girlhood ... Rahel had remained a Jew and pariah. Only because she clung to both conditions did she find a place in the history of European humanity' (RV, 258).

Arendt began this particular work in 1929, shortly after she had completed her dissertation on St Augustine's concept of love. By 1933 she had completed a draft of the book, although two chapters were added later such that the study was not finished until 1938. The work was finally published in 1957, but by then she had introduced the case of Rahel Varnhagen into her 1951 *The Origins of Totalitarianism* as part of the analysis developed in the chapter on 'the Jews and society'. Seyla Benhabib's (2003) *The Reluctant Modernism of Hannah Arendt* helped establish *Rahel Varnhagen: The Life of a Jewess* as a major work in the Arendtian corpus. Benhabib emphasises the crucial importance of the Jewish salon in the culture of *fin de siècle* eighteenth-century Berlin society. For a brief period, the Jewish salons were places within which the public and private intersected in a new kind of social space. 'The salons', Benhabib writes, 'are also spaces in which friendships are formed: these friendships are more personal than political, but here again the lines are not clear; the salons are spaces in which personal friendships may result in political bondings'. These 'bondings', she goes on to argue, may result in friendships that are exclusively neither private nor public, but primarily civic: '[B]oth the polis and the salons contribute to the formation of "civic friendship", either among a group of citizens or among a group of private, like-minded individuals who can gather for a common political purpose' (20).

Although the Jewish community was at the heart of this salon culture, the salons brought together a mixed society of aristocratic and middle-class intellectuals and artists. What bound them together was that none of them fully belonged to respectable society. It was a social space within which Varnhagen's ambivalent status as part-pariah and part-parvenu was not entirely disadvantageous: a space within which a new ideal of humanity – the joy of conversation, the search for friendship, and the cultivation of intimacy within a setting that combines the public and the private – was generated and nourished. In what Arendt calls 'the vague, idyllic chaos which the Jewish salon of those days represented' (RV, 127), Varnhagen's own salon – situated in her attic room on Jägerstrasse – was preeminent. Attended by almost all the important intellectuals of Berlin – notably, Schleiermacher, Schlegel and Wilhelm von Humboldt – it became the intellectual hub of what we would now think of as German Romanticism.

While respectful of the salon culture, Arendt recognised its extreme vulnerability. The Jewish salon, she argued, 'had good luck for three decades', but 'was the product of a chance constellation in an era of social transition'. As such it did not signify 'that the German Jews had attained to social rootedness'. The opposite, she argued, was the case: 'precisely because the Jews stood outside of society they became, for a short time, a kind of neutral zone where people of culture met' (RV, 127). Within that zone they remained relatively safe: their exceptionalism provided them with some limited security. It was, ironically, as they became *un*exceptional – as they began to be assimilated – that they no longer had the protection of that neutrality and were perceived as a threat. This is the dilemma that constitutes Varnhagen's tragic fate: remain an outsider and risk being perceived as a 'pariah' or become a 'parvenu' and risk being excluded as a threat.

Varnhagen, insisted Arendt, cannot be abstracted from history, because her fate as a Jewish woman is implicated in the social and political transitions of her time. If history had provided Varnhagen – briefly – with a space for 'civic friendship', then it also provided her with the experience of inescapable exclusion. Friendship was not – and could never be – a means of escaping history. Written against the reality of the relentless rise of Nazism, *Rahel Varnhagen: The Life of a Jewess* bears testimony to the fragility of friendship and the vulnerability of the conditions necessary for friendship to flourish. She was prescient in foreseeing – if not the full horror of Nazism – the conjunction of historic forces that would render that unique and unprecedented version of fascism a possibility. It was with Varnhagen's condition as a Jewish woman – located at a particular point in time – that Arendt identified; and it is because of the nature of that identification that Arendt described Varnhagen as 'my closest friend, though she has been dead for some one hundred years' (quoted in Young-Bruehl, 1982, 56).

Arendt, in this early work, sought to derive meaning from a particular life – a life over which the person who lived it had no ultimate authority. Varnhagen, as Arendt shows, was born into a pre-existing web of human relationships within which her words and deeds initiated processes which, as well as affecting, were also affected by innumerable wills and actions of other actors and speakers. Varnhagen was not – and could not be – the author of her own life story because the processes she initiated were boundless, irreversible and unpredictable in their consequences. Nor, in seeking to derive meaning from Varnhagen's life, was Arendt claiming authorship of it. She was seeking, rather, to interpret it from her own historically located position as a Jewish woman living, like Varnhagen, through a period of immense social transition and political upheaval. Central to that interpretation was the significance of – and, crucially, the fragility of – friendship. For Varnhagen, as for Arendt, friendship promised some stability and continuity in a world of inescapable uncertainty. Indeed, it was that inescapable uncertainty that made friendship meaningful. But – and this is Arendt's central insight – it was that same uncertainty that renders friendship inescapably fragile. The world of human plurality that, in all its boundlessness, irreversibility and unpredictability, makes friendship possible renders it also chronically vulnerable from within and without.

Plurality brings with it the possibility of freedom and agency, which Arendt saw as necessary elements in friendship. But she also saw the need for continuity amidst the uncertainties that are inherent in a world of boundless plurality. The power of promise meets the challenge of plurality through engagement and complementarity. In the following four chapters, the twin themes of plurality and promise – of freedom and continuity, of uncertainty and security – are explored through four friendships that shaped Arendt's life and informed her work. They also trace – in retrospect – the arc of her movement from one world of ideas to another world of ideas. Her flight from the old world to the new world denoted, for her, a geographical shift of location, but was indicative also of a wider geopolitical shift in the world order. The implications of that geopolitical shift reverberated through Arendt's writing and had a profound influence on her life and work and on her personal and political commitments.

4

Arendt and Heidegger: The Struggle for Recognition

I think that one day, when it comes to Arendt and Heidegger ... we will need to talk openly, fittingly, philosophically, with due seriousness and at appropriate length, of the great shared passion that bound them together over what might be called 'a whole life', across or beyond continents, wars, the Holocaust.

Derrida, 11 January 1995, quoted in Peeters, 2013, 244

Unavoidable questions

Why did a Jewish woman – forced to flee Germany and then France in the face of Nazi persecution – choose to maintain a lifelong relationship with a man who had been actively and enthusiastically involved in pursuing anti-Semitic Nazi policies and who remained throughout his life unrepentant regarding that involvement? Any attempt to address this question is complicated by the fact that we cannot be sure when, or indeed whether, Arendt was aware of the *full* extent of Heidegger's active pursuit of those policies. Nevertheless, that involvement was sufficiently well known – and, indeed, a cause of scandal and outrage among academics and intellectuals not only in Germany but internationally – for the question to be unavoidable. We may quibble over the extent of Arendt's knowledge, but her awareness of Heidegger's complicity and culpability is beyond question. Nor was it something she ever sought to refute or deny. Indeed, there can be no denying that, as Richard Rorty (1990) puts it, 'Heidegger was a Nazi, a cowardly hypocrite, and the greatest European thinker of our time'.

However, there is a second complication which is more challenging. It is the concern expressed by Derrida, in the quotation at the head of this chapter, regarding the need to find the right angle of approach in addressing the question of Arendt's relationship with Heidegger. Continuing this line of thought, Derrida claims that 'this lifelong passion deserves better than what generally enshrouds it – an embarrassed or discreet silence on the one side, or, on the other, vulgar rumour or whispering in the corridors of academia' (Derrida, quoted in Peeters, 2013, 244). The 'vulgar rumour or whispering' may have diminished in volume since Derrida reportedly spoke these words in a 1995 seminar, but the problem of finding a way of talking 'openly, fittingly, philosophically' about this relationship has not gone away.

The broad outline of the relationship between Arendt and Heidegger has been common knowledge since the publication in 1982 of Young-Bruehl's biography, *Hannah Arendt: For Love of the World*. However, the correspondence between Arendt and Heidegger was not published until 1998 and only published as an English translation in 2004. Moreover, the published correspondence is both partial and one-sided, with only a quarter of the published letters having been written by Arendt. As Benhabib (2003, 225) points out: 'We do not know what happened to the rest of her letters. Did Heidegger destroy them in his efforts to conceal the affair? Did Arendt get rid of her own correspondence? Whatever the circumstances, Heidegger's voice and presence dominate the volume.' Given the limitations of the archive, the relationship continues to generate speculation.

Is the relationship to be understood as the eruption of Arendt's female side (Ettinger, 1995; Sherratt, 2013)? Was it a case of exploitation to which Arendt's youth and ambivalence regarding her own Jewish identity rendered her particularly vulnerable (Wolin, 2001)? Is it an instantiation of the power of redemptive forgiveness over vengeance (Kristeva, 2001; Maier-Katkin, 2010)? The assumptions underlying each of these questions undoubtedly contain an element of truth. Arendt's early encounter with Heidegger may have been a kind of chaotic self-surrender; Heidegger was exploitative and Arendt did throughout her life have a complex relationship with Judaism and, perhaps, with her own Jewish identity; and there may be something to be said for her having 'forgiven' Heidegger. She may have been – and, like most of us, probably was – sometimes daft, often confused regarding her identity, and occasionally drawn towards simple and other-worldly solutions to complex and worldly problems: precisely the qualities that would have rendered her, at eighteen years of age, susceptible to the predatory and exploitative practices of an older, authoritarian and charismatic character such as Heidegger.

Whatever interpretation we place on the relationship between Arendt and Heidegger should take account of a number of incontrovertible facts: the relationship was lifelong though intermittent; Arendt herself was instrumental in maintaining and ensuring its continuity; and the terms of the relationship changed significantly over time. Moreover, as Dana Villa (1996) has shown, they shared in their intellectual preoccupations 'something like a common problematic ... despite radical differences in emphasis and ultimate concern' (136). This was not a youthful indiscretion – or even a great lost love – that Arendt chose to expunge from her memory. Nor was it a passion that she occasionally dipped into as a diversionary stimulus. It was a relationship that she doggedly pursued – increasingly on her own terms – throughout her life. It was inextricable from the sense she had of herself. The irony is that Arendt's complex and troubled relationship with Heidegger – that prompts many commentators and critics to question or even challenge the esteem in which she is generally held as a public intellectual – was for Arendt herself a crucial element in her own self-esteem and sense of self-worth. Arendt, in maintaining lifelong contact with Heidegger, was not colluding in a chronic dependency relationship, but insisting upon and expressing her *in*dependence.

From the outset Arendt sought recognition from Heidegger: recognition of her full potential and of her achievements. Her insistence on a lasting friendship was above all a struggle for such recognition, since friendship was for Arendt conditional upon the mutual recognition by each friend of the equality and freedom of the other. To have given up on the possibility of a relationship based on friendship – through, for example, denial or incrimination – would have been to give up on that struggle. Arendt's insistence on holding open that possibility was neither an exercise in self-obeisance nor a self-sacrificial act of forgiveness. On the contrary, it was both self-assertive and self-preserving. The struggle for recognition was hard fought and – in the end – hard won by Arendt. But it had less to do with heart-over-head, cultural self-questioning or the recourse to Christian forgiveness than with the need for recognition as a precondition for self-realisation.

Shared passion

Arendt was barely eighteen when, in 1924, she entered the University of Marburg, a year after Heidegger had been elected to an extraordinary professorship in philosophy. Seventeen years older than Arendt, Heidegger was yet to publish his ground-breaking *Sein und Zeit* (*Being and Time*) but was already a hugely influential and charismatic figure. Karl Lowith, a student of both Husserl and Heidegger, described Heidegger as 'a small dark man who knew how to cast a spell in so far as he could make disappear what he had a moment before presented'. His lectures, Lowith added, 'consisted in building up an edifice of ideas which he then proceeded to tear down, presenting his spellbound listeners with a riddle and then leaving them empty-handed' (Lowith, 1994, 42–3, quoted in Sherratt, 2013, 194). Heidegger was also married – to Elfriede Petri – and had two sons: Jörg (born 1919) and Hermann (born 1920).

On 10 February 1925, Heidegger wrote to Arendt. It is not clear whether this is the first written correspondence between them, but it clearly marks a significant shift in the relationship. Heidegger refers to a visit Arendt had already made to his 'office hour', a time Heidegger presumably scheduled for individual tutorials with his students. However, we do not know how many times or on what basis Arendt and Heidegger had met prior to this particular 'office hour' visit. What is clear from the letter is that Heidegger is already establishing the terms of the relationship. The letter opens with an urgent demand: 'I must come see you this evening and speak to your heart'. While insisting that 'Everything should be simple and clear and pure between us' and that 'I will never be able to call you mine', he is clearly drawing her into a relationship that is far from 'simple and clear and pure' and over which he is assuming control. The subtext of the letter is not so much an invitation as a command to enter into a clandestine relationship with no strings attached: 'I will never be able to call you mine, but from now on you will belong in my life, and it shall grow with you' (AH, 3–4).

In none of the surviving letters from Heidegger in this earliest stage of the correspondence is there any sense of the particularity of the person with whom he is corresponding. Arendt is an 'innermost, purest feminine essence' (AH, 3), a 'girlish essence' (AH, 4), a 'womanly existence' (AH, 5). He is the protector: 'I can take care that nothing in you shatters; that any burden and pain you have had in the past is purified; that what is foreign to you and what has happened to you yields' (AH, 5). She is – or could be – the representative of 'womanly Being': 'May masculine inquiry learn what respect is from simple devotion; may one-sided activity learn breadth from the original unity of womanly Being' (AH, 5). He is intent upon defining her womanhood: 'Only when you are happy will you become a woman who can give happiness, and around whom all is happiness, security, repose, reverence, and gratitude to life' (AH, 4). Moreover, womanhood is to be found not in 'the forced academic activity of many of your sex', but in the 'preservation of one's innermost womanly essence' (AH, 4). Arendt is drawn close by being kept at a distance – 'distance that lets nothing blur' (AH, 5) – and in being kept at a distance gains the clarity of an abstraction.

By the end of February 1925 Heidegger has been shocked into the realisation that something had 'happened': 'The demonic struck me ... Nothing like it has ever happened to me'. Admittedly, between those last two sentences is inserted the usual sublimatory prose – 'The silent prayer of your beloved hands and your shining brow enveloped it in womanly transfiguration' – but Heidegger acknowledges that he has been 'struck'. (AH, 6) A month later – in a letter dated 21 March 1925 – Arendt is still 'the young girl', but is no longer just a daydream: 'I daydream about the young girl who, in a raincoat, her hat low over her quiet large eyes, entered my office for the first time, and softly and shyly gave a brief answer to each question – and then I transpose the image to the last day of the semester – and only then do I know that life is history' (AH, 9). Heidegger signs off this letter with 'I love you still'. Arendt is no longer *just* the passive female object within Heidegger's field of vision. She has within six weeks of the correspondence commencing become a presence.

However, she is not as yet a voice. Three days after the previous letter, Heidegger – now on his semester break – writes to inform Arendt that his younger son has pulled a tendon as a result of a skiing accident and that their next planned rendezvous may not therefore be possible. He signs off this letter with 'Best' and as 'Your Martin' (AH, 10). Five days later, Heidegger sends a brief missive informing Arendt that their meeting is off. This letter is simply signed off 'Best, M' (AH, 10). A fortnight later – 12 April 1925 – he writes 'in a frenzy of joy at your impending arrival' and thanks her for a card she has sent him. He is now simply 'Your M' (AH, 10–11). However, with the new semester about to start, Heidegger begins to turn his attention back to Arendt. He is anxious that she attends two days of lectures he is delivering as part of the Hessian Society for Art and Science at Kassel. On 17 April he writes to inform her of how they might meet at some point over the two days during which he will be delivering his lectures. He proposes to see her 'during the break on Monday evening'. He will be 'lodging near Wilhelmshohe Castle, very exclusive', while she can stay at the 'Stift' (i.e. a seminary or cathedral chapter). He does not know whether he will have time to pick her up when she arrives. However, after the Monday lecture he will, he informs her, 'take leave of my acquaintances and hosts and get on the No 1 tram to Wilhelmshohe, the last stop'. She will – 'discreetly' – take the next tram: 'Then I'll take you home'. He signs off this missive with 'See you soon' and, again, as 'Your Martin' (AH, 11–12).

While Heidegger was holidaying with his wife and two young sons during the spring semester break, Arendt was with her mother, stepfather and stepsisters in Königsberg. She spent some of her time writing a self-reflective – and self-dramatising – piece entitled 'Shadows', which she handed to Heidegger in Kassel. It is a relatively short piece of prose, but Arendt bound it as a booklet with a cover of thin blue-purple handmade cardboard (AH, 222). The contrast between Heidegger's situation and Arendt's is stark: he nested in a nuclear family and with the authority of a senior academic with an international reputation; she a first-year university student living in a house with her mother and a step-father and step-siblings with whom she had little in common. It is hardly surprising, therefore, that what she wrote evokes a sense of deep loneliness and longing. She writes about herself in the third person and characterises this self-as-another in terms that echo Heidegger's own characterisation of her as a 'girlish essence' emerging into 'womanly Being'. She writes of 'her quiet, barely awakened youth', of 'her helpless, betrayed youth' and of 'the shy austere morning of her young life' (AH, 12, 13, 14). 'Perhaps', she concludes, 'her youth will struggle free of the spell, perhaps her soul will realize what it is to speak out and to be released under a different sky' (AH, 16).

Heidegger responds to 'Shadows' by reassuring Arendt of his 'belief in the genuine, rich impulses of your existence'. He affirms, that is, her need 'to be realised under a different sky'. He assumes that the different sky in question lies over Marburg where under his tutelage he sees her flourishing: 'You were so happy when you arrived, sparkling and free, just as I hoped you would be on your return to Marburg. I was dazed by the splendour of this human essence' (AH, 17). Arendt, however, remains an 'essence': splendid but objectified. On that basis the relationship settles into a pattern of meetings, the erotic intensity of which were presumably heightened by the secrecy surrounding them. Arendt is in Heidegger's gaze. He notes her presence at his lectures, while also drawing her attention to his familial responsibilities regarding his sick children and Elfriede: 'I can't imagine how the household will be maintained. Surely some kind of help can still be found' (AH, 38). By the end of 1925 the relationship seems to have settled into what might be described as an 'extra-marital affair'. This settlement – managed with manipulative flair by Heidegger – seems to have been accepted by Arendt.

Arendt's side of this early stage of the correspondence has – as far as we know and for whatever reason – not survived. As Benhabib (2003, 225) points out: 'Whatever the circumstances, Heidegger's voice and presence dominate'. But Arendt's actions spoke louder than words. After a year and half of her secretive affair with Heidegger, Arendt moved to Heidelberg to study with Karl Jaspers. It is unclear whether in transferring her studies Arendt was pushed by Heidegger or pulled by her own desire for 'a different sky'. Possibly both. But in one of the few letters that survive from this early stage of correspondence, Arendt achieves authority – and voice – through her assessment of the situation: 'What I want to tell you now is nothing but, at heart, a very frank assessment of the situation. I love you as I did on the first day' (AH, 50). That is frank and straightforward. What follows is difficult and coded: 'But the desolation that fate kept in store ... would have blocked my path, which is wide and not a leap, runs through the world'. What did fate keep in store? What blocked her path? Why is the path wide and not a leap? We do not have the evidential wherewithal to answer these questions, but we do know that Arendt left Marburg and that in doing so she distanced herself geographically from Heidegger.

She maintained her relationship with Heidegger during her time in Heidelberg. But the geographical distance between them provided her with some psychological space within which to gather her resources. Since entering into the relationship with Heidegger, her sense of self – and of self-worth – had been shaped and moulded by his perception of her. Notwithstanding the complexities and tensions of conducting the affair at a distance, Arendt must have experienced a sense of freedom at Heidelberg. Their meetings became more sporadic and the relationship – although maintaining its emotional charge – seems to have become less relentless in its intensity. The final break in the relationship came when Arendt met Günther Stern in 1929 and married him later that year. Stern had been a student of Heidegger and had later been the victim of what in retrospect can be seen as Heidegger's characteristically unhelpful, ungenerous and self-important attitude towards fellow academics (AH, 37–8). The experience of having had to handle Heidegger's ego was one Arendt and Stern shared. Heidegger's treatment of Stern was sufficiently important to Arendt to warrant her alluding to it in a letter she wrote to Heidegger on the day of her wedding to Stern: '[A]s a way out of my restlessness, I have found a home and a sense of belonging with someone about whom you might understand it least of all' (AH, 51). (The dating of the letter is open to question, but if her use of 'today' in the letter is taken literally then it was indeed written on her wedding day.)

The fact that Arendt wrote to Heidegger on or even close to her wedding day hardly bode well for the marriage. Nor, indeed, was her characterisation of the marriage 'as a way out of my restlessness' a particularly promising start. Arendt's feelings towards Heidegger remained highly ambivalent. In the letter in question she writes: '[D]o not forget that our love has become the blessing of my life' (AH, 51). And she concludes the letter with what is clearly an invitation to maintain at least some communication between them: 'And I would indeed so like to know – almost tormentingly so, how you are doing, what you are working on … I kiss your brow and eyes' (AH, 51). Arendt signs off as 'Your Hannah' (AH, 51). In a further letter that seems to have been written the day after her marriage, Arendt refers to having just bumped into Heidegger quite by accident that same day and neither having initially recognised the other. Putting to one side the bizarre coincidence of this chance encounter, one is struck by the emotional turmoil expressed in the letter: 'So many things that had left me utterly confused came together. Not just, as always, how the sight of you always rekindles awareness of my life's clearest and most urgent continuity, of the continuity of our – *please* let me say it – love' (AH, 51).

What sense are we to make of this troubled and deeply troubling relationship? It seems to have little if anything to do with what Arendt came to think of as 'friendship'. It was premised not only on multiple inequalities, but also on Arendt's willingness to adopt – and adapt herself to – Heidegger's idealisation of her. Even if we judge that idealisation not to have been distorting, there can be no denying that it was hugely controlling. In spite of his endless insistence on enabling her to flourish, Heidegger curtailed her freedom and ensnared her in a relationship that it is very difficult not to define as exploitative. Arendt no doubt benefited intellectually from her conversations with Heidegger – and the erotic charge between them was clearly transformative for them both. But judged from a perspective for which Arendt came to have huge respect – namely, that of common sense or *sensus communis* – her relationship with Heidegger was something from which, and for her own good, she needed to escape.

The strange – and strangely reported – encounter between Arendt and Heidegger on the day after her marriage is perhaps emblematic of this early phase of their lifelong relationship. That encounter was characterised by lack of *recognition*. Heidegger failed to recognise Arendt; and Arendt failed to recognise Heidegger. Being recognised is, of course, different from being seen, in that it involves an appreciation of that which is distinctive in the object of perception. In his *The Struggle for Recognition: The Moral Grammar of Social Conflicts*, Axel Honneth (1995) wrote: 'Persons can feel themselves to be "valuable" only when they know themselves to be recognised for accomplishments that they precisely do not share in an undifferentiated manner with others' (125). Such recognition gives individuals the confidence to both articulate their needs and exercise their abilities: '[T]his sort of confidence, these unanxious ways of dealing with oneself, constitute aspects of a positive relation-to-self that can only be gained through the experience of recognition' (174). That experience, maintains Honneth, 'is dependent on prerequisites that human subjects do not have at their disposal, since they can only acquire this freedom with the help of their interaction partners' (174). If there is no one to recognise us we remain unrecognised, and – in remaining unrecognised – we lack the conditions necessary for individual freedom and self-realisation: we may be part of the visual field that constitutes the world of appearances, but remain undifferentiated within it. Our value – insofar as we are deemed to have any – is a function of the category that we are perceived to represent.

That is precisely the situation that Arendt found herself in when idealised as an 'innermost, purest feminine essence' (AH, 3), a 'girlish essence' (AH, 4), a 'womanly existence' (AH, 5). To be viewed in such a way may be immensely seductive, but is very different from being recognised. Recognition assumes differentiation. To be recognised is not only a matter of being seen, but of being seen as different; not only a matter of being heard, but of having one's own distinctive voice attended to. Arendt was, as the saying goes, seen but not heard. 'There is', as Jonathan Rée (2000) makes abundantly clear, 'nothing more personal than a voice'. Voices, he shows, are 'destined for other people: you speak, primarily, in order to be heard. And the idea of being heard, of possessing a voice or having it ignored or suppressed, of demanding, validating, giving or offering a voice – the voice of the people, the voice of God – nearly coincides with that of human and civil rights' (1).

Arendt failed to achieve that voice – that recognition – in the early stage of her relationship with Heidegger. But she craved it and struggled for it. Her carefully bound copy of 'Shadows', which she delivered to Heidegger while attending his lectures as his clandestine lover, bears testimony to that resolve. So, 'to talk openly, fittingly, philosophically, with due seriousness' of what Jacques Derrida calls 'the great shared passion' between Arendt and Heidegger is to speak of Arendt's struggle for recognition within that relationship. To be recognised by Heidegger was, for Arendt, to be *recognised*. Eighteen years were to elapse before she resumed that struggle.

Nazi years

In what might be read as a coda to the first phase of their relationship, Heidegger wrote to Arendt a letter dated 'Winter 1932/33'. Heidegger had by this time – in 1928 – been appointed as Husserl's successor to the highly prestigious chair of philosophy at the University of Freiberg. Heidegger's letter begins abruptly: 'The rumours that are upsetting you are slanders'. The rumours in question related to his alleged anti-Semitic discrimination against Jewish students and colleagues. The purpose of the letter is to rebut the accusations implicit in these rumours. By way of clarifying how he had behaved towards Jews, Heidegger provides what he terms a number of 'facts'. He justifies his alleged lack of availability on the grounds that 'I am on sabbatical this winter semester and thus in the summer I announced, well in advance, that I wanted to be left alone and would not be accepting projects and the like'. He then claims that, in spite of this, 'the man who comes anyway and urgently wants to write a dissertation is a Jew, while another man who comes to see me every month to report on a large work in progress (neither a dissertation nor a habilitation project) is also a Jew'. He has also been sent 'a substantial text for urgent reading' by a Jew. He has also, he claims, in the last three semesters, supported two applications for fellowships from Jews and supported a further fellowship for a Jew to study in Rome. 'Whoever', insists Heidegger, 'wants to call that "raging anti-Semitism" is welcome to do so' (AH, 52).

What is interesting about this response to the letter from Arendt – which for whatever reason does not as far as we know survive – is that Heidegger seems acutely aware of those of his academic associates who are Jewish. He has clearly identified them as such. This no doubt says a lot about the 'racially' defined context within which he was operating, but may also say something about Heidegger's own mind-set. It is also of interest that he interprets anti-Semitism entirely in terms of his interactions with individuals. There is no suggestion in his response that anti-Semitism may have its roots in ideology or history. If he were seriously rebutting the charge of 'raging anti-Semitism', then one might imagine he would have adopted a broader perspective. Instead he adopts an irritated and peremptory tone. 'This exchange', as Benhabib (2003, 226) puts it, 'remains one of the few instances in which Heidegger shows a temper and some anger'. Whatever letter Heidegger received from Arendt clearly rattled him.

Although the 'facts' contained in Heidegger's letter may have been accurate at the time of writing, they remain an extremely partial account of his dealings with fellow Jewish academics and his role as a senior academic during this period. Having been elected rector of the University of Freiberg on 21 April 1933, he became a member of the Nazi Party on 3 May. His inaugural address as rector at Freiberg was delivered on 27 May and began, after his Nazi salute, with the following homage to Hitler and the alignment of the German academy with the fascist state: 'The assumption of the office of rector is an obligation to the spiritual leadership of this university ... But this spirit achieves clarity, distinction and power only and above all when the leaders, Führer, are first led themselves – led by the relentlessness of the spiritual order that expresses its history through the fate of the German nation' (quoted in Sherratt, 2013, 116).

The anthem of the Nazi Party was printed on the back of the programme notes for the ceremony. The singing of the anthem was followed by the Nazi salute and the shouting of '*Sieg Heil*'.

Although Heidegger handed in his resignation as rector on 23 April 1934 – a point that is often made in mitigation of his support for Nazism – he remained a member of the Nazi Party to the end of the Third Reich (Benhabib, 2003, 227). During his tenure as rector he forbade a number of Jewish colleagues from entering the university or using its facilities, including his erstwhile teacher and mentor Edmund Husserl. During that tenure Heidegger clearly had the full confidence of the Nazi regime as is evidenced by a report of a meeting held in April 1933 between a small group of Nazi professors and the new Nazi secretary for higher education at the Ministry of Home Affairs in Karlsruhe. According to the report prepared by one of the professors present in these discussions, 'Heidegger ... enjoys our full confidence, and we would therefore ask you to regard him for the present as our spokesman here at the University of Freiberg' (Ott, 1993, 143–4). In 1945, partly as a result of a negative report from Jaspers regarding Heidegger's anti-Semitism, Heidegger was forced into retirement without licence to teach. Although the prohibition against his teaching was lifted in 1949 and Heidegger resumed his teaching at the University of Freiburg in 1951, it is difficult to find any grounds upon which to disagree with Benhabib (2003, 227) in her assessment of Heidegger during this period as 'a conniving opportunist'.

Heidegger's deeply conservative background and upbringing may go some way towards explaining his uncritical and indeed enthusiastic embrace of Nazism. He was born in 1889 – the same year as Hitler – in the small Bavarian town of Messkirch, which was dominated by its Roman Catholic heritage. The local peasant economy was based mainly on agriculture and crafts, although Heidegger himself was born into the lower middle class as a consequence of his father being a sexton at the local church. On leaving school, Heidegger entered a Jesuit seminary, served as a soldier during the last year of World War I, and in 1917 married Elfriede Petri. After the war he studied with Edmund Husserl and was employed as his assistant at the University of Freiberg. Husserl thereby became Heidegger's academic mentor and worked with him until 1923 when he obtained a post at the University of Marburg. It was there that from relatively humble origins and a rural background he achieved a reputation across Germany as a compelling lecturer and philosopher. He was also on the point of completing what in retrospect is generally judged to be one of the great works of the Western philosophical canon. He was influential and was achieving power within the university sector, but he was also relatively young and inexperienced. He had always lived in closed and rule-bound societies – Messkirch, the Jesuit seminary, the army – and was arguably ill-prepared for the demands of the post of elected rector at the University of Marburg. None of this in any way excuses Heidegger, but it may go some way towards explaining his opportunistic acquiescence to the cult of charismatic leadership and nationalistic fervour that Nazism employed as key element in its totalitarian armoury.

'Heidegger the fox'

In 1946 – some thirteen years after their last previously recorded correspondence and four years prior to the resumption of their correspondence – Arendt published an article entitled 'What is existential philosophy?' in which she adopted a critical position in relation to Heidegger's work. She begins her critique by noting what she calls Heidegger's 'terminological façade' and his 'obvious verbal tricks and sophistries' (EU, 176). She then identifies what she sees as Heidegger's central insight; namely, that the self has no substance other than its own existence. She argues that 'Heidegger claims to have found a being in whom essence and existence are identical, and that being is man. His essence is his existence ... Man has no substance; he consists in the fact *that* he is' (177). This formulation, she adds, 'puts man in the exact same place that God had occupied in traditional ontology' (178). If the 'essence' of the self is its absence of 'substance', then being and nothingness are inextricably linked. Man – like the God of Heidegger's Jesuit seminary – is the great 'I am' and nothing but the great 'I am'.

Arendt then proceeds to draw out what she sees as some of the implications of this central insight. The first such implication is that Heidegger has clearly turned the theistic world of his Judeo-Christian upbringing upside-down: 'Heidegger's is the first absolutely and uncompromisingly this-world philosophy' (179). This judgement regarding the unique and unprecedented nature of Heidegger's philosophy seems exaggerated if not hyperbolic, but it does allow Arendt to draw out a second implication regarding the unavoidable alienation of the human condition as understood by Heidegger: 'The crucial element of man's being is its being-in-the-world, and what is at stake for his being-in-the-world is quite simply survival in the world. That is the very thing that is denied man, and consequently the basic mode of being-in-the-world is alienation, which is felt as both homelessness and anxiety' (179). If man is the master of his own being, then the price he pays for that mastery is chronic and inescapable alienation: 'The essential character of the Self is its absolute Self-ness, its radical separation from all its fellows' (181).

The third implication Arendt draws from what she sees as Heidegger's big idea is that it opens itself to 'mythologising and muddled concepts like "folk" and "earth" in an effort to supply his isolated Selves with a shared, common ground to stand on' (181). In retrospect this is a clear reference to Heidegger's Nazi affiliations, although at the time the reference to 'folk' and 'earth' may have been less obvious. In terms of the conceptual distinctions she was developing at the time, Heidegger's mode of thought is unpolitical and possibly even apolitical. Heidegger's philosophy, she concludes, leads to 'some kind of nature-oriented superstition', whereby human beings are alienated from that which defines their humanity: 'If it does not belong to the concept of man that he inhabits the earth together with others of his kind, then all that remains for him is a mechanical reconciliation by which the atomized Selves are provided with a common ground that is essentially alien to their nature' (181). Heidegger has, as Arendt sees it, entrapped himself in an elegant system of thought from which there is, and can be, no escape: no recognition, that is, of human plurality and the power implicit in that plurality.

Six years after the publication of this piece – and shortly after she has resumed contact with Heidegger – Arendt enters into her diary what she calls 'the true story of Heidegger the fox' (AH, 304). It is a relatively short entry written as a fable in which Heidegger is depicted as a somewhat incompetent fox that fails to realise he is himself caught in a trap into which he is seeking to lure others. However, 'nobody could really fall into his trap, because he was sitting in it himself' (AH, 305). The fox then hits on the idea of making the trap as beautiful as possible in order to entice others into it. Many were enticed into the trap: 'If one wanted to visit him in the den where he was at home, one had to go into his trap' (AH, 305). But, according to Arendt's fable, the sad irony was that everybody could walk out of the trap except the fox. The even sadder irony was that the fox failed to realise the extent of his own entrapment: '[T]he fox living in the trap said proudly: So many fall into my trap; I have become the best of all foxes' (AH, 305).

In these two pieces – one her public assessment of existentialism and the other a private diary entry – Arendt is clearly positioning herself not only in relation to but also *against* Heidegger's way of thinking. Neither critique is directly *ad hominem*: the 1946 article deals with Heidegger's thought and the 1952 diary entry deals with a metaphorical or mythical Heidegger. However, in both cases Arendt is undoubtedly and emphatically putting Heidegger in his place. Both pieces were written as Arendt was either about to resume or had recently resumed contact with Heidegger. Perhaps, in order to re-enter the trap and be assured of being able to walk out unscathed, Arendt had to get the measure of Heidegger. In both these very different pieces Arendt is intent upon establishing an intellectual and philosophical distance between herself and her former lover. In so doing she was perhaps – and perhaps unwittingly – fighting for the renewal of their relationship based, this time round, on the kind of mutual recognition that informs what she understood by friendship.

Troubled reunions

In 1950, then, a second phase in Arendt's and Heidegger's relationship begins. During a trip to Europe she met with Heidegger in February of that year and also visited him and his wife, Elfriede, at their home in Freiburg. This would seem to have been a difficult meeting. Elfriede by now knew of her husband's earlier relationship with Arendt. Writing to Arendt in the immediate aftermath of this meeting, Heidegger feels it necessary to interpret and to some extent justify his wife's attitude. He claims that the purpose of what he calls 'the exchange' was to 'enter the pure element of conscious trust among us three'. He insists that Elfriede's words 'were aimed *only* at *that*; they were not meant as a demand for you to make any confession of guilt to her'. While not acknowledging his own guilt, he does admit to 'the taint that had necessarily marked it because of *my* silence'. However, he immediately exonerates himself by means of a tortuous argument that his silence was not an abuse of Elfriede's trust, but an affirmation of the trust between himself and his wife: 'In fact, it was because I knew that my wife would not just understand but also affirm the joyousness and the richness of our [i.e. Arendt's and his] love as a gift of fate that I pushed her trust aside' (AH, 58). In other words, it was simply because Heidegger was so sure that Elfriede would be understanding of his infidelity that he did not bother to tell her about it!

Arendt responded immediately by letter from the hotel where she was staying in Freiburg. She wrote that she had come to Heidegger's home 'without knowing what your wife expected of me'. She had been 'shaken by the honesty and urgency of the reproach', but had chosen to remain silent not just 'as a matter of discretion, but also as a matter of pride'. She then adds that her refusal to respond to whatever reproach had been levelled against her by Elfriede was also 'a matter of love for you – not to make anything more difficult than it must be'. Finally, in an allusion to her transfer of studies from Marburg to Heidelberg, she declares: 'I left Marburg exclusively for you' (AH, 60). Shortly after sending this letter to Heidegger she wrote to Elfriede addressing her as 'Mrs Heidegger'. She briefly puts her side of the story, but without any attempt at self-justification. She offers no excuses: 'You did not expect one, after all, and I could not provide one, either'. She claims not to have realised that any explanation was required, 'because I did things later in connection with this affair that were so much worse that I did not remember the early things at all'. Explaining these later 'things', she writes: 'You see, when I left Marburg, I was quite firmly determined never to love a man again, and then later I married, somehow indifferent as to whom I was remarrying, without being in love. All this changed only when I met my current husband' (AH, 61).

The letter from Arendt to Elfriede also contains a forthright reference to the latter's Nazi sympathies and anti-Semitic convictions: 'You never made a secret of your convictions, after all, nor do you today, not even to me. Now, as a result of those convictions, a conversation is almost impossible, because what the other might say is, after all, already characterized and (forgive me) categorized in advance – Jewish, German, Chinese' (AH, 61–2). This issue is raised by Arendt not in an accusatory fashion, but by way of an invitation to talk about the matter further on condition that any such talk would be undertaken on Arendt's terms: 'I am ready at any time, and I said as much to Martin, to talk about such issues in an objective, political way – I like to think I know a few things about them – but only on the conviction that personal, human issues are kept out of it' (AH, 62). Arendt seems to be saying that she is willing to discuss racism and nationalism, but not if the assumption of racist and nationalist categories constitutes a precondition of discussion. Such a discussion would, therefore, be 'almost impossible' (as she put it) with those for whom such categories are non-negotiable. Nevertheless, Arendt closes this letter with the statement that 'We will see each other again soon' and with the request that Elfriede accepts the letter 'as a greeting and as thanks' (AH, 62).

This is a remarkable letter. We need to recall that Arendt had, at the age of eighteen, entered into a romantic and presumably sexual relationship with a married man who was considerably older than her and who, as her academic supervisor, exercised a position of power over her. She was also a German Jew who had been forced to flee her homeland as a result of a fascist regime that had been supported both by the woman whom she was addressing and the husband of that woman. Yet, it is Arendt who undoubtedly takes control of this complex situation. She clarifies the issues and keeps open the possibility of future dialogue. She also enters and exits Freiburg on her own terms in a hired car and stays at a hotel of her own choice. Heidegger, on the other hand, is entrapped in Freiburg having been granted retirement from the university and been ostracised from the wider community of scholars within and beyond Europe as a result of his support of and collaboration with the Nazi regime. Arendt's letter seems to suggest that she realises the significance of the shift in the power relation between herself and Heidegger. There is no record of Elfriede's response, and beyond this initial interchange in the second phase of their correspondence the vast majority of letters that have survived are those written by Heidegger. His subsequent correspondence suggests that he chose to ignore that subtle but irreversible shift.

In the ensuing correspondence Heidegger is intent upon establishing a sense of accord between Arendt, Elfriede and himself. Just a few days after Arendt had sent her letter to Elfriede, Heidegger informs Arendt that 'the spontaneous harmony between my wife and you is something that will last'. Given the tenor of Arendt's letter, 'spontaneous harmony' seems somewhat optimistic, as does Heidegger's following comment that 'all that remains is a minor resolution of a misunderstanding whose real root may be in the superficial talk of others' (AH, 65). If the 'misunderstanding' in question relates to Elfriede's 'convictions' as alluded to in Arendt's earlier letter, then something more than 'a minor resolution' would surely have been required. Heidegger seems intent upon disregarding these differences and creating a sense of comfortable unity in which Arendt and Elfriede will both love him while remaining in harmony with each other. A month later he implores Arendt to 'stay close to Elfriede' and again fails to acknowledge the complication of the situation and the complex emotions of all those involved: 'I need her love, which bore everything in silence through the years and still has room to grow. I need your love, which, mysteriously maintained in its early seeds, brings hers from its depths'. He even wants to draw Arendt's second husband, Heinrich Blücher, into this harmonious fantasy world: 'In the same way, I also want to nurture in my heart a silent friendship with your husband, who became your companion in those years of suffering' (AH, 71).

In these letters Heidegger is also constantly inviting Arendt into what she, in her 'true story of Heidegger the fox', termed his 'nature-oriented superstition'. Here his desire for a return to organic nature complements his need for harmony and symmetry in the triangular relationship between himself, his wife and Arendt. In the letter in which he tells her to 'stay close to Elfriede', he also writes: 'Hannah, when the city tears at you furiously, think of the straight firs towering up before us, into the light air of midday in the winter mountains' (HA, 72). In a later letter he asks: 'Hannah, have you seen the brown of a freshly ploughed field in the light of dusk?' (AH, 76). Arendt was by this time firmly established in New York as a cosmopolitan intellectual. Insisting upon this dichotomy between the city 'that tears at you furiously' and 'the straight firs towering up before us', Heidegger hopelessly misplaces Arendt. Of course, Arendt may have colluded in this fantasy. On the evidence available, she does not seem to have seriously challenged it. Nevertheless, Heidegger's constant allusions to Arendt as a child of nature are – as well as being mawkish – almost comically inappropriate.

While seeking to infantilise Arendt – 'the woman is hidden in the girl, the girl in the woman' (AH, 79) – Heidegger was also attempting to use her as means of re-establishing contact with former colleagues. An ongoing theme during this phase of the correspondence is his lack of contact with Jaspers, with whom Arendt is – as Heidegger knows – in regular contact. He complains that Jaspers did not write to him during the war years, which is hardly surprising given that Jaspers' wife, Gertrud, was a Jew and that Jaspers was highly critical of Heidegger's support for the Nazi regime. He further complains that Jaspers did not refer to him by name in the relevant volume of his recently published three-volume *Philosophy* (AH, 83–5). A little later in the correspondence he writes: 'Jaspers writes you regularly ... He has not answered my two letters from April'. He then complains about 'a rather unpleasant review' of his work that had been written by a former student of Jaspers and adds that 'it is generally assumed that Jaspers is behind it' (AH, 95–6).

In what can be seen as an instance of the self-entrapment alluded to by Arendt in her fox fable, Heidegger clearly required access to Arendt's international networks but could not bring himself to acknowledge the intellectual achievements that had established her as an influential figure across those networks. Responding to the announcement of the publication of her *The Origins of Totalitarianism*, he remarks: 'I wanted to ask about my writings in the previous letter, because I was surprised you had not mentioned any of them' (AH, 103). When, shortly after, he receives from her a copy of the book, his response is: 'We thank you for your book, which, with my poor English skills, I cannot read'. He then adds insult to injury by telling Arendt that 'Elfriede will be very interested in it, but at the moment we and the house are too agitated' (AH, 105). His obsessive regard for his own work and academic career are in stark contrast to his almost complete silence regarding her work and achievements. He is in such a state of denial regarding her public success that he cannot tolerate any evidence of it.

In May 1952 Arendt again visits Heidegger in Freiburg, attending one of his seminars and meeting with both him and Elfriede on several occasions. At one of the meetings Elfriede, far from displaying 'spontaneous harmony', erupted in a display of anger and jealousy. Following that meeting Heidegger wrote a brief letter to Arendt informing her that his cold was getting worse and that he felt tired. He added: 'It is best if you *do not write* now and *do not come visit* either. Everything is *painful and difficult*. But we must bear it' (AH, 112). After that the correspondence is much more sporadic. In 1954 Arendt provided advice and professional support in preparing an English edition of Heidegger's *Being and Time*, taking it upon herself to enter into a correspondence with the translator on points of detail. At the same time she informed Heidegger about her ongoing work on *The Human Condition*, but he made no mention of this in the ensuing correspondence. In 1960 she sent him the German edition of the book (which she herself had translated), telling him that it 'owes practically everything to you in every respect' and that 'if things had worked out differently between us ... I would have asked you if I might dedicate it to you' (AH, 124). There is no evidence in the surviving correspondence that he either acknowledged this gift or responded to her comments regarding the dedication. At this point the correspondence virtually dried up, although in April 1965 he sent her a belated thank-you card for 'greetings, good wishes, and gifts' sent to him on his seventy-fifth birthday (AH, 124).

If it was indeed recognition that Arendt was seeking, then her attempt to renew their relationship on the basis of a mature friendship was hardly a rip-roaring success: she had come to him on her own terms as a strong woman who was gaining fulfilment in both her private and public lives; he had refused to acknowledge the achievements that had contributed to her sense of self-fulfilment and, in addition, had sought to impose his own terms on the relationship. Those terms included a seemingly impossible rapprochement between his ex-lover (Arendt) and his wife (Elfriede) and the tacit assumption of harmonious accord between the three of them. Arendt's public presence was acknowledged only insofar as it was useful to Heidegger in his attempt at academic rehabilitation. In all other respects it lay entirely outside his field of vision.

Heidegger was adept at establishing no-go areas and protecting them by means of elaborate smokescreens of fantasy and romance. The jangling asymmetries that characterised the relationship between Arendt, Elfriede and himself were spirited away into an impossible 'harmonious symmetry'. Similarly, his own colossal failures of judgement and acts of disloyalty and betrayal towards former colleagues were shrouded in a thick fog of self-justification, self-pity and disingenuous claims regarding his own naivety: 'I am neither experienced nor talented in the domain of the political' (AH, 76). Far from resolving the question posed by Benhabib (2003, 225), Arendt's post-war reunion with Heidegger highlights its intractability: 'How could she justify to herself, as a persecuted Jewish émigré and public intellectual who reflected deeply and brilliantly about Jews, Germans, and the Holocaust, her continuing friendship, affection, and loyalty to this man?'

A kind of settlement

That, of course, is Benhabib's question – and *our* question as we struggle to understand this seemingly tangled relationship – but it was *not* Arendt's question. The moral problem as experienced by Arendt presented itself in very different terms. The question for her was not 'How can I justify to myself my continuing friendship, affection, and loyalty to this man?', but 'Given the irreversibility of my original encounter with this man, on what terms should I live out the consequences of that encounter?' Her answer to her own question would seem to have been something like: 'On the terms defined by friendship'. So, the struggle for *recognition* was unavoidable, since without it there could be no friendship as Arendt understood friendship. She achieved that recognition in what might be seen as the final phase of their relationship, but at considerable reputational cost. It is the final cost of that struggle for recognition that perhaps Benhabib – and we – question from our various retrospective positions. However, Arendt could – like the rest of us – only live life forward. She chose always to live with the unpredictable consequences of her own actions. Exit, for Arendt, was not an option.

The final phase of their relationship commenced in July 1967 when Arendt delivered a lecture on Walter Benjamin at the University of Freiburg. Heidegger knew about the lecture in advance and was present. This, as far as we know, was the first time they had met since 1952. The lecture – delivered in the main lecture hall of the university by a leading public intellectual – was a reversal of the circumstances under which they had first met: then, the young Arendt caught the attention of the renowned philosopher as he stood at the podium; now the elderly Heidegger not only caught the attention of, but was addressed directly by Arendt as she began her lecture (AH, 129). Arendt and Heidegger had kept in intermittent contact over the years and he had sent her a sixtieth birthday greeting the previous year (AH, 127–8). Also, by this time, Arendt was sixty and Heidegger was seventy-seven. Both were established but highly controversial figures: he a great philosopher who had actively supported the Nazi regime during World War II, and she a Jewish public intellectual who was considered by many to have betrayed the Jewish people through her coverage of the Eichmann trial in 1961.

The correspondence then resumed with many more of Arendt's letters surviving during this final phase and with a fairly regular flow of letters between them. The correspondence is much more relaxed, focusing largely on Heidegger's work but also on areas of mutual philosophical interest. Heidegger also acknowledges, at the beginning of this final phase of their correspondence, Arendt's achievements: '[F]or the insightful, your lecture was effective simply because of its level and its structure. Such work is increasingly vanishing from our universities, along with even the courage to describe things as they are' (AH, 129). This was hardly a eulogy, but it was at least an acknowledgement – and an endorsement – of her intellectual accomplishments. His ensuing letters lack the mawkish tone of some of his earlier correspondence and her side of the exchange is much more confident. Insofar as Elfriede is mentioned, it is by way of mutual 'regard' rather than any attempt to fictionalise their triangular relationship into a non-existent loving harmony.

In 1969 Arendt and her husband visited Heidegger and his wife. The visit seems to have been amicable on all sides. Later the same year Arendt delivered a radio broadcast in tribute to Heidegger on his eightieth birthday. In it she paid tribute to Heidegger's mode of thought: 'Heidegger never thinks "about" something; he thinks something' (AH, 152). Such thinking, she claimed, may set itself tasks and address problems: '[I]t always has some specific issue, of course, that it is currently occupied with or, more precisely, excited about – but one cannot say it has a goal. It is constantly active, and even the marking out of paths is more a matter of opening up a dimension than of reaching a goal that is first sighted and then aimed at' (AH, 152). In contrast to 'the old oppositions of reason and passion, of mind and life', Heidegger embodied 'the idea of a *passionate* thinking, in which thinking and being alive become one' (AH, 153). Heidegger in other words was, for Arendt, the supreme teacher, who modelled what thinking is and how – at best – thinking works.

Towards the end of her broadcast script she touched on the issue of Heidegger's wartime record. She appeared to switch tack, no longer arguing for the unity of thinking and being, but for their disunity. Heidegger, she argued, briefly – 'ten short, hectic months 35 years ago', as she put it – changed 'residence' from the world of thought in which he was at home to the world of human affairs in which he was a stranger. She claimed that Heidegger recognised his 'mistake' and that, having done so, he 'risked considerably more than was common at German universities back then'. He then, she claimed, 'let what he had experienced take deep root in his thinking' (HA, 160–1). This is a clear reference to Heidegger's own self-justification based on the fact that he had resigned as rector of the University of Freiburg after one year.

Arendt chose to overlook Heidegger's continuing membership of the Nazi Party, the anti-Semitic discrimination he had practised against Jewish colleagues, and his continuing failure to account for his convictions and behaviour during this period: either she was being highly selective regarding the facts of the case or she had allowed herself to remain in ignorance of those facts. This later endorsement of Heidegger is – in comparison to her 1946 essay, 'What is existential philosophy?' – remarkable in its lack of critical engagement with Heidegger's legacy. In a briefer statement published after Heidegger's death, Arendt's vindication of him is if anything even more explicit: 'May those who come after us, when they recall our century and its people and try to keep faith with them, not forget the devastating sandstorms that swept us up, each in his own way, and in which something like this man and his work were still possible' (AH, 163).

Arendt's friendship with Heidegger was hard-won and complex. Perhaps until the end it entailed elements of the erotic. It was dutiful – on her behalf – and in its final phase would seem to have provided each of them with the pleasure of talking together about the ideas that each of them had struggled with for a lifetime. The friendship managed – rightly or wrongly – to survive the huge differences that divided them. It finally provided Arendt with the recognition she had craved. Had Arendt been able to read the letter that Heidegger addressed to Hans Jonas after her death she might well have felt that at last she had won the struggle for recognition. In what was hardly a ringing endorsement, but at least an acknowledgement of Arendt's public presence, Heidegger wrote: 'Hannah was the center of a large, diverse circle'. On the highly restrictive scale of Heideggerian magnanimity, this faint praise amounted to an endorsement *cum laude*.

If we learn anything from this relationship about the nature of friendship, it is that friendship is a complex compound. Arendt's friendship with Heidegger grew out of an intensely erotic and troubled relationship. It was not a complete and perfect friendship as idealised by Montaigne, but in many ways an incomplete and imperfect friendship: a muddle in which anger, disappointment, resentment, but also an intuitive and undeniable affinity played their part. It built on that residue of erotic passion and its accompanying guilt and hurt. It is a relationship that could be categorised in very many ways. That it developed into friendship was largely as a result of Arendt's perseverance and sheer stubbornness. Insofar as it was a friendship, it was not one based on political solidarity. On the contrary, it endured radical political difference. Throughout their lifelong relationship Arendt displayed a sense of almost dogged duty towards Heidegger, but her overriding need was to gain his recognition. She needed him to recognise her as she recognised him. In the end she gained a begrudging recognition, but at a huge cost.

5

Arendt and Jaspers: Becoming Worldly

To see and understand the others helps in the achievement of clarity about oneself, in overcoming the potential narrowness of all self-enclosed historicity, and in casting off towards far horizons. This risking of boundless communication is once again the secret of becoming-human, not as it occurred in the inaccessible prehistoric past, but as it takes place within ourselves.

Jaspers, 1994, 387

Life before Arendt

To move from the correspondence between Arendt and Heidegger to that between Arendt and Jaspers is to move from the half-light to the full blaze of communicative transparency. If Arendt's friendship with Heidegger constituted a lifelong struggle for recognition *within* their relationship, then her friendship with Jaspers was based on their mutual need for dialogue that recognised the world *beyond* the parameters of their relationship. Their friendship was framed by their mutual concern for the world. Throughout the forty-three years of their recorded correspondence (from 1926 to 1969) they engaged with world events and refined their own position in relation to those events through a process of continuing critical dialogue. It is a rare record of a sustained correspondence between two public intellectuals who shared a desire to understand the mid-twentieth-century world through which they were living.

Jaspers' early life prior to his meeting Arendt was characterised by his chronic ill health, his relationship with his family and with his brother in particular, and his deep commitment to Gertrud Mayer, whom he married in 1910. He was a man full of contradictions: an intensely private man who lived and flourished through his relationships with others; a German patriot who demanded that post-war Germany acknowledge its own guilt and restore itself from the basis of that acknowledgement; a psychiatrist who rejected the psychiatric categorisation of mental disorder; a philosopher who sought to de-philosophise philosophy. For Arendt, Jaspers personified a philosophical outlook that insisted on 'the fact that not Man, talking to himself in the dialogue of solitude, but men, talking and communicating with each other, inhabit the earth' (MDT, 90).

Jaspers was born in 1883 in Oldenburg, which is located in the north-western region of Germany. In 1901 he began studying law at the University of Freiberg. However, his studies were interrupted by his being diagnosed as suffering from bronchiectasis (an obstructive lung disease). Jaspers used this interruption as an opportunity to persuade his family (and his father in particular) that his association with the law faculty had been an error of judgement and that he wished to pursue his academic studies through empirically grounded scientific inquiry. His ultimate goal as he saw it was philosophy, but he saw his own route to that goal not through the study of law but through the natural sciences. With his family's financial and moral support he switched to studying medicine at the University of Heidelberg. While Heidelberg remained his main base, he also spent some time at the Universities of Munich, Berlin and Gottingen, before passing the medical state examination in 1908 with a doctoral dissertation on the theme of 'homesickness and crime': the interplay, as we might now see it, between belongingness and criminality.

Between the diagnosis of his medical condition and the completion of his doctoral thesis, three significant occurrences had intervened that were to shape his life and intellectual career. The first and most significant of these was his meeting with Gertrud Mayer on 14 July 1907. He was twenty-four and she was four years older. Within a month they became secretly engaged and openly married on 29 September 1910. Later, as part of an autobiographical sketch that Jaspers presented on a German television network in 1966–1967, he recalled his first meeting with Gertrud as a lightning strike: 'During this visit something like a bolt of lightning struck us both. This occurred in the very first moment when Gertrud, still with her back toward me, got up and turned to face me. It was as if in this moment two people met who had been bound to each other since time immemorial' (Jaspers, 1994, 524).

Gertrud opened Jaspers to the world. 'Their friendship', as Suzanne Kirkbright (2004, 51) noted, 'released Jaspers from his solitary lifestyle'. But – because Gertrud was a Jew and he a Gentile and they were both Germans living in the first half of the twentieth century – it also meant that he was bound into a commitment that would require some hard choices. Dismissed by the Nazi regime from his post at Heidelberg University in 1937, his plans to take up posts in Oxford, Paris and Basel all failed – in part because of the difficulties of gaining an exit visa for Gertrud. In 1943 there was an official ban on the publication of his work.

Yet Jaspers' commitment to Gertrud never wavered. Nor is there any indication that it became begrudgingly dutiful. Among his papers that were discovered after his death was the draft of a eulogy for Gertrud that he had prepared in the event of her death – she died five years after him and the eulogy was read out at her funeral:

> In loving struggle we wandered through this wondrous, magnificent and terrible life, bound to one another within this world from the first moment of our meeting, entirely different from each other in the basic tenor of life, in feelings, in our psychology, and yet united even to the point of mutual contradiction within that transcendent of which it is not possible to speak in an appropriate manner.
>
> Jaspers, 1994, 526

The second significant occurrence was his encounter with the visual arts that infused his relationships and his work with a new vigour and creativity. Jaspers first visited Paris with Gertrud in 1912. Here – at the museum in the Jardin du Luxembourg – he had his first encounter with the Impressionists: Manet, Monet, Pissarro, Renoir and Sisley in particular. Later that year Jaspers visited the International Art Exhibition in Cologne where he viewed work by van Gogh, Cézanne and Gauguin. Jaspers was by no means a newcomer to art, since his father was a serious painter and he had been brought up with a deep respect for the visual arts. But his introduction to Impressionism, which was at the time still highly controversial, was deeply liberating in new and unexpected ways. He saw in the texture of van Gogh's paintings – in, for example, the pattern, pace and intensity of brushstrokes – the need that the artist felt to depict reality through her or his expression of that reality. It was a reality hit head-on: an intersubjective collision rather than a reality that one made prior sense of and then objectively depicted.

What Jaspers discovered in the work of van Gogh had a profound effect on his view of psychotherapeutic practice and the working out of his philosophical ideas. He developed a sceptical attitude towards forms of therapeutic practice that allotted specific cases in relation to pre-specified categories: a scepticism that resulted in his becoming increasingly distanced from Freudian modes of analysis. His preferred approach to analysis was deeply inductive and grounded in an understanding of the particularities of each specific case. Jaspers' intense 'seeing' of the immediacy of van Gogh's art played back into his thinking about intersubjectivity – about what it means to understand another human being. Human 'being' – the experience of being human – can only be understood in its irreducible specificity.

His way of seeing – and experiencing – particular works of art also contributed to what might be seen as his major conceptual contribution to philosophy: namely, his notion of 'limit situations'. Such situations, as he argued in the second volume of his three-volume *Philosophy* (Jaspers, 1969–1971), never change and present themselves as insurmountable and non-negotiable walls that constrain and limit us. Such situations cannot be modified or explained through deduction: they can only be elucidated through depiction; they have to be confronted; they go with the mortal territory of humanity. Far from being deterministic, such a view suggests that only by acknowledging our mortal limits can we begin to control our own destinies and in so doing take possession of our lives. Human agency is contingent upon the agent's awareness of the provisionality and conditionality of all human action.

When we look at the great works of van Gogh's middle period – for example, his *Sower* of December 1882, his *Weaver* of March 1884 or *The Potato Eaters* of April 1885 – we are faced with the 'limit situations' of the peasants whose working lives he was depicting. Within the ultimate 'limit situation' of mortality itself are the further limitations imposed by grinding poverty and the deprivations occasioned by such poverty: lack of mobility, lack of choice in anything other than the basic necessities, and an almost complete lack of opportunity other than the opportunity for endless repetition. What Jaspers took from van Gogh was the need to see human situations prior to any attempt to analyse them: the analysis would – and could only – emerge from the seeing. It is only by encountering our 'limit situations' that we begin to take control of our own existence.

The third occurrence was the death of his younger brother, Enno, in 1931. The two brothers had never enjoyed an easy relationship. In 1907 – when Enno was eighteen and Jaspers twenty-four – Enno wrote to his brother accusing him of avoiding direct contact with others and implying that he was using his illness as a means of avoidance. Jaspers, on the other hand, increasingly saw Enno as profligate and ill-disciplined – or, as he put it in a letter to his parents in 1926: 'He cannot do anything with himself and is seized by a greed for entertainment, activity and adventure that are only to be satisfied with financial means that are considerable' (quoted in Kirkbright, 2004, 104–5). Each was to some extent the other's alter ego, but the relationship never seems to have settled down into amicable complementarity. On the contrary, the differences increased and the tensions intensified as they grew into adulthood.

After two bankruptcies and an increasing dependency on heroin, Enno confronted the ultimate 'limit situation' and opted for what he presumably saw as the only available exit route – suicide. Jaspers had tried to support him through his heroin addiction and the severe financial problems that in turn had serious consequences for the family finances. However, in what was to be the final year of Enno's life, Jaspers suggested to his sister that they should refuse the sum of money requested by Enno from the family estate and instead provide a more limited allowance. Within a month Enno had poisoned himself. Jaspers was unable to attend the funeral as a result of his own ill health – an absence that Enno would no doubt have interpreted as a further act of avoidance by his elder brother.

Only in 1966 – twenty-five years after the event – did he share with Arendt the circumstances relating to his brother's death:

> My brother committed suicide with heroin, which, if you have the connections, you can acquire in the illegal drug trade. He lost consciousness after a few hours and noticed before he did that he was unable to swallow. My mother, observant as she was, realized what was happening but put off calling a doctor and said nothing to my father. Then she called a friend of Enno's who was the director of the hospital in Oldenburg and said to him: 'Gerhard, you must pump out his stomach. This is what Enno wanted.' And Gerhard proved himself a loyal friend.
>
> AJ, 652–3

From mentor to friend

By the time of Enno Jaspers' death in 1931, Arendt had moved to Berlin with her first husband, Günther Stern, and begun work on *Rahel Varnhagen: the Life of a Jewess*. Jaspers was still very much her mentor, having taken over her doctoral supervision in 1926. However, by the early 1930s the relationship had begun to shift towards something more akin to friendship. Paradoxically, one of the main factors influencing this shift was a disagreement between them – or, more specifically, Arendt's honesty in making explicit their difference of viewpoint. On this particular occasion the difference arose as a result of Jaspers having sent Arendt a book he had written on Max Weber and that was published in 1932 with the subtitle 'the German essence in political thought, in scholarship, and in philosophy'. In a letter dated 1 January 1933, Arendt thanked him for the book and then went on to say that although it did not bother her that he had portrayed Weber as 'the great German' it did bother her that he found 'the German essence' in Weber and identified that essence with 'rationality and humanity originating in passion'. She had 'the same difficulty with that as . . . with Max Weber's imposing patriotism itself'. As a German Jew she identified primarily with the Jewish people so that any notions of 'the German essence' or of German 'patriotism', while irrelevant to her personally, were in her view politically naïve and intellectually muddled (AJ, 16).

Arendt's willingness to speak her mind – together with Jaspers' open and generous response to her doing so – paved the way for what would become a continuing dialogue that enabled them to go on formulating and reformulating their opinions on, among other things, the political fate of Germany, Israel and the United States. Within this dialogue each required and received honesty and respect from the other: in expressing her reservations regarding the book he had sent her, Arendt showed that she could be something other than a former student and junior colleague, while in responding with openness Jaspers showed that he could be something other than a former supervisor and mentor. The common ground of intellectual dissent was where they discovered and developed their lifelong friendship. Theirs was a deeply pedagogical friendship in which each learned from – and taught – the other.

Following Jaspers' dismissal in 1937 from his post at the University of Heidelberg, Arendt maintained throughout the war years intermittent contact with him and his wife. Throughout the war years – and, indeed, until his relocation to Basel, Switzerland, in 1948 – Jaspers and his wife were in a highly vulnerable position personally, while he was also professionally and academically marginalised. During this period Arendt supported them by sending food parcels from the United States. It was partly as a result of these acts of kindness that Gertrud and Arendt also formed an enduring bond of friendship. What united Jaspers and Arendt was their shared experience of the horrors of Nazism, but each of them had different perspectives on that experience. It was – that paradox again – those differences of perspective that forged their friendship. They were each in very different places, and the differences mattered in terms of how they made sense of what they both saw as the near-death experience of civilisation as they knew and valued it.

By the time Arendt and Jaspers were able to resume a regular correspondence – at the end of World War II – she was already adopting a tragic world view. In her working through of the ideas and analyses that informed *The Origins of Totalitarianism*, she was developing a critique of totalitarianism as a unique and catastrophic intervention in human affairs, while in *On Revolution* she was to judge the French and Russian revolutions as tragic failures that had sought to achieve liberty at the expense of freedom. In what she saw as the inevitable choice between liberty from the sheer necessity imposed by abject poverty and the constitution of a free and vibrant polity, both these iconic revolutions had opted for the former – and in so doing had each led to its own version of 'terror': either, the terrorism of Robespierre or that of Stalin. This was – arguably – a bleak and in many ways a deeply conservative view of the world. It was – inarguably – a tragic one.

Although seemingly a more conservative character – reserved, formal and cautious – Jaspers was more comedic in outlook. He naturally favoured fortune and providence over fate. Arendt – although more gregarious and risk-taking – was more inclined to scepticism on the big issues that concerned them: the future of Germany, the legitimacy of Israel and the role of the United States. Her unerring sense of the tragic looked to him for some modification and shading into hope. His more hopeful outlook was in turn modified and finely shaded by her worldly scepticism. Whereas he was inclined to optimism, she was disposed to caution. As her mentor he feared that her horses would run away with her, but it was she who, as their friendship flourished, helped him to rein in his own horses of hopefulness. Their friendship was based on a finely-tuned complementarity of differing outlooks and dispositions whereby each went on learning from the other – the means by which they communicated not only with one another but about the world they both knew and were seeking to understand.

It was the boundless communicative capacity of Jaspers' way of thinking and philosophising that Arendt drew attention to in her public utterances regarding his significance as a public intellectual. In her 1946 article 'What is existential philosophy?' – which had been highly critical of Heidegger's work – she argued that Jaspers had transformed philosophy into an active process of philosophising whereby 'philosophical "results" can be communicated in such a way that they lose their character as results' (EU, 183). The 'results' become the occasion for further conjecture, discussion, argumentation, thereby rendering the philosophical process endlessly inclusive and inconclusive. His way of doing philosophy assumed equality between those engaged in the philosophical discourse: 'Jaspers does not retain even the Socratic priority of the questioner, for in communication the philosopher moves, as a matter of principle, among his equals, to whom he can appeal and who can in turn appeal to him' (EU, 183). The assumption of equality between those engaged in the process of philosophising is not, in other words, a contingent factor – but is constitutive of that process and, as such, 'a matter of principle'.

In a later article published in 1957, she characterised him as someone for whom '[t]hinking becomes ... a kind of practice between men, not a performance of one individual in his self-chosen solitude'. Jaspers, she continued, was 'the first and only philosopher who has ever protested against solitude, to whom solitude has appeared "pernicious" and who has dared to question "all thoughts, all experiences, all contents" under this one aspect: "What do they signify for communication?"' With Jaspers, she maintained, philosophy had 'lost both its humility before theology and its arrogance toward the common life of man' (MDT, 86). He had, in her view, brought philosophy down to earth and placed it firmly in the realm of human exchange and discourse.

In an address given in 1958 when the German Peace Prize was awarded to Karl Jaspers, she returned to this theme of the 'realm' of philosophy:

This realm, in which Jaspers is at home and to which he has opened the way for us, does not lie in the beyond and is not utopian; it is not of yesterday nor of tomorrow; it is of the present and of this world. Reason has created it and freedom reigns in it ... It is the realm of *humanitas*, which everyone can come to out of his own origins.

MDT, 80

In the final paragraph of that address she claims to speak as one whom Jaspers had led into this realm. This is, of course, a reference to his having supervised her doctoral studies and been her early mentor, but it also clearly refers to their friendship as being a means of actualising that realm through their continuing dialogue that was always concerned with what was 'of the present and of this world'.

Old Europe

For both Arendt and Jaspers philosophy was inextricably entwined with politics, and politics was, in turn, inextricably entwined in their own life histories. The pressing concerns of their time – the future of Europe and the reconstruction of Germany, the establishment of the state of Israel and the emergence of the United States as a world power – raised questions that were, for them, not merely of academic interest but of personal significance and public consequence. It was the impact of those questions on their own lives, together with their own insistence on confronting and addressing them, that enabled Arendt and Jaspers to pronounce from their own experience on world events and thereby achieve the authority of public intellectuals.

Each was differently placed in relation to those events: Arendt as a German Jew rendered stateless by the geopolitics of post-World War II Europe and finally gaining US citizenship; Jaspers as a German Gentile married to a Jew and finally gaining refuge in Switzerland. Both had their own reasons to have to think through what it meant to be German and Jewish, what Israel signified as both the Jewish homeland and as a new state within the emergent world order and how the United States should shape its increasingly powerful role in the world. Yet, for both of them that process of thinking through – a process that Arendt characterised as 'worldliness' and Jaspers as 'encompassing' – was a philosophical and political necessity. Their lifelong dialogue was among other things a serious and sustained attempt to address that need by clarifying their own positions and disagreements and sharing their experiences: a sharing that increasingly involved their spouses as their own friendship reached out to their own families and their wider circle of friends.

German nationalism was, as already noted, one of their early points of disagreement. At the time of the early exchange regarding Jaspers' recourse to the notion of 'the German essence', Arendt was still a German citizen. Even then, in 1933, she rejected Jaspers' attempt to counter the growth of fascism through a reconstruction of German 'patriotism' based on the idea of a national 'essence' or 'German character'. How as a Jew – albeit still a German Jew – could she possibly make sense of such an argument as a viable strategy for resisting the rise of fascism? As part of that early exchange Arendt pits her own experience against that of her mentor:

> I am of course a German in the sense that I wrote of before. But I can't simply add a German historical and political destiny to that ... Germany in its old glory is your past. What my Germany is can hardly be expressed in one phrase, for any oversimplification – whether it be that of the Zionists, the assimilationists, or the anti-Semites – only serves to obscure the true problem of the situation.
>
> AJ, 18–19

After World War II, in a letter written in 1947, Jaspers picks up on the themes of the earlier exchange. Their ongoing dialogue has various strands which they develop across time and sometimes with a considerable span of intervening correspondence on other matters. So, after the catastrophes of World War II, which they have experienced in different ways and in different places, Jaspers returns to one of the earlier strands and begins to redevelop it: 'I think constantly now, with my heart, about what my being a German means. Until 1933 that was never problematic for me. But now ...: The whole world shrieks at one, so to speak: You are a German' (AJ, 94). Jaspers then shifts from the question of his own German identity to that of Jewish identity, linking the latter to 'the idea of God': 'What a Jew is seems clearer to me than what a German is. Biblical religion and the idea of God and the idea of the Covenant are crucial to the Jew' (AJ, 94).

Responding to this letter – and in the course of many practical details regarding the publication of his lectures, her current writing schedule and the food parcels which she sent to the Jaspers each month throughout the war years – Arendt pits her own experience as a non-religious Jew against his notion of what it means to be a Jew: 'Historically, you are correct in everything you say. But the fact remains that many Jews such as myself are religiously completely independent of Judaism yet are still Jews nonetheless' (AJ, 98). In effect she rejects his characterisation of what it means to be a Jew, but she does so without any hint of acrimony. Similarly, he receives her rebuttal without any attempt to defend his position or win the argument. Indeed, they both seem to revel in clarifying rather than resolving their disagreements, since in so doing they are also clarifying their own positions and defining their own identities.

After Jaspers relocated to Basel in 1948 – thereby achieving some geographical and presumably psychological distance from Germany – his feelings towards his country of birth shifted but remained deeply ambivalent. In a letter written to Arendt from Basel in early 1949, he tells her: 'The news from Germany is not good. Here, at a distance, sympathy increases and anger subsides – but there is no denying that I do not belong among *those* Germans' (AJ, 128). He then goes on to say that there is, nevertheless, 'something in the German character that I love above all else and that one perhaps loves best when one floats about homeless in the world' (AJ, 128). Of course, the two statements are not incompatible, since what he is distancing himself from are 'those Germans' rather than the generality of Germans. Nevertheless, what he claims to 'love above all else' – namely, 'the German character' – is precisely the kind of idealised abstraction that Arendt had taken issue with back in 1933.

By 1952 Jaspers was becoming increasingly disillusioned with the post-war Adenauer administration and, in particular, its refusal to acknowledge the collective guilt for the Nazi crimes: a refusal which, as he saw it, reflected a general inability – or unwillingness – of most Germans in the immediate post-war years to understand their own implication in what had happened. In a letter sent to Arendt towards the end of that year he wrote: 'What it comes to in the end is that I will never cease claiming you as a "German" (you know that, of course), although ... I am, along with you and many other Germans, "not a German," namely, not in the political sense (even though I am a German according to my passport, but that gives me no pleasure)'

(AJ, 204). He is, of course, in part referring here to the fact that although still a German citizen he no longer lives in Germany. However, the statement carries the added significance that he no longer takes any pleasure in that citizenship and that, in spite of his being a German citizen in name, he no longer feels himself to be German 'in the political sense'. The ambivalence still hovers around in that he seems to be saying that he is and is not a German, without quite defining in what sense he is and in what sense he is not. But the further distancing of himself from the politics of post-war Germany is clear and unambiguous.

Jaspers' statement also hinted at the differences and commonalities that shaped their correspondence and in some ways defined their friendship: he, with his old German passport, now living in Switzerland; she, with a new US passport, now living in the United States; both, as he saw it, with their cultural roots in Germany. In a letter written in 1959 to Heinrich Blücher, Jaspers was still hankering after an idealised Germany that could be distinguished from 'the people visible in the Federal Republic today' and expressed disappointment at Arendt's indifference towards it:

> From Germany – which in her conversation she likes to confuse with the people visible in the Federal Republic today – she has pulled away even more, is more indifferent toward it. That pains me somewhat. I feel she is mistaken about herself, even though she truly has, together with you, achieved a state in which she exists with her feet on the ground, even though deprived of the ground of her origins.
>
> AJ, 383–4

In spite of what might have been read by Blücher as an implied criticism of his wife, the tone of Jaspers' letter was not in any way rancorous or colluding. It is more about Jaspers' regret than any failure on behalf of Arendt. It was signed off with 'warmest greetings' and, as Jaspers points out in a postscript to the letter, was actually typed up by Arendt who was visiting him and his wife on one of her visits to Europe – a fact which testifies to the emotional honesty and openness between them. It also testifies to the inclusivity of their friendship in which their spouses became increasingly involved in the ongoing correspondence. The friendship became, in Jaspers' term, 'encompassing'.

But Arendt was persistent in pushing their friendship towards what she termed 'worldliness'. The world, for Arendt, is inscribed in everything. Germany, for Arendt, was what it was: not an idealised abstraction, but 'the people visible in the Federal Republic today'. The people of Germany were what constituted Germany. So when from the vantage point of New York and in the new year of 1960 she wrote to Gertrud Jaspers (with the assumption, as always, that Jaspers himself would be privy to the correspondence), she did so with grave misgivings regarding what she saw as the state of the people of Germany as she had witnessed them in her recent visit:

> A very perceptive woman of my age said to me in Frankfurt: It's as if we were walking on swampland again. I'm afraid that is only too true. We talked about the abyss between official Germany ... and the people. The so-called people are profoundly unhappy despite the wildest prosperity; they're malicious, secretly hoping that everything will fall apart, even if that means they have to suffer. They're full of resentment against everybody and everything, but especially against the so-called West and democracy. This is all unarticulated; there is no movement, no focal point, but the atmosphere it creates is dreadful.
>
> AJ, 384–5

Assimilation and identity

The views that Jaspers had been developing in his ongoing correspondence with Arendt found public expression in his 1961 *The Question of Guilt*. In this publication he highlighted the recognition of collective guilt – and of co-responsibility for the crimes committed under the Nazi regime – as a necessary condition for the reconstruction of Germany within a reformed Europe: '[T]he fact of my being German – that is essentially, of life in the mother tongue – is so emphatic that in a way which is rationally not conceivable, which is even rationally refutable, I feel co-responsible for what Germans do and have done' (Jaspers, [1947] 1961, 80). Because he is himself a German, argues Jaspers, he is implicated in the crimes committed under the Nazi regime; and because he is implicated he shares responsibility; and because he shares responsibility the question of his guilt arises and must be addressed. The fact that he himself was not involved in committing these crimes and that he and his wife were placed at grave risk as a result of the anti-Semitic policies pursued by the Nazi regime is, Jaspers implies, of no relevance. He may not be a criminal, but 'the fact of my being a German' makes him responsible.

Again, Arendt and Jaspers were differently positioned with regard to how restoration should be achieved: his emphasis on remorse as a precondition of participation in the restorative process was at odds with her emphasis on participation as a precondition of political responsibility. While his notion of participation presupposed a prior agreement regarding collective responsibility, hers presupposed nothing other than a willingness to engage from one's own position of difference. However, both agreed that the Adenauer administration had failed to ensure that Germany confronted the full implications of its own Nazi past – and that one of the consequences of that failure of moral and political leadership had been to compromise Germany's future. Reluctantly, Jaspers conceded what Arendt had much earlier judged to be the case – that political hope in and for the future was not to be found in Germany.

So, where was political hope to be found – hope, that is, in a new politics that would offer the possibility of new beginnings within a post-World War II world? Israel was one such possibility, but a possibility that again highlighted some of the major differences between them – differences that formed another important strand in their continuing correspondence.

In 1952, ten years after completing her biography of Rahel Varnhagen, Arendt sent a manuscript copy of this work to Jaspers asking his advice on whether the work should be published. In his response Jaspers acknowledged that 'this book is powerful and significant' (AJ, 192), but expressed the view that, if Arendt were to publish it, it would be 'at the risk that in the light of the highest standards a shadow will fall on you' (AJ, 196). His minor reservations concerned 'an excess of repetition' and 'the lack of a detailed chronological table' (AJ, 192), but his major reservation concerned Arendt's treatment of Varnhagen as a person. He argued that Arendt had failed to let her subject speak 'from her core' because she had interpreted her entirely through the lens of her 'Jewishness': '[Y]ou let this figure speak, but not from her core, that is, not as this human being herself who is not in her nature a Jew but who passes through this world as a Jew and therefore experiences the most extreme things, things that happen not only to Jews' (AJ, 193). Varnhagen, in other words, is 'in her nature' first and foremost 'this human being herself' and only secondarily a Jew.

From Jaspers' perspective, Arendt had diminished Varnhagen by collapsing her entire identity into that of 'a Jew'. He recommended, therefore, that she 'reduce Rahel's Jewishness to one element in your presentation and let the greatness of her soul stand in the foreground' (AJ, 195). In effect, he was suggesting that Arendt distinguish Rahel's 'Jewishness' from 'the greatness of her soul' – that Arendt assimilate Varnhagen's distinctive 'Jewishness' into her common and undifferentiated humanity. Since for Jaspers 'the idea of God and the idea of the Covenant are crucial to the Jew' (AJ, 94), Varnhagen – for whom neither idea was of central importance – could be interpreted as having dissolved her 'Jewishness' into her generalised humanity. Her 'Jewishness' was an accident of birth – a contingency – that could and should be 'naturalised', just as the Jewish diaspora could be assimilated into the 'natural' world order. From this deeply assimilationist perspective, the emergence of an independent politicised Jewish state posed a severe threat.

Responding, Arendt began with her thanks for his 'good, long letter' and her tribute to 'your wonderful thoroughness, your illuminating patience, your listening and responding at the same time and both at once' (AJ, 196). She conceded his points regarding the technical and stylistic shortcomings of the work and emphasised that it had been written some time ago prior to her more recent work. Having reflected upon his comments, she had – she declared – made a decision: 'I won't publish the book' (AJ, 197). (A reworked version was published in 1958.) She then proceeded to set out at some length her views on Zionism and Jewish assimilation. The book had been written, she wrote, 'from the perspective of a Zionist critique of assimilation, which I had adopted as my own and which I still consider basically justified today' (AJ, 197). She then goes on to argue that the picture of Varnhagen is 'in all its essential features' the one put forward by Varnhagen's husband who was so assiduous in erasing her Jewish identity and legacy in her later years.

'Judaism', as she pointed out, 'doesn't exist outside orthodoxy on the one hand or the Yiddish-speaking, folklore-producing Jewish people on the other' (AJ, 199). The simple fact of being Jewish does, however, affect one's existence regardless of orthodoxy or folklore. As she did not make explicit but was implicit in her comments, the simple fact of being designated Jewish was a matter of life and death for those living under Nazi occupation – a fact of which Jaspers was himself well aware given his own marital situation. For the

Jew, Arendt implied, 'Jewishness' is not a contingent factor that one might place at a safe distance from one's humanity. On the contrary, it is how one's humanity is perceived and therefore intrinsic to one's being in the world. One may choose one's religious affiliations and commitments, but one cannot choose whether or not to be a Jew. So, for Arendt, assimilation of the Jewish diaspora was not an option and the establishment of an independent politicised Jewish state provided at least the possibility of hope. In spite of the sensitivity of the issues addressed and the candid exchange of viewpoints, the tone remains one of deep mutual respect as Arendt signs off this round of their correspondence 'with warmest and fondest greetings'.

A couple of years later in 1954, the theme re-emerged. In the course of another long letter on various subjects, Jaspers again raises the issue of assimilation. He explains how his friend Ernst Mayer had spoken about him to his sister when they were both students and how his sister had initially rejected the idea of meeting him on the grounds that 'he may be anti-Semitic' (AJ, 246). However, they did meet up, and, Jaspers continues, 'when I met Gertrud, at the end of the semester, after she had held out against a joint visit for a long time, our fate was decided within an hour. And I'm supposed to decry assimilation?' (AJ, 246). Gertrud was, of course, his lifelong partner with whom – as we have already seen – he immediately formed an intense bond 'within an hour' of their first meeting. Jaspers' rhetorical question – 'And I'm supposed to decry assimilation?' – suggests that he sees their immensely fulfilling marriage as both an instance and a vindication of 'assimilation'.

Arendt could well have met the question on its own terms – she was, after all, a Jew married to a non-Jew and, like Jaspers and his wife, she and her husband were both of German origin. But she chose not to do so. Instead, she takes him back to the idea of Jewish identity based on 'historical and social experiences with a group of people' (AJ, 248). Jews are Jews not primarily by virtue of their religion, but as a result of their shared history and experience. That is where she located her Jewish identity, which could not in her view be assimilated into any other category. Her Jewishness was what it was. 'As far as assimilation is concerned,' she argued, 'the situation was politically and socially impossible . . . But precisely because it was politically and socially so complex it offered, on an individual level, remarkable opportunities of a human and intellectually productive sort'. From Arendt's perspective, 'German Jewry was truly a great thing', but only because of the necessary and irreconcilable tensions implicit in the phrase 'German Jewry': those nouns in apposition – 'German' and 'Jewry' – were a restatement of the problem, not a solution to the problem (AJ, 248).

Notwithstanding his views on assimilation – and possibly because of his grounding of Jewish identity and history in 'the idea of God and the idea of the Covenant' – Jaspers became increasingly supportive of the state of Israel throughout the 1950s. In 1956 he wrote to Arendt claiming that 'Israel is becoming the touchstone of the Western world. If the West abandons Israel, it will suffer the same fate as Hitler's Germany, which let the murder of the Jews happen. The danger remains frightful. For now, I think, we can be satisfied with Israel's actions – moderate, intelligent, and courageous, as the best Western countries are' (AJ, 308). A year later he is again extolling the virtues of Israel's 'moderation and intelligence':

> Then there is politics. We would seem to be of one mind. Ever since November I've been affected by politics in a way I haven't been since the Nazi period. The main reason is no doubt that we are finally seeing something that we can respect, perhaps admire: Israel's bearing and policy. It is clearly winning the approval of all decent people ... The 'greatness' of Israel's accomplishment is the uniting of moderation and intelligence with boldness, self-sacrifice, and the capability to match words with deeds ... My feeling is something like this: The destruction of Israel would mean the end of humankind – and probably in fact bring about its destruction.
>
> AJ, 310–11

In response to what she calls his 'wonderful long letter', Arendt tactfully points out that they are not 'of one mind' on this particular issue: '[Y]ou express your "feeling" that "the destruction of Israel would mean the end of humankind," and that doesn't seem justified to me even as a feeling'. Indeed, she adds, it is not even certain that 'it would mean the end of the Jews'. She then proceeds to outline a further disagreement between them: 'We're also not in agreement about the significance of the Jews for Europe, their political significance right now. That has changed decisively in the last twenty years' (AJ, 313). With the creation of Israel and the decimation of the Jewish population across Europe, the critical mass of European Jews no longer constituted a significant political presence. She might have added that, insofar as the Jewish diaspora had a geopolitical epicentre, then this was more likely to be the United States – of which she was now a citizen – than Germany, which had rendered her stateless.

In spite of these differences – or perhaps because of them – there was an intuitive understanding between Arendt and Jaspers. Each of them possessed – in different ways and differing proportions – their own complex mix of realism and naïvety, which made for a certain complementarity in their relationship. That complementarity enabled Jaspers to provide Arendt with the support she desperately needed in the period following the publication of *Eichmann in Jerusalem* in 1963. He understood that the purpose of her reportage had been to tell the truth not to court publicity, but he also understood that she had been naïve not to realise that her truth-telling would be viewed as an act of aggression by those adversely affected by truths she chose to tell – and that she would, therefore, inevitably face the full blaze of hostile publicity. He understood, also, how Arendt's particular blend of hard-headed realism and naïvety – so different yet not entirely dissimilar to his own – had on this occasion rendered her highly vulnerable: 'You can't tolerate human baseness', he wrote in 1963, 'and you prefer personally to avoid the public eye. Now you are experiencing both at once'. He continued, in a superbly sympathetic yet critical reading of her report of the Eichmann trial:

> I have read your book now from the first to the last line. I consider it marvellous in its subject matter. It bears witness, in its intent, to your uncompromising desire for truth. In its mind-set, I find it profound and full of despair ... And then I think ... how infinitely naïve not to notice that the act of putting a book into the world is an act of aggression against 'life-sustaining lies.'
>
> AJ, 531

Pax Americana

By the time Arendt replied, President John F. Kennedy had been murdered. Writing in November 1963 – on the day that Lee Harvey Oswald, who had been apprehended for shooting Kennedy, was himself shot to death by Jack Ruby, a nightclub owner – she tells Jaspers and Gertrud that she is 'writing still under the shock of Kennedy's murder'. Immediately, she identifies the inconsistencies surrounding the two related cases of murder that, as she puts it, 'are not only horrible but also, and worse still, completely foggy': the fact that Oswald was murdered by 'this underworld character, of whom the radio was just saying, as though by the by, that he was well known to the police in Dallas (was on a good footing with them?), has made everything much worse' (AJ, 534).

Less than a week later she writes again, this time with a chilling assessment of the situation: 'It seems as if a mask has suddenly been torn off the face of this country. And behind it we see an abyss of potential violence and pure bloodthirstiness that we had not guessed was there to this extent' (AJ, 538). She goes on to tell them that she has 'heard that students at the University of Texas said, or, rather, screamed "That's what happens to a nigger-loving president, and that's what'll happen to every nigger lover!" And school children reacted with wild, spontaneous applause when they heard the news. What's at stake is no more nor less than the existence of the republic' (AJ, 533).

The stakes were high, she concluded, because Kennedy's presidency had represented a way of doing politics – 'an openness to the arts and sciences, a respect for the life of the mind, a conscious and consistent attempt to give intellectuals a voice in the political arena without influencing or exploiting them' – that represented the possibility of new beginnings (AJ, 538). Following what she saw as the antipolitics of McCarthyism, Kennedy's administrations had offered the kind of political hope that many had invested in the state of Israel. Yet, the reality in both cases was proving very different. The circumstances surrounding Kennedy's death had highlighted the deep-rooted racist and virulently anti-communist elements in American society.

It had also, as far as Arendt was concerned, exposed the willingness of government not only to collude with but also protect and even promote those elements. Eight months after Kennedy's murder, her initial sense of the 'fogginess' surrounding his death had settled into a conviction that the 'fog' was a deliberate attempt at obfuscation – or, worse still, state deception: 'Kennedy's murder has never been solved. The only thing that seems established is that it couldn't have been Oswald' (AJ, 558). Arendt, in other words, was flatly rejecting the official account of the circumstances surrounding Kennedy's death. She also rightly surmised that the report of a presidential commission headed by Chief Justice Earl Warren (the 'Warren Report') would maintain the opposite:

namely, that the murder had been solved and that Oswald had been solely responsible for committing it. (For a contemporary assessment of the evidence available, see Shrenon, 2013.)

Jaspers tended not to respond in detail to Arendt's analyses of the situation in the United States. He was clearly interested in and exercised by the issues she raised, but was reluctant to pass judgement. He clearly felt that Europe owed the United States a great deal by way of loyalty for its intervention in World War II. This seems to have influenced his response to her strong views on the student protest movement and the Vietnam War. She shared with him her respect for the student protest movement which – as she saw it in early spring 1965 – had grown from the civil rights movement: 'Their organization is superb. In Berkeley they've achieved everything they set out to achieve, and now they can't and don't want to stop' (AJ, 583). Regarding the Vietnam War, Arendt not only referred to it as 'this insane Vietnam policy' but also rejected its implicit claim 'to the Pax Americana that Kennedy warned so strongly against' (AJ, 621). On both issues Jaspers was in broad agreement, acknowledging in the case of Vietnam that she was 'unfortunately right' (AJ, 623). However, he felt that as a European he was not in the same position as Arendt with regard to criticising the United States: 'I think we Europeans should keep our mouths shut ... It behoves us to show respect for the state to which we all owe our existence and relative security' (AJ, 623). Jaspers was still of the old world of Europe and – as he saw it – in some ways beholden to the new world of which Arendt was now a member.

She now had the authority to speak back to both the old world from which she had been exiled and the new world within which she was now a public figure. Jaspers remained to the last her most significant and enduring connection with the old world of Europe. Although Arendt and her husband were part of the intellectually vibrant New York Jewish community, many of whom had been uprooted from Europe, Jaspers and Gertrud remained for her the most tangible link to the Europe within which she had been born, brought up, and educated – and from which she still drew philosophical sustenance and a sense of intellectual identity.

Jaspers was still *there* – a citizenly presence in the Europe of which she was no longer a citizen. Their friendship had developed from a formal teaching relationship, through a mentoring relationship during which each became mentor to the other, into a friendship based on mutual care and boundless communication involving not only themselves but also their spouses. Their friendship was a complex layering of learning together, sustaining and supporting one another personally and professionally, and talking with one another primarily through their extensive correspondence but also face to face on those few occasions that Arendt was able to visit him and his wife. Their friendship was not just another layer of their lives. It was the root system that ran all the way down and all the way across the layers and allowed each of them to flourish.

Footprints and legacies

On 26 February 1969 Arendt received a telegram from Gertrud Jaspers: 'Karl died 1:43 PM. Central European Time'. He had died – at the age of eighty-six – on Gertrud's ninetieth birthday. Arendt took a flight to Basel to be present at the private funeral. She also took part in the official memorial service at the University of Basel. In her brief speech she tried to define what she had found distinctive and exemplary in Jaspers as a human presence. She said it was the man and not his books that was the true exemplar – because, as she put it, 'Jaspers exemplified in himself, as it were, a fusion of freedom, reason, and communication'. Moreover, he did so in such a way that 'we from henceforth cannot think of these three things – reason, freedom, and communication – as separate but have to think of them as a trinity' (AJ, 685).

In fusing reason, freedom, and communication, Jaspers was also exemplifying the interdependency of ethics, as the study of how to live well, and morality, as the study of how we should treat other people. Learning how to live well by respecting one's own capacity for reason and freedom involves respecting that same capacity in others and acting accordingly. For Arendt, Jaspers' unique contribution had been to show through both his life and his work how the integrity of ethics and morality required a *tertium aliquid*: namely, communication. It was this third element that set him apart as a philosopher in and for the world. 'It would', she said, 'have been easy to imagine him as a statesman', adding that 'for almost a quarter century he was the conscience of Germany' (AJ, 685). By insisting on the interdependence of reason, freedom *and* communication, Jaspers had revealed how ethics and morality necessarily raised questions that carried political import: 'He was born for the ways of a democratic republic, and he took the greatest pleasure in human exchange that was conducted in that spirit' (HAJK, 685).

Arendt's footprint across the latter half of the twentieth century and into the twenty-first century is much more clearly defined than that of her great friend, Jaspers. Nevertheless, his legacy is still widely acknowledged. Although no longer hugely influential, both his 1913 professorial thesis, *General Psychopathology* ([1913] 1997), and his 1922 *Strindberg and van Gogh* ([1922] 1977), with its development of a 'pathographic analysis', continue to be important reference points in the broad field of psychodynamics. His approach to therapeutic practice – whereby patients are diagnosed, not as instances of a pre-specified category, but as unique cases whose individuality must be understood and respected by themselves as well as by the therapist – can also be seen resurfacing in current approaches to cognitive therapy. He understood from his early engagement with the paintings of Van Gogh that sticking a label on something prior to fully understanding it – by which time the label may be of little help – militated against the possibility of achieving any such full understanding. Psychiatric and therapeutic practice, as he understood it, was interpretive – as opposed to just clinically diagnostic. It involved an understanding of the individuality of the individual in the particular social and historical conditions within which the individual was located. (For a recent example of the continuing relevance of Jaspers to the field of psychopathology, see Fuchs *et al.*, 2014; Stanghellini and Fuchs, 2013).

Jaspers has also exerted a continuing influence on the history of ideas as these relate to what, in his 1953 *The Origin and Goal of History*, he termed 'the Axial age': the period, that is, from 800 to 200 BC, during which both religious and secular thought underwent what Jaspers saw as a kind of revolutionary surge that was to have a major and lasting impact on Western society. This was, as Jaspers interpreted it, a liminal period during which many of the enduring religions of the world emerged and the idea of democracy was born. His analysis of the causes, circumstances and contingencies that gave rise to 'the Axial age' is now of less significance than the implications of this periodisation for those with an interest in the beginnings of religious traditions and the ways in which those beginnings have played out through history over the last two millennia. Jaspers saw this periodisation as a pretext for reconciling diverse religious and secular traditions within a unified Europe whose new beginnings he traced back to 'the Axial age' – the historic axis, that is, upon which the world continues to turn. (For recent examples of the continuing relevance of the notion of 'the Axial age', see Armstrong, 2006; Bellah and Joas, 2012.)

For Jaspers the significance of 'the Axial age', as he conceived it, was its '*summons to boundless communication*' (Jaspers, 1994, 387). If the great traditions of religion and culture turned on a common axis, then communication across and between religious and cultural divides was both possible and desirable. Jaspers was arguing that the problem of the meaning of 'the Axial age' is something quite different from that of its cause. What it means for us in the here and now is that communication is a necessary condition for becoming human: 'This risking of boundless communication is once again the secret of becoming-human, not as it occurred in the inaccessible prehistoric past, but as it takes place within ourselves' (Jaspers, 1994, 387). In identifying Jaspers' endless capacity for human exchange and communication as his defining characteristic, Arendt was highlighting the one quality that would also define his continuing intellectual legacy.

Through their lifelong friendship, Arendt and Jaspers realised the ideal of 'boundless communication' both within their relationship and through their continuing engagement with the world of human affairs, which was central to that relationship. What was happening within the world – as it affected both themselves and others – was of supreme importance to them both. They brought the world into their friendship while at the same time using their friendship as a means whereby each of them clarified her or his relation to the world. They were worldly in different ways. Both had thought deeply about the world. But she had travelled and experienced it more widely than he – although, as she might well have been the first to point out, not necessarily more deeply. He contributed to their relationship – over and over again – a kind of wisdom. Arendt needed that wisdom just as he needed – from his more sedentary position in Basel – her spontaneity of response. They were both – in their different ways – spectator and participant in the history of their time.

6

Arendt and McCarthy: Becoming Ourselves

When you entered the room and you were talking to her [McCarthy], something was always happening. She was so intelligent. And, you know, very eccentric in many ways. As I guess every person is when you really get to know them. Her mind was always full of something fresh and new. It was a great pleasure to be around her. I miss her terribly – every day.

Elizabeth Hardwick, quoted in Kiernan, 2000, 742

The past in the present

Mary Therese McCarthy, as she was christened, first met Arendt in Manhattan in 1944. She was in her early thirties and Arendt in her late thirties. McCarthy was still in the second of her four marriages, while Arendt was in her second and final marriage. McCarthy knew nothing at first hand of Arendt's 'old' Europe and Arendt was still working her way into McCarthy's 'new' America. Their differences of background were stark. But beneath those differences there were very important commonalities: both had, as children, experienced parental bereavement and upheaval; both had run away from home (and returned); both were young and aspiring female writers and intellectuals in what was a fiercely male-dominated world; both were also complicatedly at odds with their heritage – McCarthy as a lapsed Catholic and Arendt as a non-religious Jew. Arendt could hardly be described as an apostate, since she had not been brought up within the Jewish religious tradition. Nevertheless, the fact of her being a Jew was central to her identity, such that her experience of cultural bifurcation resonated with McCarthy's more direct experience of apostasy. Both, in short, were exposed from early childhood to life-changing events over which they had little or no control. Their friendship was framed by this shared experience of vulnerability and uncertainty – but also by the different ways in which these two extraordinarily self-willed and intellectually courageous women coped with that experience.

McCarthy wrote about her youth and young adulthood in a number of books, some of which were a composite of feature articles for various publishing outlets, and one of which was published posthumously (McCarthy, 1992, 1957, 1987). Her novels – particularly her 1942 *The Company She Keeps* – are also a complex mix of autobiography and fiction. Her own past pressed heavily upon her because having been orphaned at a young age she had few verifiable reference points. She had to rely entirely on her own often hazy recollections, on conversations with her brother and on press cuttings to disentangle fact from false memory. There was always the nagging feeling that she may have blocked out or simply failed to notice what in retrospect might be important – or that she might have skewed her memory so as to make her past more palatable or bearable. This left her with both a great respect for facts and a predisposition towards fiction. If in her own past the distinction between fact and fiction was far from clear, then she needed the facts in order to get things straight and the fiction in order to fill in the gaps. So, tracing McCarthy's early years prior to her first meeting with Arendt is not simply a matter of establishing the facts, but of understanding how her deep-seated mistrust of what she took to be the facts was crucial to what she was and what she became. It is not the facts of the case but their fuzziness that shaped McCarthy. There were, for her, no clear and incontrovertible foundations to her life. Each memory was susceptible to endless interrogation and reiteration. She was forever drafting and redrafting herself.

McCarthy was the oldest of four siblings who were orphaned when she was six. Her parents both died within a week of one another in 1918. They were early victims of the influenza pandemic of 1918–19 that in its overall death toll probably rivals AIDS and the Black Death. The children were taken in by their paternal great aunt and by her new husband who lived in Minneapolis. McCarthy's 1957 *Memories of a Catholic Girlhood*, which is partly a composite of earlier autobiographical articles and partly a commentary on those accounts, reveals something of the abuse that she and her brothers suffered during this period and the impact of that abuse on her writing and her relationships. But over and over again she cuts into her narrative of these early years to interject a note of caution regarding the veracity of her own account. With reference to her father, she writes: 'He read to me a great deal ... and I remember we heard a nightingale together, on the boulevard, near the Sacred Heart convent. But there are no nightingales in North America'. Then a little later she adds: 'Many of my most cherished ideas about my father have turned out to be false'. What is noteworthy is the specificity of what she retrospectively suggests is a false memory: she remembers hearing the song of the nightingale 'on the boulevard, near the Sacred Heart convent'. The unreliability of her memory was tagged not to a sense of not-remembering, but to the specificity of what in retrospect she judged to be false memory.

However, McCarthy was in no doubt that she – and particularly her brother who was nearest to her in age – had been physically abused by her great aunt and her husband. The following incident occurred after a supposed theft by McCarthy of her youngest brother's toy – a tin butterfly: '[T]he boys were ordered to bed, and then, in the lavatory, the whipping began. Myers [the great aunt's husband] beat me with the crop, until his lazy arm tired; whipping is hard work for a fat man, out of condition, with a screaming, kicking, wriggling ten-year-old in his grasp'. The great aunt then 'took his place, striking harder than he, with a hairbrush, in a businesslike, joyless way' (McCarthy, 1957, 77). The abuse involved not only these extreme cases of physical violence, but also systems of control that included oppressive health, cleanliness and disciplinary regimes, together with a prohibition on reading anything other than a limited number of prescribed texts. 'The basis', wrote McCarthy, 'of my aunt's program for us was in truth totalitarian: she was idealistically bent on destroying our privacy' (McCarthy, 1957, 70). The regime was one of uncompromising efficiency: '[I]f we were forbidden companions, candy, most toys, pocket money, sports, reading, entertainment, the aim was not to make us suffer but to achieve efficiency ... From the standpoint of efficiency, our lives, in order to be open had to be empty' (McCarthy, 1957, 71).

The tin butterfly incident was the culmination of six years during which McCarthy and her brother had on several occasions run away with a view to being admitted to an orphanage, a fate which seemed preferable to their life with their great aunt and Myers. On each of these occasions they were taken in by their paternal grandmother, who, while not condoning their actions, offered them brief sanctuary for a day or two before their enforced return. After the tin butterfly incident McCarthy was taken in by her maternal grandparents on a permanent basis. McCarthy acknowledges her own uncertainty regarding the exact reasons for this move, but related it both to the tin butterfly incident and to the fact that in retrospect it would seem that her great aunt and her husband had in effect been embezzling the considerable sum of money that her maternal grandfather had been paying them to cover expenses relating to the children's upbringing. At this point the children were split up, with McCarthy and the brother to whom she was closest being sent to different boarding schools.

By the age of eleven McCarthy had lost both parents within a week of one another, been mentally and physically abused by those responsible for her care and protection, and been separated from her siblings. The abrupt change in her circumstances occasioned by her grandparent's intervention was the stuff of fairy tales: their house overlooking Seattle's Lake Washington was a world away from the life she had endured in Minneapolis. Her grandfather was a Protestant and her grandmother a Jew, but neither took their nominal affiliations particularly seriously. McCarthy moved from a situation that had taught her that survival depended on being red in tooth and claw to one in which order and civility were the prevailing norms. As her most recent biographer put it:

> There were no onerous tasks to perform. No threats of corporal punishment. When she opened her mouth to voice an opinion, no one made fun of her. From the wallpaper on her bedroom walls to the linens on her bed, every item was costly and chosen with an eye to pleasing the senses... Her clothes were no longer threadbare... Never again would she be forced to eat a turnip or suck the white cord from the scrawny neck of some ancient boiled hen.
>
> Kiernan, 2000, 44

But the past had left its mark on McCarthy. The torments of Minneapolis had set her apart and now she was separated from the siblings with whom she had shared that torment. She was isolated, watchful and unclear as to the events leading up to her seemingly miraculous relocation to Seattle. Her experience of life had been fatalistic in both its unpredictability and chronic uncertainty. Minneapolis had taught her that the only available choices – such as running away with her brother – were necessarily wilful and morally reprehensible. To be good one had to renounce choice and abandon agency. Moral agency was a contradiction in terms, in that morality demanded the eradication of agency. 'Goodness' thereby became a foreign – or, at least, a highly problematic – concept. This perhaps partially explains McCarthy's lifelong predisposition towards controversy and self-assertion. To have the experience in one's formative years of being literally beaten into submission presumably leaves one either broken or determined to assert oneself at any cost. It also perhaps explains McCarthy's affinity with Arendt who was also to some extent an instinctive controversialist. But at eleven years of age, it simply set McCarthy apart in ways that both she and her grandparents must sometimes have found difficult. At that early age, as Kiernan (2000, 46) puts it, 'she had grown not only older but wiser in ways that the adults around her could not imagine and had no wish to explore'.

Although her maternal grandmother was Jewish and her maternal grandfather a Protestant, McCarthy had been brought up a Catholic. Her mother had converted to Catholicism after her marriage and she had attended a Catholic school in Minneapolis. Her grandfather clearly wished to honour his dead daughter's wishes while presumably hoping for some continuity in her educational experience. Consequently, she was enrolled in a convent school where she became a weekly boarder. The school was very different in both its ethos and its intake from her previous school and this seems to have intensified her sense of isolation and difference. In her second year – and not fully understanding the consequences of her actions – she announced that she had lost her faith. She was then sent to a coeducational Seattle public school, where she failed most of her courses, and then to a single-sex Episcopal boarding school. Here she was wayward and rebellious – narrowly missing expulsion on at least one occasion – but began to flourish educationally under the influence of teachers and fellow pupils who appreciated her distinctive qualities.

She remained ambivalent regarding the legacy of her early Catholic education and her Catholic upbringing. Looking back on her school in Minneapolis – possibly the worst school, in terms of academic prestige, she had attended – she wrote: 'Our ugly church and parochial school provided me with my only aesthetic outlet, in the words of the Mass and the litanies and the old Latin hymns, in the Easter lilies around the alter, rosaries, ornamental prayer books, votive lamps, holy cards stamped in gold and decorated with flower wreaths and a saint's picture' (McCarthy, 1957, 18). The same school had also given her a taste for meritocracy: 'Catholics of our neighbourhood were children of poor immigrants bent on bettering themselves ... There was no idea of equality in the parochial school ... [E]quality, a sort of brutal cutting down to size, was what I was treated to at home. Equality was a species of unfairness which the good sisters of St. Joseph would not have tolerated' (McCarthy, 1957, 19).

At the same time McCarthy was acutely aware of the biases and prejudices implicit in the version of Catholicism to which she had been exposed in Minneapolis, and – crucially – the capacity of that version for generating intolerance, bigotry and self-righteousness: '[R]eligion is only good for good people ... Only good people can afford to be religious. For the others, it is too great a temptation – a temptation to the deadly sins of pride and anger, chiefly, but one might also add sloth' (McCarthy, 1957, 23). If religion had provided her with a sense of beauty within the ugly and demoralising circumstances of her early life in Minneapolis, it had also provided her with a keen sense of the injustices that can flow from the assumption of religious authority. It had, in short, left her instinctively rebellious against all forms of authority, while at the same time desperately craving the attention of those in authority: a heady mix in any context, but – in the milieu of 1940s and 1950s New York – an intoxicating brew that was both intellectually challenging and erotically charged.

Complicated complementarities

From school McCarthy went on to graduate from Vassar College, New York, in 1933. In that same year she married Harald Johnsrud, an actor who also aspired to write plays. Three years later, in 1936, her first marriage ended, and in 1937 she became the lover of Philip Rahv, who was one of the founding editors of the highly influential literary journal *Partisan Review*, and who remained a lifelong friend. After leaving Rahv, she married the writer and critic Edmund Wilson in 1938 – seven years after the publication of his pathbreaking (1931) *Axel's Castle* and just two years before the publication of his hugely ambitious (1940) *To the Finland Station*. Her marriage to Wilson – with whom she had one son, Reuel Wilson – lasted until 1946 when she entered a third and penultimate marriage to Bowden Broadwater.

When McCarthy first met Arendt in 1944 she was, therefore, although still in her early thirties, at the centre of the New York literary scene, with an ex-lover co-editing one of the major international journals, and a husband who had already gained a reputation as one of the most influential and innovative literary critics of his day. She was contributing to leading intellectual journals – *The Nation*, *The New Republic*, *Harper's Magazine* and *The New York Review of Books* – and was part of the inner circle of *Partisan Review*. However, she was also nearing her second divorce and still struggling to establish her own literary and journalistic reputation in what was an almost entirely male-dominated culture. She had – rather like Rahel Varnhagen as depicted by Arendt – placed herself at the centre of a social, literary and intellectual circle in relation to which she was part parvenu and part pariah. She survived by working exceptionally hard, by carefully crafting her prose, but also by ensuring that she herself was noticed and that her opinions were couched in terms that would guarantee that they gained the attention of any gathering of which she was a part.

Not surprisingly she was seen by some as attention-seeking and flippant. Diana Trilling, who was married to the literary and cultural critic Lionel Trilling, was very clear in her views regarding McCarthy during this period of her life:

> I took my politics too seriously to be amused by Mary. She was stupid politically. Irresponsible. She did harm. She presented herself to the world as the most responsible of people but she was irresponsible really. And she was awfully smug about her liberal bona fides. They don't impress me very much; they were too easily come by. I like a little hard thinking instead.
>
> Quoted in Kiernan, 2000, 119–20

Interestingly, Trilling – born Rubin – was the daughter of Polish Jews, so when it came to 'liberal bona fides' she was speaking with some authority. Whether an upstart or an outcast, McCarthy was treated with caution by many and patronising disdain by others. Among the latter was Isaiah Berlin – diplomat and eminent British academic of Russian-Jewish origin – who pronounced the following succinct but withering verdict on her achievements: 'She was a great wit, but she was not a great thinker' (quoted in Kiernan, 2000, 119).

Arendt's initial response to McCarthy seems to have been not dissimilar. At a party in New York in 1945 – in the context of conversation about the hostility of French citizens to the Germans occupying Paris – McCarthy said she felt sorry for Hitler who was so absurd as to want the love of his victims. The remark was ill-judged: another instance, perhaps, of McCarthy alienating others by seeking to impress them. Arendt was incensed, declaring herself to have been 'a victim of Hitler, a person who had been in a concentration camp'. She then turned to Philip Rahv, at whose house the party was being held, and asked (no doubt rhetorically): 'How can you have this kind of conversation in your home, you, a Jew?' In fairness there may been a degree of self-dramatisation on both sides. After all, Arendt was in some ways as much a parvenu as McCarthy in the emergent celebrity culture of the New York intelligentsia, and, like McCarthy, needed to impose herself and her identity on the gathering. Only three years later – on a subway station platform after Arendt and McCarthy had attended a meeting together – did the two women overcome this early setback. According to McCarthy, Arendt simply turned to McCarthy on the platform and said: 'Let's end this nonsense. We think so much alike'. McCarthy apologised for her original remark and Arendt acknowledged that there had been a degree of overreaction in her own response given that she had never been in a concentration camp but only in an internment camp in France (Young-Bruehl, 1982, 196–7).

What followed was a lifelong friendship that proved to be immensely important and mutually beneficial to both women. Ostensibly, at least, McCarthy was more a fox than a hedgehog, and Arendt more a hedgehog than a fox: McCarthy seemed to know many things, while Arendt knew one big thing. But Isaiah Berlin's neat antithesis – referring to a line by an ancient Greek poet, Archilochus – is subject to the same criticism that he directed at McCarthy: strong on sharp wit, weak on complexity of thought (Berlin, 1953, 3). Arendt's work does indeed suggest a big idea developed through very different texts and across several decades. But it also suggests an immense responsiveness to the boundless plurality in the world around her: a responsiveness that has more than a whiff of the fox about it. Similarly, McCarthy clearly came across as extremely foxy to many of her contemporaries, but she too had a trajectory and a project that was hedgehog-like in its single-mindedness. When Albert Camus wrote in 1958 'that a man's work is nothing but this slow trek to rediscover through the detours of art those two or three great and simple images in whose presence his heart first opened', he might well – in spite of the masculine pronouns – have been thinking of either Arendt or McCarthy (Camus, 1979, 26). Each, in her own way, circled round – and returned to – the same preoccupations that were grounded in their early experiences of the world.

They complemented one another in complicated ways. Arendt needed to understand the 'new' world that she had entered; McCarthy needed to understand the 'old' world from which Arendt had emerged. Each was in a sense the other's shadow – perhaps, even, the other's fantasy. As Carol Brightman points out in the introduction to their correspondence, theirs was 'a friendship that border[ed] on romance, not sexual romance, but not entirely platonic either' (AM, xxix). Repeatedly, they expressed the desire to be in one another's presence; spoke of how much they missed one another and how much they were looking forward to one another's visits; and signed off their letters with deep expressions of love for one another. There was nothing exclusive about the relationship – spouses and partners were included in many of the fond greetings – but clearly each took immense delight in being with the other. For McCarthy, in particular, knowing that Arendt was there – and being reassured that she was there – was of immense importance. But increasingly Arendt, too, relied on McCarthy for reassurance and human comfort, particularly after the death of her husband in 1970.

At one level – the level of utility – the friendship operated as a mutual support system within the highly competitive professional world in which they both operated. The support was rarely overt – for example, neither reviewed the other's work or publically championed it – but may for that very reason have been more effective. Although overlapping, their networks were different and extensive. They were able to keep one another informed of what was happening or not happening across those networks; share confidential views and opinions regarding some of the key players and their relationships; encourage one another when the negative reviews rolled in and celebrate one another's successes. A great deal in their correspondence is 'gossipy', but the gossip served the very important function of mutual advancement – and sometimes sheer survival – in the tough world of freelance journalism, reviewing and writing that they both inhabited.

At another level they simply took great pleasure in one another's company. It is difficult not to see in their friendship an element of the mother–child relationship: McCarthy finding in the older Arendt the pleasure of stability that she had lost with the death of her mother, and Arendt finding in the younger McCarthy the restlessness that she had experienced as an adolescent and towards which she felt a kind of protective sympathy. Of course, this dichotomy is no more useful than the fox-hedgehog dichotomy if pushed to its limit. But it reminds us that their shared experience of insecurity, isolation and uncertainty in early life impacted upon both their later lives and that no doubt it did so in complicatedly different ways. It was not only their complementarities but also their differences that provided the mutuality and reciprocity that each needed and in which each took pleasure. In the world in which each of them had grown up, 'need' and 'weakness' were in many ways synonymous: strength was equated with self-reliance. To be able to acknowledge within their own relationship their mutuality of need – while recognising each other's strengths and differences – was for each a supremely adult way of becoming strong together.

Being oneself is extremely difficult, particularly when – as in the case of Arendt and McCarthy – one becomes a public and to some extent controversial figure relatively early in one's life. But this is an aspect of intersubjectivity that we all experience and can therefore relate to: how to balance self-perception and the self as perceived by others. In the case of both Arendt and McCarthy the tension between the 'I' as subject and the 'me' as object must have been particularly acute. How can one 'be oneself' when the presentation of one's own self is reflected back as in a hall of mirrors? This was the question to which their lifelong friendship might be seen as an answer. Their friendship was about becoming themselves: each helped the other to become herself; each was useful to the other in the professional and social circles within which they moved; and, crucially, each took pleasure in the other. Each was a better person than she might have been had they not, on that subway platform, drawn a line under the past and moved on. Their new beginning was a friendship within which each was able to complement and strengthen the other.

'Workmanlike friendship'

McCarthy was particularly good – as someone for whom English was her first language – at picking up on Arendt's sometimes idiosyncratic use of English.

Arendt was writing in her third language – after German as her first, and French as her second – and at times she seemed to be using English words to bend themselves around concepts that were more readily available in her mother tongue. Of course, Arendt knew very well what she was doing in moulding the English lexicon to the conceptual requirements of her argument. But McCarthy – for whom language mattered a great deal – highlighted the occasional tensions between expressive and communicative intent in Arendt's use of English.

Why, for example, in the piece on Walter Benjamin collected in *Men in Dark Times*, did she deliberately use a phrase such as 'the consistence of truth', when the word 'consistence' jarred and the sense so obviously required the term 'consistency': 'I don't know what this means – consistency in the sense of firmness, thickness density or in the logical sense of agreement or connection, absence of contradiction? ... In a recipe, you say "Stir until the mixture is of the right consistency." ... Such a key term ought to be pinned down for the reader' (AM, 224). The fault, McCarthy tactfully added, probably lay with the translator of her piece (which had originally been written in German and translated by Harry Zohn) rather than with her own usage.

Arendt's reply showed no signs of defensiveness or of any collusion in shifting the blame to the translator of the piece. The bulk of her reply dealt with other matters and when she turned to McCarthy's comments on this particular work she simply stated that she was 'very happy about your comments'. She brushed aside the idea that it was a fault in translation, pointing out that this was the one piece in the entire volume that she had rewritten for the English edition. So, as she put it: 'consistence versus consistency is my fault'. Picking up on the homely culinary metaphor, Arendt repeats her originally intended meaning: 'I meant "stir until the mixture is of the right consistency" and used "consistence" because consistency is usually in the sense of logical consistency'. She had, as she put it, succeeded in convincing her editor and the copy-editor of this idiosyncratic usage 'probably because neither ever read a cook book' (AM, 232).

In the same letter McCarthy had provided Arendt with a very open and honest response to *Men in Dark Times*. It was, she said, 'a series of fairy tales' of the personages depicted; it was 'maternal' towards its subjects; it was German and had made her think about 'how you/they are different from us'. It expressed a particular notion of 'workmanly friendship, of apprentices starting out with their bundle on a pole and doing a piece of the road together. All this gave me much pleasure, as well as surprise'. But it was this notion of 'workmanly friendship' that, for McCarthy, gave this particular work a distinctly Germanic feel: 'It's the only work of yours I would call "German"'. Again, Arendt only slighted demurred. She was not sure why McCarthy saw the book as 'German', but she agreed 'about the fairy tale quality of the portraits'. She agreed with her point about the portraits – or 'silhouettes' as she preferred to call them – depicting a particular kind of 'workmanly friendship'. But – she maintained – 'I do think about people in these terms' (AM, 225).

In other words, Arendt tended to see people as emblematic of human qualities that might be inferred from their particular dispositions; and she saw the particular people she had portrayed – or 'silhouetted' – as emblematic of the qualities and dispositions necessary for 'workmanly friendship'. It is ironic that Arendt was spelling this point out to McCarthy, whose full and generous response to the style and spirit of her friend's work was emblematic of precisely those qualities and dispositions. Every writer – particularly one working in her third language – needs a keen critical ear for the way in which the words sound, how they hang together in meaningful conjunction, or jar, and how they are received within the echo chamber of the mind. Writing, as Arendt knew, is expressive and transgressive. But it is also, as McCarthy knew, communicative and subject to conventions. You can and must, as Arendt knew, make language your own – but you must also, as McCarthy was well aware, have respect for its strictures. Not to put too fine a point on it: rules matter.

McCarthy fulfilled her role of 'workmanly friendship' through what at times feels like a kind of exasperated pedantry. But what fellow writer worth her salt would not have responded with gratitude to McCarthy's nagging reminder of the requirements of our necessarily down-to-earth trade: 'Restrictive clauses are always set off by commas. The distinction between which and that hasn't always been made in English, and in the old days the shift from one to another was often determined by euphony ... But today the distinction is more rigorous. Exceptions are made when the "that" could be distinguished from the other kind of "that"...' (AM, 121). And so this lesson in the niceties of linguistic usage continues (in this case as a response to the manuscript of the concluding chapter of Arendt's *On Revolution*):

Is your translation of Livy right? I'd think very tentatively, that the 'quibus' indicates that he means that a war is just to those for whom it is necessary, which gives a different shade of meaning. As for 'les malheureux sont la puissance de la terre', words fail me, but I think you could do better. 'The poor are the earth's might'? No. 'The poor are the mighty on the earth'? 'The wretched are the mighty on earth'?

AM, 122

This is an object lesson in 'workmanly friendship' – and Arendt understood and took it as such. For her part, she understood and acknowledged that McCarthy's best-selling novel, *The Group* – eleven years in the making and so very, very different from Arendt's own oeuvre – was 'beautifully written (the inner balance of the sentences is extraordinary) and often hilariously funny' (AM, 145). (Only a prose writer of consummate skill could set the tone so beautifully and wittily as McCarthy does in the opening sentence of that novel.) If Arendt was the supreme architect of big ideas, McCarthy was a superb craftsperson for whom Arendt had great respect. Neither was unduly in awe or disparaging of the other. Each took pleasure in the achievements of the other – the hedgehog settling down quite comfortably with the fox. It was as a result of this deep companionability that McCarthy was able to bring to fruition Arendt's posthumous *magnum opus* – her unfinished *Life of the Mind* – and, in so doing, fulfil the final duties of 'workmanly friendship'.

Strength and fragility

Just as McCarthy understood some of the linguistic pitfalls that Arendt ran the risk of toppling into, so Arendt foresaw some of the emotional hazards towards which her friend – prior to her fourth and final marriage – seemed on occasion to be heading. While showing such a clear sighted, sharp witted and – some would say – cynical attitude towards human and sexual relationships in her fictional work, McCarthy displayed in her intimate relationships with men a marked tendency towards vulnerability, impetuosity and – some would say – lack of judgement. Much the same might have been said of Arendt prior to her marriage to Blücher. Arendt, in other words, knew where McCarthy was coming from. But Arendt's foresight was couched – and, it would seem, conceived – in the spirit not of prudishness and censoriousness but of prudence and circumspection. Again, it was an expression of 'workmanly friendship' – 'of apprentices ... doing a piece of the road together' (AM, 225).

A fairly early instance of Arendt's steadying influence – ten years into their friendship – relates to a period during which McCarthy's third marriage was coming under intense strain. In 1955, while in Paris, McCarthy suffered a miscarriage of the child she had conceived with her then husband, Bowden Broadwater. Shortly after the miscarriage and the temporary rift with Broadwater that followed, Arendt flew to Venice to be with her friend, with whom she then travelled to Milan to a conference where Arendt was delivering a lecture. In the aftermath McCarthy became entangled in a relationship with John Davenport, who proved to be both allusive and deceitful. Travelling to Italy by way of London with the express purpose of meeting up with Davenport, she discovered from a mutual acquaintance that Davenport had lied to her about his family connections and had entirely misrepresented his own standing within the professional and social circles in which he mixed. The mutual acquaintance – Mr Hughes, whom McCarthy had been led to believe was Davenport's cousin – put McCarthy straight.

Shortly after her meeting with Hughes – and having arrived in Italy – McCarthy reported to Arendt her version of the conversation:

> 'Cousin? Did he tell you that?' and he laughed, rather irritably. 'I'm not his cousin. I'm no relation to him,' I looked absolutely stunned, and he went on, in a hesitant way. 'I think I had better tell you that John is a pathological liar.' Well, Hannah, that was how it started. His ancestry. All that was lies about him and his 'gentle birth' ... Then there was the drinking. It was much worse, said Hughes, than I could possibly imagine ... There was nothing much you could do for him, Mr Hughes said, because of the lying, you never knew where you were with him. He also stole. Books and small objects.
>
> AM, 45

McCarthy's account ended on an even more serious note – serious, that is, for McCarthy's reputation and social standing (this was, after all, 1957). McCarthy had been compromised: 'He *had* talked about me, though not to Hughes; other people had told Hughes about it and said he ought to be stopped from talking so about a married woman. The fortunate thing, said Hughes, was that he was known to be such a liar that in this instance no one believed him' (AM, 46). The emphasis on the 'had' suggests that McCarthy had half anticipated this betrayal of their intimacy. Somewhere between London, where she had met Hughes, and Italy, where she wrote to Arendt, McCarthy had crafted a story and, in crafting it, no doubt partially distanced herself from its revelations. But the rawness remained in the sense of humiliation that emerges in her account and in her fear that Davenport's boasts might, in spite of Hughes' reassurances, be believed – or that she might be tainted by association.

Arendt's response is well pitched. McCarthy's husband – Bowden Broadwater – had been round to Arendt's and Blücher's home the previous Sunday and Arendt tells her friend about the gathering and says 'he seemed to be in very good shape and I liked him' (AM, 48). Having thereby established – albeit implicitly – that her letter was not about 'taking sides', Arendt focuses on McCarthy's account of her discussion with Hughes and his revelations regarding Davenport. In her letter she manages – through the kind of humour she no doubt shared with McCarthy – to steady her friend while not demonising Davenport. In putting Davenport in his place she employs gentle satire rather than the melodramatics of moral condemnation and thereby offers McCarthy an alternative perspective on both Davenport and the humiliating and anxiety-inducing situation in which she found herself:

> Mary, dear, I am afraid you came in too close a contact with the English variety of the 'lost generation' – which apart from being a cliché is a reality … [T]o lie about one's origin and to play the aristocrat in England is, it seems to me, as much satire on the English and amusement about their standards as it perhaps is also the attempt to lie yourself into something you are not.
>
> AM, 48–9

Arendt then goes on, in similar vein, to suggest that Davenport and his ilk are not particularly good liars. They lie about facts rather than feelings and so can all too easily be found out. Perhaps, suggests Arendt, Davenport wanted to be found out. She even comes close to suggesting that there may have been a latent goodness in Davenport in his tacit acknowledgement that what 'is really not permissible is to drag other people into one's own amusements … So, you had to be frightened away' (AM, 49). Arendt acknowledges that there was 'a great deal of cruelty in all this', but that the cruelty might have been an expression of love in that he was protecting her from himself: '[Y]ou can't expect somebody who loves you to treat you less cruelly than he would treat himself'. Arendt manages to salvage a modicum of respect for Davenport (his 'cruelty' may have been a kind of inverted 'love'), while at the same time acknowledging McCarthy's good luck – and better judgement – in escaping from this potentially destructive relationship (AM, 49). Arendt's cool and measured response endorsed her friend's decision to end the relationship, while leaving her with a sense of self-respect: the man McCarthy had fallen for was not right, but not all bad; she, in falling for him, had not been a complete fool and simpleton; they were not right for one another, but it was time to move on.

McCarthy's marriage to Broadwater was by now under immense strain. Two years later – in 1959 – he flew to Europe with McCarthy's son Reuel to join her for a holiday tour of Vienna and Prague. From there they accompanied her to Poland on the first leg of a State Department trip. They were met in Warsaw by the public affairs officer at the US embassy, James Raymond West. Before Bowden and Reuel returned to New York a fortnight later, West had already told McCarthy that he wanted to marry her. He too was married so the situation was complex on both sides. By the following October McCarthy was anxiously pushing for a divorce, Broadwater was resisting her demands, and Arendt was reluctantly being drawn into the increasingly entangled and bitter relations between McCarthy and her husband. Again, Arendt makes no attempt to pass judgement on her friend's actions. Instead, she seeks to mediate between McCarthy and Broadwater and to help each see the other's point of view.

In response to a telephone conversation in which McCarthy insisted that her marriage was over and that she wanted a swift divorce, Arendt wrote to McCarthy explaining that she had spoken with Broadwater and said to him: 'If you give her the divorce *now*, you will still be friends, if not, you will embitter everything unnecessarily'. She then went on to offer very similar advice to McCarthy: 'If you start proceedings now against his wishes you will have to take into account that he will try to make things harder at every single step ... You will only have made an enemy – something which he is not now' (AM, 98). Having appealed to Broadwater to compromise, she then made the same appeal to McCarthy – and in both cases the appeal was based on the desirability of retaining friendship. Marriages end and desire fades, but friendship can and should endure.

Responding by letter, McCarthy insists that she 'is not going to accept the notion of waiting on Bowden's pleasure' (AM, 99). She adds: 'I am more deeply in love with Jim than ever and vice versa, and it is simply too ridiculous for us to be the passive foils of other people under the circumstances' (AM, 100). In reply, Arendt points out the obvious – namely that her estranged husband 'is not only not omnipotent but utterly powerless'. It is, she adds, precisely under these circumstances of utter powerlessness that people 'dream up some possibilities of power'. As to any suggestion that she should withdraw her friendship from Broadwater because of McCarthy's enmity towards him, Arendt is quite clear regarding the ethics of friendship:

> I talked to him as a friend and I did not lie. For me the fact is that you brought him into my life, that without you he would not have become – not a personal friend which, of course, he is not – but a friend of the house, so to speak. But once you placed him there, you cannot simply take him away from where he is now.
>
> AM, 103

Broadwater had become a friend: not a friend like McCarthy, but a friend nevertheless, someone welcome in the home. Such friendship could not simply be set aside. It demanded at the very least a certain duty of care and a suspension of any easy recourse to judgement: 'As long as he does not do something really outrageous which he has not done so far and really turns against you which he has not done either, I am not going to sit in judgement'. She points out the obvious: 'That his life is in ruins is quite obvious to anybody who is willing to have a look at him and his situation'. She presents McCarthy with the worst possible scenario, while absolving her of responsibility for that unlikely scenario should it occur: '[I]f he were to commit suicide which, I think, is not probable but not altogether impossible either, I would be the first to tell you that you are not to blame' (AM, 103). Towards the end of the letter, she pushes the argument further: '[I]t strikes me that you can forget so easily that you trusted him enough to be married to him for fifteen years ... [I]t seems to me rather obvious that you both are victims of your own, self-chosen past' (AM, 104).

It is a tribute to McCarthy that she accepted her friend's blunt appraisal of the situation as an expression of friendship. Just as McCarthy pulled back and provided a 'workmanly' perspective on her friend's stylistic idiosyncrasies, so Arendt pulled back and provided a 'workmanly' perspective on her friend's predicaments and entanglements. Each provided the balance and circumspection, the ballast and sense of proportion – the common sense – that the other needed and at times lacked. Arendt was headstrong in her prose – McCarthy reined her in; McCarthy was impetuous in life – Arendt pointed out the pitfalls. Together they made a good – if highly unlikely – team.

Common sense

It was on the subject of common sense that their correspondence first took philosophical wing in a letter written by Arendt in 1954. Developing ideas that would be elaborated more fully in her 1958 *The Human Condition*, she argued that common sense is crucial because it constitutes 'a kind of sixth sense through which all particular sense data, given by the five senses, are fitted into a common world, a world which we can share with others, have in common with others' (AM, 23). Common sense can be lost through introspection or what Arendt called 'the logical faculty'. Both involve a retreat from the world into either introspection or objectification. For Arendt the world is neither entirely 'in our heads' nor entirely 'out there'. It is the intersubjective space within which we relate to one another through our five senses – hearing, sight, smell, taste and touch – and in so doing constitute our common world. Common sense was, for Arendt, vital to that process: lose it and 'there is no common world any longer' (AM, 23).

Since we acquire common sense – as Arendt understood it – neither through internal dialogue with ourselves nor through the application of technical rationalism, its acquisition necessarily relies on what happens between people. Common sense, in other words, is a *practice* that requires a discursive tradition to ensure its sustainability: a tradition that relied for its continuity on conversation, correspondence and mutual commitment. We cannot *do* common sense in isolation, which is precisely why we designate it as *common*. Nor can we reduce it to a technique or method that is independent of social and cultural context. Without associative frameworks – such as institutions, families and friendships – common sense cannot come into play; conversely, without the interplay of common sense, such frameworks lose their associative potential and become either dysfunctional or chillingly bureaucratic.

Sophia Rosenfeld (2011) has argued that Arendt is central to our understanding of the 'political history' of common sense, since, for her, common sense provided 'a foundation and goal for a politics that began with the active participation of "the people" in community making'. It thereby 'set the stage, at least potentially, for true democracy' (248). Unlike ideology, which aims at control through homogeneity and the eradication of human difference, common sense 'is ultimately a noncoercive but vital form of social glue suitable for a pluralist and talkative world'. It is 'the ground on which true democracy forms and the product that true democracy creates' (252). Arendt thereby 'provided her readers with a vision of a kind of participatory democracy in which the common sense of ordinary folk could accomplish wonders' (254): the kind of participatory democracy in which people could become themselves, achieve their potential, and flourish as both persons and as citizens.

The correspondence between Arendt and McCarthy provides ample evidence of the cultivation of common sense through the continuity of friendship. Carol Brightman, in the introduction to the Arendt-McCarthy correspondence, which she edited, writes that McCarthy had told her in 1989 (the year of her death) that 'common sense . . . was something she and Hannah had aplenty, contrary to what most people might think, "because strangely enough it is very unconventional. Conventional people," she insisted, "usually have absolutely zero common sense"' (AM, xxii–iii). The correspondence also shows how their common sense was mutually beneficial, with one providing the necessary resources of common sense in those situations where the other lacked those resources. That is how common sense – and friendship – work; or, rather, what makes for 'workmanly friendship'.

Indeed, it is difficult to see how McCarthy would have managed her life had it not been for Arendt's steadying influence at crucial junctures. Similarly, Arendt's capacity to cope with the highly charged environment of New York intellectual society – not to mention the Eichmann trial and its aftermath and the death of her husband in 1970 – owed a great deal to the emotional support, gossipy insights, streetwise savvy and political *nous* of McCarthy. Each was – when the chips were down (to use one of Arendt's trademark phrases) – willing to need the other and to acknowledge that need. Neither equated need with neediness or with dependency. They were strong and, as McCarthy pointed out, 'unconventional' individuals who were not afraid of needing one another – and who, by seeking to meet one another's needs, grew and flourished in their respective personal and professional fields.

The capacity to accommodate mutuality of need is one of the hallmarks of genuine friendship – and, indeed, of any genuinely democratic politics. The emphasis here, of course, is on *mutuality*. If the need is entirely one-sided – and remains so – 'friendship' may not be the appropriate term to apply to the relationship in question. But a friendship in which neither friend was able to trust the other sufficiently to express her or his need would be a threadbare affair; just as any democracy that labelled those in need as feckless scroungers would undoubtedly be in a sorry state of democratic decline. The assumption that meeting other people's needs in some way contributes to their neediness is a fallacy. To address the needs of the other – on the other's terms – is to open up the possibility for human growth and development, which in turn opens up the possibility of mutuality and reciprocity. That is the premise upon which genuine friendships and strong democracies are based.

But the tenor of these remarks is not the tenor of Arendt's and McCarthy's correspondence. They did not analyse their relationship or use it to conceptualise – or reconceptualise – friendship. They just got on with it. This again may tell us something about the nature of friendship: friendships are not the application of some theory of friendship, nor do they rely on an ongoing reflective meta-dialogue between the friends regarding the nature of their friendship. Friendships, in the main, do not have to explain or explore the deep codes of friendship upon which they are based. There is a great deal that is appropriately and courteously *implicit* in friendship. What matters – or mattered in the friendship between Arendt and McCarthy – is the continuity and, at the last, the sense of dogged duty, that makes possible the shared repository of memory and experience that constitute the strong lines of that continuity.

Duty beyond death

On receiving a telegram from Arendt telling her that Blücher had died the previous day, McCarthy immediately flew from Paris to New York. It was

November 1970. Blücher had been seventy-one when he died, and Arendt was just sixty-four. McCarthy was fifty-eight. The significance of age differentials – and, indeed, of how age matters – shifts over the course of a lifetime. Perhaps the age gap between Arendt and McCarthy gained a different significance now that Arendt was widowed, but there is little evidence to suggest that this was the case. Arendt – not in good health herself, newly widowed and with a punishing schedule of public lectures – no doubt felt her age. But McCarthy was pushing herself to the limit in her various writing assignments – literary journalism, coverage of Vietnam and Watergate, not to mention her earlier forages into Italian art history – and she too must have been feeling her age (see McCarthy, 1956, 1959, 1970, 1974a, 1974b). They were both getting older.

Four years later in 1974 Arendt suffered a heart attack while delivering a lecture in the highly prestigious Gifford Lectures at the University of Aberdeen in Scotland. Again McCarthy flew from Paris to be with her in the hospital where she was first placed in the intensive care unit. Following Arendt's heart attack and now back in Paris, McCarthy moved into common-sense mode, advising her friend on what she understood to be an appropriate health regime. Her tone was not unlike the one she had adopted when focusing on Arendt's use of written English: straightforward, slightly schoolmarmish, but as always well meaning, down-to-earth and useful. 'Please, now, my dear', she writes to Arendt, who is still in hospital, 'obey the doctor and direct your *will* to recuperation rather than to resistance. And enjoy at least the rest, enforced though it is'. No doubt aware that Arendt had resumed smoking as soon as the oxygen tent was removed, and anxious that she may have been resisting the advice offered by medical and nursing staff, McCarthy added: '[N]o doctor, I presume, would prescribe an agitated life, two packs of cigarettes a day, and running while carrying heavy objects'.

Of course, it has its funny side: McCarthy of all people lecturing Arendt on how to behave. But McCarthy *cared* – while, at the same time, being aware that her expressions of care may be missing the mark or simply open to misinterpretation. Moreover, she herself was in an agitated state following some less than favourable reviews of her most recent novel *Birds of America* and her more recently published works of non-fiction, *The Mask of State* and *The Seventh Degree*, on Watergate and Vietnam (see McCarthy, 1971, 1974a, 1974b). So when – five months later and following a meeting between them – Arendt did not turn and wave to her friend prior to walking through the airport departure gate to board her plane for New York, McCarthy became twitchy: 'It was sad to watch you go through the gate at the airport without turning back. Something is happening or has happened to our friendship, and I cannot think that in noticing this I am being over-sensitive or imagining things. The least I can conjecture is that I got on your nerves' (AM, 364). McCarthy cared enough – after twenty-five years of friendship – to show her own vulnerability. But there is also in the tone of the statement a sense of having been slighted – a tone, that is, of injured pride that stops short of blame but is nevertheless mildly accusatory.

Arendt replied immediately: 'The notion that you would ever go [sic] on my nerves never crossed my mind. I do not know why I did not turn back at the airport; I was very sad, your notion of my splendid solitude notwithstanding. I am of course lonely as everybody would be in my situation.' Her tone then shifts slightly. She is clearly not in a mood to appease her friend and turns the same tone of injured pride back on McCarthy: 'You may be right or wrong in being suspicious of your friends, but you could not very well be suspicious of *me* – or could you? And what have I done to provoke that?' The subtext is clear enough: if your pride has been injured then so has mine! But then the tone shifts again as Arendt reassures McCarthy of her love: 'For heaven's sake, Mary, stop it, *please*. I say that of course for my own sake and because I love you, but I think I also may say it for your sake' (AM, 364–5). McCarthy cannot resist in her next letter to scratch away at the sore – 'I just thought you were cross with me about all sorts of minutiae, as though whatever I did or suggested doing rubbed you the wrong way' (AM, 367) – but the incident was soon overtaken by the rich exchange of experience and opinion that characterised their correspondence as a whole.

Nevertheless, the incident does reveal the complementarity of strength and vulnerability in both women. It also shows how McCarthy in particular wanted – and needed – to do right by Arendt. Her friendship with Arendt had been the still point in the emotional turmoil of making her way from her second marriage through to her final stable and satisfying marriage with West. She no doubt had a great deal to beat herself up about with regard to these failed marriages and her other well-publicised affairs. Her celebrity status – as author of novels that by the standards of the time were risqué, of autobiographical accounts that were raw and uncompromising, and of non-fiction that was highly critical of government policy – had provided her with financial independence and public recognition. But no doubt it also confirmed the negative perception she had of herself in her more insecure moments: sharp rather than intelligent, contra-suggestible rather than seriously critical, a bit of a parvenu. Her friendship with Arendt, on the other hand, provided her with a context within which being herself and being good were not mutually exclusive but at best mutually supportive.

So, every other Sunday Arendt and McCarthy talked on the phone, Arendt mostly in New York, and McCarthy mainly in Paris. Their talk went on and on – sustaining and sustained by their friendship – up until 4 December 1975, when Arendt suffered a fatal heart attack in her New York apartment. The funeral was held at Riverside Memorial Chapel, New York. During her oration, McCarthy declared that Arendt's self-imposed task had been:

> to apply thought systematically to each and every characteristic experience of her time – *anomie*, terror, advanced warfare, concentration camps, Auschwitz, inflation, revolution, school integration, the Pentagon Papers, space, Watergate, Pope John, violence, civil disobedience – and, having finally achieved this, to direct thought inward, upon itself, and its own characteristic processes.
>
> Quoted in Brightman, 1993, 589–90

At the time of her death Arendt was two-thirds of the way through her final work, *The Life of the Mind*. She had completed the first two sections on 'thinking' and 'willing' (which had formed the basis of the first series of the Gifford Lectures delivered in Aberdeen the year before), and the notes for the final section – 'judging' – lay on her desk with the first page of the final section of this hugely ambitious work still in the typewriter. McCarthy put aside her own half-finished draft of her next novel *Cannibals and Missionaries* (finally published in 1979) and began the personally demanding and intellectually arduous task of editing and annotating this final work of her friend. In doing so, as she pointed out in her 'editorial postface' to that work, she was maintaining the dialogue:

> It has been a heavy job, which has kept going an imaginary dialogue with her, verging sometimes, as in life, on debate ... I do not think I shall truly

miss her, feel the pain in the amputated limb, till it is over. I am aware that she is dead but I am simultaneously aware of her as distinct presence in this room, listening to my words as I write, possibly assenting with her musing nod, possibly stifling a yawn.

LM, II, 249–50

It took McCarthy three years – 'a heavy job' – to complete the task of editing and annotating Arendt's sprawling but magnificent *magnum opus*. Without that effort we would never have known the full architectonic ambition of Arendt's final work. McCarthy showed immense courage in taking on the task and a great sense of duty towards her friend in fulfilling it. Duty and courage found their fulfilment in McCarthy's friendship with Arendt, but they were also part and parcel of her moral constitution. She died on 25 October 1989, almost fourteen years after Arendt. As Frances FitzGerald, a much younger friend and distinguished author, said: 'She was the bravest woman I ever met. In every respect. She would try anything. She was absolutely afraid of no one. And nothing. It wasn't that she was arrogant, either. It wasn't that at all. Watching her die, you realised how brave she was' (quoted in Kiernan, 2000, 742). All one might add to that beautiful tribute is Elizabeth Hardwick's judgement, as quoted in the statement heading this chapter: 'She was so intelligent. And, you know, very eccentric in many ways.'

Of the four friendships discussed in this book, this is the only one between two women, and the only one in which Arendt is the older of the two friends. That is not to say that most of Arendt's friends were men or that most were older. She had many female friends, including Anne Mendelssohn, who was her oldest friend, and many friends her own age and younger, some of whom had been her former students. Nevertheless, the differences between this friendship and the other three do provide some interesting points of comparison. The relationship between Arendt and McCarthy, although suffering an early setback, did not have to overcome the initial differentials of status that were clearly in evidence in the early stages of her relationships with Heidegger and Jaspers. Moreover, the issue of Arendt's seniority only occasionally surfaces, as when, for example, she displays a slight sense of maternalism in response to McCarthy's occasional episodes of vulnerability. Otherwise, it was a remarkably equal relationship in which neither sought to control the other and where advice, when offered, was honest and impartial. Nor does there seem to have been any sexual rivalry between the two. On the contrary, they enjoyed the company of one another's partners, drew them into their shared friendship as and when appropriate, and affirmed one another's life choices. The power of their friendship lay in its capacity to support each of them in becoming fully herself.

7

Arendt and Blücher: Flourishing Together

As if one had always seen woods, but never a tree in its full majesty. A very strange growth pattern, as many trunks issue from one root, growing in a circle, and then coming together again at the treetops . . . The trunks like weathered rock.

AB, 257

Eros and *philia*

Martha Arendt – Arendt's mother – was not entirely happy with her daughter's choice of second husband. Arriving in New York in 1941, she lived with Arendt and Blücher until her death in 1948. Seven years is a long time for mother, daughter and son-in-law to live together in two cramped furnished rooms under the strain of the mother's disapproval, particularly so when they were already coping with the strains of statelessness, becoming proficient in a foreign language and earning a living. For much of the time they must have felt they were skating on very thin ice. But none of them could risk the ice breaking. Too much was at stake: Arendt was deeply in love with Blücher but also felt an immense sense of duty to her mother; Blücher was deeply in love with Arendt and would not have wanted to force on her an impossible choice between her mother or him; and Martha needed a home and loved her only daughter and wanted the very best for her. So, in spite of the cramped conditions under which they lived, they somehow made it work. Moreover, Arendt – complex to the last – needed a partner who did not fit too comfortably into the norms of domesticity as understood by her mother, but who nevertheless provided the emotional security that she needed and that she associated with home.

The correspondence between Arendt and Blücher is necessarily intermittent because they corresponded only when apart. So, unlike Arendt's other correspondence, the letters between her and Blücher miss out on some of the big events in Arendt's life. However, the correspondence between them following Martha Arendt's death does survive and reveals some of the tensions that both of them had lived with since their arrival in New York. Arendt was in New Hampshire staying with a friend when she heard by telegram of the death of her mother who had been visiting her stepdaughter in London. Writing to Blücher, she acknowledges her mixed emotions, which were clearly tangled up with her sense of obligation towards her mother and guilt regarding her husband at having agreed to her mother's request to stay with them:

> Naturally, I am both unhappy and relieved at the same time. It's quite possible that all this was the biggest mistake of my life. I couldn't have simply turned down her request, because it came from a love and a wholeheartedness that I always admired ... When I think about you in all this, my head starts spinning ... I was always resolute about one thing, mainly never to have mother move in. But then the gas ovens came ... world history.
>
> AB, 92

The letter, with its twists and turns and sense of emotional turmoil, sounds like a *cri de coeur*, particularly when – immediately after the passage just quoted – Arendt asked Blücher to place a brief notice regarding her mother's death in a weekly German-Jewish newspaper ('Don't make it too big, but also not too small, and don't economize') and announces that she would like to wear black for a few months ('do you mind if I do? Please tell me') (AB, 92). She is at once demanding and vulnerable, self-justifying and self-reproaching, controlling and slightly out of control. It as if she were asking Blücher to steady her, ground her, stop her head from spinning.

Blücher does precisely that, but not in the way one might expect. How he steadied her tells us something important about their relationship, about why Arendt valued him, and about Blücher himself. Responding to her letter, he offered a clear appraisal of the predicament Arendt was in, introduced a little sardonic humour into the exchange, but did not entirely let her off the hook. He reminded her that from her mother's 'bourgeois standpoint' his own working-class origins were an inevitable cause of disapproval: 'She pointed out to me, a little too clearly, the limited but powerful justification of the bourgeois standpoint, which I'd always been aware of'. But, he went on, it was not her mother's snobbery towards him that most infuriated him: '[W]hat really infuriated me was the way she constantly sucked your blood, and her total lack of respect for your incredible accomplishments'. Whatever 'powerful, genuine, and clear feeling' she had once possessed towards Arendt had completely 'dissolved in a flood of insipid sentimentalities' (AB, 93). The honesty and realism of Blücher's uncompromising response was no doubt indicative of those qualities in Blücher that attracted and enlivened Arendt, but that rubbed her mother up the wrong way.

Blücher's working-class origins were central to both his self-identity and the sense of natural authority that others perceived in him. Among the sophisticated leftist leaning intelligentsia of New York, Blücher had something of the genuine article about him: a working-class intellectual, largely self-taught and with strong activist credentials. A passionately articulate conversationalist with a kind of rugged charm spiced with wit, Blücher might have been seen as Arendt's 'bit of rough'. But unlike her mother, Arendt saw that implicit in the rough edges were great resources of consistency and reliability. When the chips were down, Blücher was the sort of man that one would like to have had on one's side: steady, unafraid and decisive. After the infantilising tendencies of Heidegger and the incompatibility of temperament she had experienced in her first marriage, Blücher was a good choice.

For Blücher, too, the choice was a good one. Given his own strong personality, he needed a strong and independent woman, just as Arendt needed a strong and independent man to pit against her own single-minded determination. Moreover, although they were both fierce and uncompromising thinkers, Arendt was a writer and Blücher was a talker. So, there was not the kind of competition between them that there might have been if Blücher had been writing and publishing in the same field. As it was, they were able to support and complement one another in their different intellectual activities. They were able to provide the continuity that each craved in a world that had for both of them been characterised by chronic discontinuity.

In a letter written in 1950, and in which he outlined his approach to philosophy, Blücher explained to Arendt what he understood to be his particular strengths and limitations as a thinker: 'Yes, the good fairy proclaimed: "This boy shall have power of judgement," and the evil fairy interrupted her and finished the sentence, "but nothing else." And that seems to be that' (AB, 131). The 'nothing else' referred to the written record of his own philosophising. His talent resided in his being able to think his way through to judgements that in turn led through to action. Doing philosophy was, for Blücher, not a matter of producing philosophical texts, but of engaging in a process of thinking that leads – by way of judgement – to active engagement in, and for, the world. Blücher published nothing. But, as his letters to Arendt and what remains of his lecture notes clearly show, he was a hugely energised and energising thinker whose thinking flowed into his conversation and his teaching.

It is the symbiotic relation between their thinking that defined their friendship. No doubt sexually charged – and far from 'Platonic' – their relationship fed off ideas, sparked off their reading of particular texts, and was sustained by their ongoing conversation between themselves and across their wide circle of friends. In that sense it was a deeply Socratic relationship in which each seems to have found both erotic fulfilment and the rewards of companionship: a friendship that combined both *eros* and *philia*, while retaining the necessary tension between the two. It was a relationship born not in heaven, but in the *realpolitik* of the mid-twentieth century. To understand that relationship, we have to understand how Blücher's ideas and way of doing philosophy fed into Arendt's own thinking. The point here is not to track influences – and their attendant anxieties – but to illuminate complementarities and show how these provided the conditions necessary for Arendt and Blücher to flourish both as human beings and as public figures.

Thinking together

Blücher was born into a working-class family in Berlin on 29 January 1899. After primary school he continued his education in Reichenbach/Oberlausitz, a town in eastern Saxony situated in the south-east corner of Germany close to the Polish border to the east and the Czech border to the south. In 1917 he was drafted into the army for active service before having graduated and, in the same year, joined the Spartacus League (or *Spartakusbund*), a Marxist revolutionary movement founded in Germany in 1915 by Karl Liebknecht,

Rosa Luxemburg, Clara Zetkin and others. Following the German Revolution of 1918 it formally renamed itself the Communist Party of Germany, and the following year became a member of the Communist International (or Third International). In 1928 Blücher left the Communist Party and joined the anti-Stalinist Communist Party Opposition, which was established that year initially to modify and later to replace the mainstream Communist Party. After Hitler rose to power in 1933, the Communist Party Opposition existed only as an illegal and underground organisation.

By his early thirties Blücher had become a seasoned political activist: a Marxist and anti-Stalinist at loggerheads with both mainstream communism and the fascism that Germany embraced in 1933. He had also been married twice: briefly to Lieselotte Ostwald, whom – according to Arendt's biographer – he had married 'when he was too young to know better and divorced her not long after'; and again in 1932 to Natasha Jefroikyn, a Lithuanian who gained German citizenship by her marriage to Blücher (Young-Bruehl, 1982, 133). In addition, between 1918 and 1920 he had sought to continue his education by taking evening courses at the University of Berlin, and throughout the 1920s and early 1930s had collaborated with Robert Gilbert, musician and fellow member of the Spartacus League, on cabaret shows, operettas and various film projects. He was in, in short, an imposing – and opposing – figure: twice married, an ex-soldier, politically engaged and active within the leftist counter-culture that flourished in Berlin in the years between the wars.

Blücher's second marriage – to Natasha Jefroikyn – was again short-lived. After their marriage they lived together only intermittently and by 1935 the marriage had, according to the later divorce papers, irretrievably broken down. This was perhaps inevitable in that Blücher had, the year after their marriage, escaped to Prague – a move no doubt necessitated by Hitler's rise to power and Blücher's membership of an organisation that had been designated as illegal under the Nazi regime (Young-Bruehl, 1982, 133). There is no available evidence as to why Jefroikyn did not accompany Blücher on his escape from Germany to Prague in 1933 and then to Paris where he arrived in 1934. All we know is that he was at considerable risk as a political dissident and she had gained German citizenship. The rest is open to surmise. What is clear is that Blücher's divorce from Jefroikyn was ratified in 1938, three years after their marriage had broken down and two years after he had met Arendt.

The recorded correspondence between Arendt and Blücher commenced in August 1936 – she was twenty-nine, he was thirty-seven. It was, as Lotte Kohler in her introduction to her edition of the letters remarked, characterised by 'natural intimacy and unrestrained frankness'. Arendt and Blücher corresponded in German – their mother tongue – in an idiom that Kohler describes as one of 'unconditional partnership' (AB, ix) During her first post-World War II trip to Europe as director of Jewish Cultural Reconstruction – almost ten years into their marriage and shortly after the death of her mother – Arendt is clearly reliant on Blücher for emotional security and continuity. The trip must have stirred up complex memories and emotions, involving as it did a reunion with Jaspers and with Heidegger and his wife. In a letter sent from Heidelberg during that trip and dated early 1950, Arendt hurled at Blücher: 'Have you really forgotten what we agreed, that you would write once a week?' She continued:

> I am very upset. I simply can't understand your complete lack of sense about the most primitive human responsibilities and obligations. I cannot believe that you have so little imagination that you can't imagine how I feel, careering about the world like a car wheel that has come off, without a single connection to home or to anything I can rely on. I write all this to you as bitterly and, if you will, as embittered as it looks to me, and as it has to look to me.
>
> AB, 123

In his prompt response to Arendt's troubled letter, Blücher reminded her of his own physical condition: 'Now that luckily a second, smaller stone, and some more kidney sludge, have wormed their way out, I can confess to you how hellish the whole thing has been ... That you are very upset makes me upset too, particularly as I am supposed to have caused it' (AB, 123). He also reminded Arendt that her friend Hilde Fränkel – the mistress of the Protestant theologian, Paul Tillich, who had fled Germany and was about to publish his highly influential (1952) *The Courage to Be* – was dying of cancer and provided a lengthy update on her mental and physical state. Characteristically, Blücher met implied criticism head-on, while at the same time providing reassurance. He reassured her that he was maintaining their home, fulfilling their duties towards their friends, while at the same time managing his own health problems: 'Don't be unsettled and unhappy', he concluded the letter, 'Your home here is standing, waiting for you' (AB, 126).

At the heart of their relationship was the security that – for both of them but perhaps in varying degrees – sprang from continuity: the continuity of language through their shared mother tongue; of being and living together in a shared place; and, increasingly, of thinking in harmony with one another through their shared concern with what constitutes 'the political'. Their relationship – including as it did the necessary intimacy and privacy associated with marriage – incorporated also the core elements of friendship. Being lovers and being friends is different, but by no means mutually exclusive or even dichotomous. When – as in the case of Arendt and Blücher – their thinking becomes a kind of contrapuntal melody within which disagreements become deeply harmonised, then the categories of 'lover', 'husband/wife', 'partner', 'friend' become increasingly porous and blurred. The common and inescapable experience of thinking is the binding element that sustains our partnerships and friendships through a kind of ongoing – if nevertheless intermittent – conversation: a dialogue that sustains both the relationship and the individual identities of those involved in that relationship.

So, how Arendt and Blücher fell into step in their thinking is crucial to an understanding of how friendship interfused their relationship. Falling into step had, in their case, involved a long and risky trek across continents. It had also involved an understanding not only of how thinking works, but of what it is worth thinking about – and, crucially, of the relation between thinking and what bridges the gap between thinking and action. Blücher's contribution to this ongoing dialogue is more difficult to track because he was a great talker and teacher, but was not a writer. As noted, he published nothing in his lifetime, and the records that remain are contained within the published letters he wrote to Arendt and the records held of his work within Bard College where he taught and where his archive is assiduously maintained.

The dialogue he maintained with Arendt was crucial to the development of her thinking. Together they worked through to a common position on the idea of citizenship, on what constitutes philosophy and on the nature of political action. To understand the importance of Arendt's relationship with Blücher – and its profound impact upon her own work – we need to piece together, from the sparse resources available, Blücher's own style of thinking and his own focus of thought.

Doing philosophy

During the first ten years of their marriage, Arendt was transforming herself from a philosopher into a political thinker. This transformation was accomplished in large part through the process of producing *The Origins of Totalitarianism*. Her dedication of this book to Blücher was much more than a token gesture. He had been instrumental in her transformation from philosopher to political thinker through both his continuing discussion of the major themes of the book as it developed and took shape, and through his deep respect for her as a writer and what he termed 'the awkward beauty of true style' as exemplified in that particular work (AB, 109).

Throughout that same period Blücher was, as it were, travelling in the opposite direction intellectually: transforming himself from a political thinker and activist into a philosopher. Each was gathering past resources and taking stock of them within their current context, so that her philosophical orientation to politics and his political orientation towards philosophy were carried forward into their future work: she as a writer on the international stage, and he as an increasingly influential teacher of art history and philosophy at the New School for Social Research (from 1950 to 1958) and as professor of philosophy at Bard College (from 1952 to 1968). Both institutions were located within New York, which, notwithstanding Arendt's frequent visits to Europe, became the place they made their home.

By the early 1950s, then, their intellectual trajectories had interconnected. But their respective transitions had not been easy. While Arendt had been writing *The Origins of Totalitarianism*, he had been struggling to reposition himself intellectually with a view to gaining employment in New York. This was no easy task and took its toll emotionally. Writing to Arendt in 1950, during her first trip back to post-World War II Europe, he expressed his own sense of frustration and alienation:

> Nothing works out, in spite of many interviews. You know, I think all these people find me highly suspect. The most restrained things I say frighten them ... and they look down on me, even though I intimidate them. They have a bad conscience, and I seem to reinforce it by my mere presence ... I'm cutting myself to pieces in the process.
>
> AB, 144

The 'bad conscience' is no doubt a reference to the pervasive influence of McCarthyism – at its height between 1950 and 1956 – and to Blücher's vulnerability given the extreme anti-communist mood of the times and his own political backstory. At the time he also lacked US citizenship, which he gained a year after Arendt in August 1952.

If Blücher had been a sympathetic sounding board for Arendt in her turn towards politics, she was in turn a sounding board for him in his attempt to come to terms with the Western philosophical tradition. In 1948, in the letter in which he had responded to her news of her mother's death, he wrote: 'Something strange has happened to me: a sudden and crazed attack or, better still, an assault of productivity. Dutiful and unsuspecting ... And then came the *"brainstorm"*' (AB, 93). Later in the letter he explained the significance of the brainstorm: 'In two days and a night I saw in clear progression the new conceptual whole, the consolidation of my objective. And now, finally, my doubts are resolved and I realize that I have found new territory. I know now the continent that I discovered. Now I want to set foot on it. Or, first, to chart it' (AB, 95) What he had grasped as a kind of *gestalt* ('the new conceptual whole') he could now comprehend in terms of its constituent parts and how those parts were causally related ('in clear progression'). He had, in short, perceived a history of thought implicit in which was an argument about the nature of traditional Western philosophy: 'Kant was a servant, Nietzsche a master, Marx a despot, and Kierkegaard a slave. I am a *prospective citizen*' (AB, 95). This was the new territory that Blücher set himself to chart.

He charted it through his work at the New School for Social Research and, crucially, through his leadership and development of what he termed 'the Common Course' that he instigated and developed as part of the liberal arts curriculum at Bard College. Writing to Arendt in 1952 while she was visiting Europe on a Guggenheim Fellowship, Blücher explained how he had been contracted to 'prepare a group of teachers for the project, to work out the plan'. He then went on to outline the nature of the course he hoped to develop: 'It will be a philosophical course for *freshmen*, which will aim to teach them the meaning *of ultimate questions*, at the same time introducing them naturally to their various field of study. I want to turn it into a completely modern educational plan, which will take over from *progressive education*' (AB, 214). Originally contracted to advise on the planning of the course, prepare those who would be teaching on it and undertake some initial teaching during the first semester, Blücher in fact led it and taught on it for the next fifteen years. He thereby contributed significantly to the development of a liberal arts education tradition which remains a significant – if increasingly challenged – element within the North American higher education system (see Nussbaum, 1997).

In his final lecture for the Common Course delivered in 1967 (recorded on tape, transcribed and then edited by Blücher), he summarised what the course had tried to achieve, and outlined what he saw as two opposing approaches to philosophy. He characterised the first approach as 'no more than the general theory by which all present knowledge is organized, brought into a unity whose inherent tyranny, that is, the tyranny inherent in every system, will eventually bring it to fall' (AB, 393). We become acquainted with such systems, he argued, chiefly through ideologies which employ 'high words' to justify their 'inherent tyranny'. The second approach – the one he had tried to develop through the Common Course – sought to 'cleanse the political atmosphere from the pollution of all these high words' (AB, 394). It involves an endless process of critical thinking whereby what we think we know is constantly questioned and what we do not know is constantly acknowledged: '[P]hilosophy means nothing more than man's readiness to live in the presence of what he does not know' (AB, 393).

These two approaches presuppose very different pedagogies. In developing his own notion of philosophy, Blücher became increasingly dissatisfied with didactic modes of teaching that are premised on the notion of the student as the passive recipient of knowledge. He did not rely on pre-prepared lecture notes, but on his capacity to think through a topic as he addressed his students and sought to engage them in discussion. He modelled through his own discursive style of teaching what it was to be a philosopher: the idea was to *do* philosophy – to show it in action – rather than present it as a *fait accompli*. His own model here was, of course, Socrates, whose name he constantly evoked in the 1967 lecture. For Blücher, the Socratic legacy was not so much a method or style of philosophising as a democratic and democratising impulse: if to philosophise is to live in the presence of what we do not know, then we can all be philosophers; and if we can all be philosophers, then philosophy is a deeply democratic enterprise. 'Socrates', as Blücher put it, 'is not the philosopher-king but the philosopher-citizen, telling everybody that every man can be a philosophizing being and that one can be a good citizen – that is, a political being – without being also a philosopher' (AB, 398).

Socrates was a benign third presence in the relationship between Arendt and Blücher. In 1955 when Arendt was visiting Europe to participate in an international conference sponsored by the Congress for Cultural Freedom, Blücher wrote to her in Greece from New York: 'Keep an eye out for Socrates, I'm sure he's still lounging about somewhere there, and tell him how he amazes me' (AB, 274). Later, in her last posthumously published work, she addresses the question 'What makes us think?' with reference to 'The answer of Socrates' (LM, I, 166–79). In that section of her final work – based on the first series of her 1973 Gifford Lectures – Arendt echoes Blücher's final lecture as delivered at Bard College in 1967: 'None of the *logoi*, the arguments, ever stays put; they move around. And because Socrates, asking questions to which he does *not* know the answers, sets them in motion, once the statements have come full circle, it is usually Socrates who cheerfully proposes to start all over again' (AB, 169–70).

The footnote that she added to that statement is an even clearer tribute to her dead husband for whom any self-identification with the notion of the 'clever professor' would have been an anathema: 'The frequent notion that Socrates tries to lead his interlocutor with his questions to certain results of which he is convinced in advance – like a clever professor with his students – seems to me entirely mistaken' (LM, I, 236). Just as Arendt had become a thinker through her writing, so Blücher had become a thinker through his interaction with his students and his attempt to engage them in dialogue. Shortly after starting his work at the New School for Social Research, New York – and four years after the brainstorm – he wrote to Arendt regarding his course on art history and philosophy and his sense of fulfilment at having engaged and motivated his students: 'Big and long discussions. They won't let go of me … They form small discussion groups. They go to art exhibits together, and then tell me how much better they are able to appreciate works of art. Friendships blossom' (AB, 197).

Politics in action

If Blücher insisted on the distinction between two kinds of philosophy, then he was equally insistent on two kinds of politics: the politics of coercion and suppression versus the politics of deliberation and dialogue. Underlying this distinction is a particular view of what constitutes power and how power relates to politics. Both Arendt and Blücher viewed power as the human capacity for collective action. 'Power', as Arendt put it, 'corresponds to the human ability not just to act but to act in concert. Power is never the property of an individual; it belongs to a group and remains in existence only so long as the group keeps together' (OV, 44). The ability 'to act in concert' makes possible the development of a politics of deliberation and dialogue. Only by distinguishing the notion of 'power' from related terms such as 'strength', 'force', 'authority' and 'violence' can we begin to identify and define a genuinely democratic politics – a politics, that is, of participation and engagement; or, as Blücher put it, the politics of 'the philosopher citizen' (AB, 398).

Some of Arendt's conceptual distinctions – as McCarthy pointed out – played against common linguistic usage. Her insistence on restricting power to 'the human ability ... to act in concert' and distinguishing it from force and violence may seem to fly in the face of how power is generally understood and experienced: hence Jonathan Schell's suggestion that the politically resonant distinction to be drawn from Arendt's work is between what he terms 'cooperative power' ('based on support') and 'coercive power' ('based on force'). 'Both kinds of power', as he puts it, 'are real' (Schell, 2004, 227). But what Arendt was highlighting was that one kind of power can all too easily be used to mask the other kind of power. Democratic leaders, for example, could pursue coercive policies under cover of their own cooperative rhetoric. Unless power was clearly defined it could all too easily become a metaphor for what Arendt maintained was its antithesis: namely, coercion and suppression. Therein lay the importance for Arendt of distinguishing and defining the parameters of power. Only by distinguishing the concept was it possible to ensure that it did not become an ideological tool.

Arendt's attempt to disentangle the notion of power from what she saw as its metaphorical usage echoed the insistence in Blücher's own teaching on developing a critical attitude towards words and the way in which they may be used to mystify and entangle us in coercive ideologies. In his final 1967 lecture for the Common Course, he claimed that he and his colleagues at Bard College had sought to prepare students for the world in which they lived by focusing their critical attention on the relation between language and power. Evoking Socrates – 'trying to interpret him anew, trying to use him for our own twentieth-century purposes' – he provided a retrospect on the purpose of the course he had set up fifteen years before: '[W]e prepared ourselves for the time we live in, a century that has rightly been called an age of wars and revolution; moreover an age in which almost all words have turned into lies. Words and language are those instruments by which man can create both, lies *and* truth. . . . [W]ords have become the tools of power' (AB, 391).

It was, he argued, only through the process of becoming 'examining and critical' that we can release the collective power implicit in deliberation and dialogue:

> Our political system will change only if citizens change . . . So, let's start the old discourse, the discussion again; let's become examining and critical again, and raise all the old questions again – what is justice? what is truth? . . . [T]he precondition for this activity is political freedom as it is for every kind of higher life; this very fact makes us all, or should make us all, philosopher-citizens.
>
> AB, 399

If democracies are premised on citizenship, and citizenship is premised on a polity that is both 'examining and critical', then the practice of philosophising as exemplified in Blücher's own teaching is fundamental to democratic politics. Put more bluntly – as was Blücher's custom – philosophising requires what he called 'gall': 'Even if I could talk with all the facts in the world but didn't have the gall, I would be but a paper sword and a paper shield' (AB, 86). It was the gall – the sheer bloody-mindedness of speaking truth to self-declared power – that made all the difference between paper swords and shields and those forged from more enduring material.

Throughout his life Blücher channelled his creative and analytical abilities into his voracious reading, his teaching and other collaborative ventures, and his friendships. The correspondence between Arendt and himself – and much of their conversation when together – was conducted in their shared mother tongue. Maintaining that line of linguistic continuity seems to have been crucial. Without it neither might have had the courage to speak back to the world within which they found themselves. The correspondence between them was part of a complex process of translation – or mediation – from the relative comfort zone of their first language into the more complicated linguistic terrain of their adopted tongue. Their common language of German provided them with a space within which to flourish. From that space they were able to move out into the wider terrain within which professionally and socially they communicated and learned to express themselves in their adopted language. Without that space – the space of their love and friendship within which they were able to talk in their shared mother tongue – the conditions necessary for flourishing would have been severely constrained.

It is hardly surprising, therefore, that both Arendt and Blücher were preoccupied with how and why words matter – and, more specifically, with the relation between how words are used and how power is characterised and deployed. As a writer working in a third language – after German and French – Arendt could draft and redraft her texts, but as a lecturer working without a prepared script in a foreign language, Blücher had no such safety net. (PowerPoint, launched in 1990, was not then available as a safety net for lecturers who like to look as if they are doing the kind of thing Blücher was in fact doing.) Blücher's insistence on following his own instincts as a teacher and lecturer no doubt took additional gall. But he may well not have found those inner resources had it not been for the ongoing dialogue with Arendt: their support for one another, their testing of ideas against one another, their care for – and, yes, their nagging of – one another. Their love for one another took the form of a great friendship, just as their friendship was imbued with intense love and mutual care.

Root and branch

Implicit in Blücher's evolving ideas regarding the nature of philosophy and its relation to politics was a notion of human beings as necessarily relational, interconnective and interdependent. They are, as he put it in his 1967 lecture,

> inveterate and incurable relationists, born to relate everything to everything in various manners and different forms. This is the most

human of man's passions, and a wonderful thing, perhaps even the source of all our creative abilities. The danger is only that once man believes he has found an absolute – the kosmos, or Being, or God – he can no longer stop relating everything to this One absolute. That is, instead of keeping his system of relations open and hence uncertain, he will invent a closed system where everything is once and for all related to everything else. Isn't it marvellous?

AB, 392

The openness of what Blücher here calls the 'system of relations' is crucial to Arendt's and Blücher's lifelong relationship, within which they shared intimacies, thoughts and ideas, information, worries (often in the earlier days about money) and concerns (increasingly about their health). When they were together, they talked, became absorbed in their separate projects, met friends and acquaintances, and settled into the familiar habits and customs of being together. When they were apart they corresponded by letter, occasionally spoke on the phone and maintained a running commentary on the progress, ailments and achievements of their mutual friends in the United States and across Europe. These routines formed the bases of a relationship that was deeply intimate yet orientated towards their wider circle of friends, acquaintances and professional associates.

During Arendt's various absences from New York, Blücher became a sympathetic listener to those of their friends who were for whatever reason passing through difficulties in their personal lives. He was particularly supportive of their mutual friend Hilde Fränkel, the mistress of the Paul Tillich, who felt deeply isolated given Tillich's intermittent contact with her during the final stages of her illness. Arendt and Fränkel had met in Frankfurt around 1930 and had rediscovered each other in New York during the war years. Theirs was a deep friendship lasting until Fränkel's death in 1950. Fränkel was, as Eleanor Honig Skoller (1993, 121) puts it, 'endowed with an overwhelming naturalness that was endlessly fascinating to Arendt'. The final stages of her illness coincided with Arendt's first post-World War II journey back to Europe since her emigration from Germany and her flight from France.

Throughout that period Blücher kept in close contact with Fränkel, providing Arendt with regular updates on her friend's physical and mental state. In early 1950 he wrote to her as she was travelling through Germany:

> Hilde is in a bad way ... She is really being tormented. Her pain is so overwhelming that she has to take more and more morphine. And she says that as a result she can only live like an animal ... Most of the time she can't read anymore because she can't take anything in ... I still prevail on her, quietly and insistently, to stay alive ... She is thoroughly convinced that she will never see you again, which I dispute energetically, and I do believe she will live at least another six months. It is horribly sad, darling, to stand by and watch a person die slowly.

He concluded this section of his letter with the thought that 'she is like a dear little child that has come to harm' (AB, 125–6).

In a slightly later letter, Blücher made it clear that he saw this kind of human engagement and obligation as 'the origin of freedom'. While not alluding to Fränkel or other specific instances, he clearly had in mind the vital importance of an expansive – and expanding – relationality that was inclusive of their own relationship while recognising the wider networks of friendship that they both shared: 'That we are capable of intuiting ourselves in other human beings and intuiting them in us, to seek and to recognize, and that we are willing to do this – here lies the origin of freedom' (AB, 131). Freedom, in other words, had its origins in the human capacity for mutuality and reciprocity. It can never be simply *individual* freedom, since the freedom of any individual is dependent upon the freedom of myriad other individuals. Freedom is necessarily *collective*, in its sensitivity and responsiveness to the way in which our freedoms rely on interdependency and mutuality.

This notion of freedom was central to the deeply shared humanism that lay at the heart of their relationship and their sense of being at home together. In the final sentence of the letter in which he had outlined to Arendt what he saw as 'the origin of freedom', Blücher explained: '[T]hat is why I have established an eternal home here in this world, and not in the supernatural homeland of Zion, right in the middle of this world, with your help and that of friends, so that I too can say: "where one or some of you are gathered, there is my homeland, and where you are with me, there is my home"' (AB, 133). His home, he insisted, was not located in a 'supernatural' utopia, but 'here in this world ... right in the middle of this world'. Insofar as his home was – as he put it – 'eternal', it was because of their worldly continuities and interconnections that at once focused on and radiated out from his relationship with Arendt.

In her letters to Blücher, Arendt was constantly informing their shared worldliness through her sharp observations of places, people and events. On her 1949–50 trip to Europe she wrote to Blücher with a vivid description of war-torn Berlin: '[F]rom Spandau to Neukölln is one big field of rubble; nothing recognisable; only a few people in the streets, like an incredibly spread-out village ... In the Eastern Sector nothing has been rebuilt ... Great unemployment. People grim, dressed worse, starving, still carrying sacks on their back ... Furthermore no one has any money, unbelievable poverty. Everything problematic' (AB, 133–4). On this – her first emotionally gruelling – trip back to Europe, she began to place in perspective the extraordinary trajectory of her life up until that time. She wrote of Europe as a nightmare from which – with Blücher – she had escaped: 'I think of you and feel as if I have escaped from a nightmare, a nightmare of seeking but finding nothing' (AB, 134–5). Blücher remained for her – as she remained for him – her 'home-land'.

Five years later – in early 1955 – as visiting professor in the Department of Political Science at Berkely, she described for Blücher her first response to San Francisco Bay: '[I]t is as beautiful as a dream. The chain of mountains and hills look a little Japanese ... [A]ctually they are not chains, not a real mountain range, but round hills that seem to grow and curve independently out of each other or out of the plain. I know such landscapes only from Japanese or Chinese painting' (AB, 229). Towards the end of her teaching stint at Berkeley she described the giant redwood trees of California: '[T]hat was incredible. As if one had always seen woods, but never a tree in its full majesty. A very strange growth pattern, as many trees issue from one root, growing in a circle, and then coming together again at the treetops ... The trunks like weathered rock' (AB, 257). It was her experience not only of the human world but also of the natural world that Arendt wanted and needed to share with Blücher.

Her description of the redwood trees in their 'full majesty' might almost be taken as a metaphor for the specificity of her friendships. She had, as she put it, 'always seen woods' – always, to pursue the metaphor, seen friendship in the abstract – but to experience a particular friendship was 'incredible'. The 'growth pattern' of particular friendships, the issuing of many friendships from 'one root', the 'growing in a circle, and then coming together again': these detailed characteristics of the redwood trees evoke a sense of what friendships meant to Arendt. Her enduring friendships were 'trunks weathered like storm', each providing a tentacular branchwork of wider friendships and associations. They were the means by which the branchwork of friendship flourished and became mutually sustaining.

Arendt's friendship with Blücher was the 'one root' without which the branch-like structure was unsustainable. Blücher had neither financial resources nor an international reputation to match that of Arendt; he had no ambition to write for publication or to become a public figure; he intermittently suffered from ill health and was averse to travelling by air even on domestic flights. He was, on the other hand, generally acknowledged to be a great teacher in the Socratic tradition. He was also an inveterate reader and by all accounts a superb conversationalist who delighted in controversy and debate. He was also loyal to the two institutions that had supported him and provided him with employment following his move to New York. Notwithstanding his strange mixture of vulnerability and strength – or perhaps because of it – he was undoubtedly Arendt's 'weathered rock'.

Life after Blücher

Following Blücher's death on 31 October 1970, Arendt was distraught. She had known him for thirty-four years and been married to him for thirty of those years. Although she still had a wide circle of friends and colleagues, the fallout from her reporting of the Eichmann trial had left her isolated from some of her oldest friends and acquaintances. Jaspers had died the previous year and, although Heidegger was still alive, his sense of duty towards Arendt was – as we have seen – extremely limited. McCarthy remained loyal and supportive, but she was partnered while Arendt was now widowed. W. H. Auden, whom Arendt had known quite well but not intimately since 1958, proposed marriage to her only a month after Blücher's death. Arendt, of course, turned him down. (She nevertheless published a fine tribute to Auden in *The New Yorker* after his death three years later. See RLC, 294–302.) As she explained to McCarthy, she hated the sense of pity that Auden had aroused in her through what she saw as his inept and inappropriate proposal and his general state of dishevelment on the occasion that the proposal was made (AM, 269–70).

Blücher was unique. Unlike Heidegger, Jaspers and McCarthy, he wrote nothing for publication. Young-Bruehl (1982, 432) has suggested that, although opinion was divided as to whether this was the result of a writing block or a matter of Socratic principle, the most likely suggestion is 'that the "cannot" and "will not" each had their weight in him'. He was also unlike Heidegger, Jaspers and McCarthy in that he was part of both the old world of Europe from which he and Arendt had fled and the new world of their adopted United States. Yet he was disinclined to return to Europe after the war, and – although he remained something of an outsider in his adopted country – was content to stay in New York while Arendt travelled the world. Perhaps, as Young-Bruehl (1982, 434) has suggested, 'Blücher never really overcame his hatred of Europe's bourgeois civilization and certainly not of Germany's particular path'. He was equally dismissive of what he saw as the self-indulgence of some of his students in the United States, particularly as it related to the drug culture, which he saw as deeply anti-philosophical in its escapist tendencies: '[T]o ruin and destroy your perceptions [i.e. your senses] and then say you want to pursue the truth: are you crazy? The experiences you have you will not be able to communicate' (quoted in Young-Bruehl, 1982, 434).

He was also – to a degree that set him apart from Heidegger, Jaspers and McCarthy – hugely gregarious, while having a rare ability to enjoy his own company. When Arendt was away, he would manage and maintain their network of friends in New York, often relaying messages to them from Arendt and relaying messages back. He was much sought after as a guest and was punctilious in his care for those of their mutual friends who were ill or passing through difficult personal or professional circumstances. But he was also happy to spend days reading and preparing in his own inimitable way for his unscripted seminars and lectures. One imagines him in a prolonged state of Socratic dialogue – with himself, with the books he was reading, with Arendt and with their mutual friends. His stream of thinking was constantly bursting its banks and flooding whatever situation he was in.

The uniqueness of the man lay in his argumentativeness, which was an expression of his passion for debate, his openness to opinion and his insistence on sustaining discussion beyond the point of disagreement. Writing shortly after Blücher's death, Dwight Macdonald – radical writer and critic – wrote that there was one quality among all others that he had particularly liked in

Blücher: 'the ability to commit himself to a position, passionately, and damn the horses or the expense!' (quoted in Young-Bruehl, 1982, 432). If Blücher was competitive in argument, it was because he was committed to keeping the argumentative game going; if he was adversarial, it was because he refused to accept that the argumentative game was governed by reason alone; and if he was contradictory – and at times self-contradictory – in argument, it was because for him the game was the same game that had been played by Socrates on the street corners of ancient Athens. The game, in other words, was an exercise in truthfulness – and, as such, was deadly serious. What Dana Villa (2001, 28–9) wrote about Socrates seems a fitting epitaph for Blücher:

> Socrates does not apply to the ignorant and recalcitrant many an expert knowledge available only to the few; rather, he attempts to open the philosophical vocation to everyone. This is not to say he harbors the unrealistic expectation that the majority will become philosophers. It *is* to say, however, that he thinks neither age nor civic status is a bar to the kind of self-examination he has in mind. What matters is not class, status, education, gender, or even freedom but the capacity to think.

Although a staunch secularist, Blücher would no doubt have shared with Dante a profound contempt for the cowardly and pusillanimous who live without blame and without shame – being neither hot nor cold – and are assigned after death to Limbo. Heaven, according to Dante, excludes them – and yet they are not even in Hell. They are neither one thing nor the other. In Dante's vision, they are running about noisily in circles and constantly stung by insects. They never lived because they never exercised their willpower or their capacity to reason. In Dante's schema they are inferior to the lowest category of sinners, who at least exercised their agency on behalf of evil. Their inability to commit themselves to a position would – for Blücher – have been as great a cause of contempt as it was for Dante.

Among the papers collected in the Blücher Archive at Bard College is one in which Blücher was formulating a scale of human relationships and the human capabilities associated with that scale: 'Accepting the whole human being from within – love; accepting the whole personality from without – friendship; accepting an independent person – political relationship; accepting an individual as a member of society; accepting strangers as co-workers' (quoted in Young-Bruehl, 1982, 433). In his relationship with Arendt he had found the integration of the categories that comprise this schema. Their relationship – over the span of its years – embodied love, friendship, the political, the social and the experience of being co-workers. Their friendship was inextricably entangled with each of these other categories.

The Bard College archive includes a lecture Blücher delivered in 1968 – a year after his final lecture to the Common Course – in which he focuses specifically on the meaning of friendship:

> [F]riendship means love without *eros*. The *eros* is overcome. It was there in the beginning, but it had been overcome and it doesn't count any more. What counts is the mutual insight of two personalities who recognize each other as such; who in effect can say to each other 'I guarantee you the development of your personality and you guarantee me the development of mine.' That is the basis of all real community thinking, and such a community can only start with friends.
>
> Quoted in Young-Bruehl, 1982, 433

This feels like a personal statement. But its meaning is open to interpretation. Is Blücher saying that friendship is a compensation for the loss of *eros*? Or is he saying that friendships may evolve beyond *eros*? Or that a relationship that has its source in *eros* may nevertheless grow into friendship? What Blücher is clearly not doing is forcing a dichotomy between *eros* and friendship. He is simply affirming that our human capacity for love cannot be restricted to the confines of *eros*. Unravelling his argument back to its unstated premise, he might be saying that without friends there can be no community and that without the acknowledgement that some friendships have their origins in *eros* ('it was there in the beginning') we necessarily limit the potential of friendship. It would then follow that our erotic desires, passions and attractions cannot simply be siphoned off or left behind, but are a necessary part of our human flourishing.

That we leave Blücher with more questions than answers – and that the questions suggest an undertow of personal self-reflection – seems appropriate. From his radical activism in pre-World War II Germany to his development of critical modes of inquiry and pedagogy at Bard College and the New School for Social Research, Blücher was a relentless questioner who persistently challenged others to formulate their own questions. He was a challenger: a chatterbox to some, no doubt a gadfly to others, and a wonderfully sensitive and responsive listener to a small number of close friends. His life – like that of Socrates – was a demonstration not of the power of reason but of the impossibility of total rationality. Philosophy was in the doing of it, just as politics was always in and of the action.

Life after Blücher was, for Arendt, a consolidation of much of what she had learnt in and through their relationship. Thinking, willing and judgement were to be the great unifying themes of her final work, *The Life of the Mind*. She had learnt to think with Blücher, she had received confirmation of her own will through their relationship, and she had trusted him as a man of judgement. During the five and a half years between his death and hers she endeavoured to gather the past, to do her duty by her friends, and to bring her own thinking – which was inextricably interwoven with his – into a systematic synthesis. That she failed in the last of those tasks again seems wholly appropriate. Whatever system might be derived from Arendt's work is as open and permeable as her own way of thinking. *The Life of the Mind* – dutifully and lovingly edited by McCarthy – is one of those texts that precisely because it is unfinished remains open to the future.

Blücher's legacy lives on – not only as the husband of Arendt – but as an educator who contributed hugely to the development of the tradition of liberal arts education and to the critical pedagogies that have supported and carried forward that tradition. His, too, was an unfinished text. It was unfinished because for him philosophy took the form of a particular kind of dialogue characterised by a refusal of foreclosure and an insistence on the need to follow through into action. For Blücher – as for Arendt – philosophy was inextricably entwined with the politics of the here and now.

There can be no doubt that the marriage between Arendt and Blücher was deeply loving and erotically charged. But it was not – and Arendt would have utterly rejected the idea that it might have been – a marriage made in heaven. It was a marriage made on earth and based on an enduring friendship that was deeply caring and mutually supportive. It was also a passionately intellectual friendship, a world of words and ideas that they were forever elaborating and into which their wider circle of friends were frequently invited to help in that task of exploration and elaboration. It was a world characterised by the plurality of endless discourse through which Arendt tested and refined the core concepts of her thinking. What she understood by friendship – and what we might learn about friendship from her life and work – are all derived from that shared world. The following chapter returns to that world as she sought to formulate it in her last great unfinished work, the architectonics of which are constructed around the three pillars of thinking, willing and judging.

8

The Hermeneutics of Friendship

Aristotle, speaking about friendship, remarked: 'The friend is another self' – meaning: you can carry on the dialogue of thought with him just as well as with yourself ... Socrates would have said: The self, too, is a kind of friend.

LM, I, 189

Friendship as practice

Friendship was woven into the fabric of Arendt's life. She had a vast network of friends spread across Europe and the United States at a time long before email, Facebook, Skype, texting, Twitter or the now ubiquitous mobile phone. Her friendships were sustained through face-to-face meetings (often involving travel), regular correspondence by letter and occasional conversation by landline (which was, in comparison to today, an extremely expensive option). Friendship, in other words, involved a considerable investment of time (arranging and undertaking visits, writing and posting letters) and money (postage stamps, rail and air fares, telephone bills). Friendship was – to use McCarthy's term – necessarily 'workmanlike' in that it required a commitment to the routines and practices of friendship. Instant communication via the social media was not an option. It was necessary to think ahead, set aside time for letter writing and build into one's travel arrangements as many meetings with old and new friends as possible. While Arendt and Blücher were sufficiently well off to move into more comfortable apartments in Manhattan in 1959, they had until then been far from financially secure. Both also led extremely demanding professional lives. Yet, Arendt's commitment to maintaining her friendships and extending her network of friends was unremitting.

Given the central importance of friendship in her life, it is remarkable that in her writing Arendt developed no detailed analysis of the nature of friendship. As a writer she was methodologically and philosophically committed to making fine conceptual distinctions and developing her arguments by way of those distinctions. In her final work, *The Life of the Mind*, she summed up her position as follows: 'Everything that exists among a plurality of things is not simply what it is, in its identity, but it is also different from others ... When we say what a thing is, we must say what it is not or we would speak in tautologies' (LM, I, 183). If plurality assumes difference, then difference implies the need to make distinctions. The rhetorical method follows from the philosophical premise.

Yet, in spite of this insistence that 'when we say what a thing is, we must say what it is not', Arendt seems not to have been interested in distinguishing friendship from other forms of human relationship. Admittedly she draws on the classic distinction between *philia* and *eros*, with the latter associated in her mind with an element of self-surrender, which is antithetical to the mutuality and reciprocity implicit in friendship. She also distinguishes friendship as a form of chosen relationship from kinship as given without choice: we do not choose our parents or our lineage. But beyond these fairly routine distinctions there is little attempt to define friendship as a distinct category. Nor is Arendt particularly interested in distinguishing between different forms of friendship, such as those traditionally characterised as friendships of pleasure, utility and virtue. She seems willing to take friendship at face value.

Why this reticence in analysing friendship? Why this uncharacteristic willingness to allow it to remain conceptually fuzzy? My guess is that Arendt was less interested in friendship as a concept than in friendship as a practice – less interested, that is, in friendship than in actual *friendships*. Friendship was something she *did*. It was – for someone who had existed as a stateless migrant – a necessary condition for survival. So she drew less on the traditional distinctions between friendship and other forms of association – or between different kinds of friendship – and more on what her experience taught her about friendship. She was, for example, very clear that friendship was about continuity. In practice, therefore, there was not so much a distinction to be drawn as a scale to be borne in mind: the oldest friendships were the best and, as the years passed and some friendships matured, the older friendships moved up the scale of perfection. Not that there was any sense of 'perfect friendship' for Arendt, but there was the sense of persistence. Friendship was a long haul – a deeply rewarding and beneficial haul – but a long haul nevertheless.

So friendship necessarily involved that most unfashionable of virtues: duty. Duty has become politically suspect, associated as it now tends to be with enforced drudgery. No one would be dutiful by choice, would they? One's prime duty – in a consumerist society premised on the all-importance of individual choice – is duty to oneself. Duty and freedom are at opposite poles on this political spectrum. But, for Arendt, duty towards one's friends was a necessary means of ensuring the possibility of freedom. Her friendships had, after all, seen her through, sustained her and provided her with a modicum of security in what had been a chronically insecure world. Moreover, duty was one of the great republican ideals, as evidenced in the emphasis Aristotle placed on duties as opposed to rights. Duty on this alternative political spectrum is not the antithesis of freedom, but one of the conditions necessary for its realisation: duty is what we owe one another – what is due to us – by virtue of laying claim to a common world.

Duty meant that having arrived in New York as a stateless person you did everything you could – as soon as you could – to ensure that, for example, Walter Benjamin's work was preserved for posterity. It meant that – notwithstanding your own straitened circumstances – you sent monthly food parcels to the Jaspers who had remained in Germany. It meant that you dropped whatever you were doing to be with McCarthy when she miscarried. It meant that you prepared and delivered orations in honour of your friends as they reached key milestones in their public life, and that you similarly honoured them when they died. Duty was what made continuity possible. Arendt's sense of duty towards her friends was matched by their corresponding sense of duty towards her: supreme examples of which are McCarthy's editing of her friend's *magnum opus*, *The Life of the Mind*, and Jaspers' letters of support and encouragement in the aftermath of the Eichmann trial. Duty was also in evidence as her friends rallied around her immediately after Blücher's death in 1970, with McCarthy flying from Paris to find Arendt already surrounded by friends from New York and elsewhere. Without duty, there could be no continuity; and, without continuity, duty would become merely dutiful.

But the exercise of duty also requires impartiality. Arendt managed to maintain friendships with both Heidegger and Jaspers in spite of the fact that neither was reconciled to the other and that Arendt kept Jaspers in the dark regarding her continuing contact with Heidegger. She also insisted upon her right to maintain friendships with both McCarthy and her third husband in spite of the messy divorce proceedings underway. How to exercise the duties of friendship towards those who, for whatever reason, are in a state of discord, dispute or animosity? Arendt's position was very clear: you have a duty towards your friends regardless of their relationships with one another. You can be friends with people who are themselves not friends. You can even be friends with people who – for whatever reason – bear animosity towards one another. If continuity requires duty, then duty requires the kind of inclusive impartiality that embraces multiple and sometimes conflicting perspectives.

Arendt, then, was less interested in what friendship is than in the conditions necessary for friendship – continuity, duty and impartiality – and how, when these conditions are met, friendship enables us to survive and flourish as human beings. She was interested in how friendship provides an intersubjective context within which we can realise our potential and thereby activate the power that is always latent in human relationality: the power that she considered fundamental to democratic politics. I shall draw out the implication of this theme in the final chapter, but first we need to explore how friendship works, what drives and motivates it, wherein its potentiality for power lies. What – in the constitution of friendship – provides it with that potential? In order to address that question we need to explore in greater detail some of the major themes of what Jerome Kohn (1996, 155) has described as 'her final, tremendously ambitious, yet strange work' – *The Life of the Mind*.

Thinking and willing

Friendship, for Arendt, was inextricably entwined with her notion of thinking. Much of our thinking is conducted in solitude, but – argued Arendt – even solitary thinking involves a dialogical element or what she called 'the duality of the two-in-one' (LM, I, 187). On that basis she drew a sharp distinction between loneliness and solitude: '[S]olitude is that human situation in which I keep myself company. Loneliness comes about when I am alone without being able to split up into the two-in-one, without being able to keep myself company' (LM, I, 185). When we talk to ourselves we are thinking aloud, thereby carrying on a process that – when internalised – becomes solitary thinking and – when externalised – is manifest in the world of human affairs. In that sense thinking is Janus-faced, turning both inward towards solitary reflection and outward towards dialogue and discourse. If Heidegger represented the inward-looking aspect of human thinking, then Blücher represented its outward aspect. Friendship accommodates both. It allows for both self-reflection and for reflective dialogue. Friendship is a space within which we mediate and negotiate these different modes of thinking: a space within which people can be both self-reflective and reflectively expansive.

The link between thinking and understanding is crucial, since thinking is only hermeneutically purposeful through its focus on what is to be understood. That is not to say that thinking involves knowing in advance the object of thought, but that through thinking about and around a subject we begin to clarify what needs to be understood. Without that link between thinking and understanding, thinking drifts into daydreaming, wishful thinking or fantasising. Understanding grounds thinking in the world of human affairs. It is, as Phillip Hansen (1993, 207) puts it, 'a kind of thinking-in-action'. It guides the movement of our thinking, steering us out into the world and providing us with an objective – if nevertheless intersubjective – reality about which to think. So, the conceptualisation of friendship as a space within which people might engage in thinking raises the question of what understanding might thereby be gained. What is the hermeneutical value of friendship?

In addressing that question it is important to bear in mind the core elements that comprise friendship: self, the other and the world. The relation between these elements comprises the subtext of the four narratives of friendship outlined in the previous four chapters. Each of those friendships in different ways and to varying degrees enhanced the understanding of self, the other and the world. The friendship between Arendt and Jaspers, for example, was presented as primarily but by no means exclusively world-oriented, while the narrative of the friendship between Arendt and McCarthy highlighted the prime but again by no means exclusive importance of intersubjective understanding – the understanding, that is, of the self in relation to the other. These particular and necessarily oversimplified typifications are less important than the idea that generates them: namely, that understanding within friendship is a cyclical process involving the distinct selfhood of the two friends and their interconnectedness with the world within and beyond their friendship.

For Arendt this cyclical process – whereby selfhood is enhanced through mutuality, and mutuality through selfhood – was the defining feature of friendship: 'I first talk with others before I talk with myself, examining whatever the joint talk may have been about, and then discover that I can conduct a dialogue not only with others but with myself as well ... [This] dialogue of thought can be carried out only among friends' (LM, I, 189). By talking with friends I learn to talk with myself, and by learning to talk with myself – 'to keep myself company' – I learn to identify myself within the boundless plurality of the world. This 'dialogue of thought' enables us to understand ourselves in relation to others, and others in relation to ourselves. In so doing, it also enables us to understand the world as both intersubjective and objective reality – as 'in here' as well as 'out there'.

Such understanding is possible, argued Arendt, because the world is naturally 'phenomenal'. It is a world made manifest through *appearance*:

> The worldliness of living things means that there is no subject that is not also an object and appears as such to somebody else, who guarantees its 'objective' reality ... Living beings, men and animals, are not just in the world, they are *of the world*, and this precisely because they are subjects and objects – perceiving and being perceived – at the same time.
>
> LM, I, 19–20

We are, in other words, creatures whose being and becoming are defined through a lifelong process of differentiation. Central to that process is the innate capacity for the 'two-in-one' of solitary thought and its dialogical equivalent in the conversation between friends. Without that capacity we would be unable to become ourselves in the world and unable to make sense of others sharing the world with us.

In the second volume of *The Life of the Mind* Arendt locates this process of individuation in the human capacity for 'willing'. The will, she argues, is the source of the individual's specific identity. Because the architecture of her last work remains incomplete, the relation between her key concepts is never fully explained. However, she clearly saw thinking and willing as distinct, while at the same time related. While thinking prepares us for the ongoing task of mediation and negotiation in a world in which each is both appearance and spectator, willing enables us to determine how the self is asserted within this phenomenal world: 'Just as thinking prepares the self for the role of spectator, willing fashions it into an "enduring I" that directs all particular acts of volition. It creates the self's *character* and therefore was sometimes understood as the *principium individuationis*, the source of the person's specific identity' (LM, II, 195). Through this identity-forming assertion of the self into the world of human affairs, the will becomes 'the spring of action'. The will – 'the self's *character*' – actualises thought.

The lynchpin of Arendt's conceptual system is what – as a secular Jew drawing on Augustine's defence of the Christian doctrine of the Trinity – she termed 'independent substance'. She used the term to elucidate what she saw as the unity in complexity of the 'phenomenal' world: a world of mutuality predicated on independence. Friendship, she argued, is paradigmatic of that unity in complexity: 'two men who are friends can be said to be "independent substances" insofar as they are related to themselves; they are friends only relatively to each other. A pair of friends forms a unity, a One, insofar and as long as they are friends … The point here is that such a mutually predicated relationship can occur only among "equals"' (LM, II, 98). It is because friends are equal and different – and their equality and difference are defined in and through their friendship – that they are able to achieve greater understanding of one another and of the world within which their 'two-in-one' is a constitutive element.

'Enlargement of the mind'

The tripartite structure that Arendt had envisaged for *The Life of the Mind* focused on 'thinking', 'willing' and 'judging'. In the event only the first two of those three conceptual building blocks was put in place, with the result that the work lacks not only a detailed discussion of the third element but also an overarching argument as to how the three concepts are related within the overall scheme. In posthumously editing the work, McCarthy included as an appendix to the second volume excerpts from Arendt's lectures on Kant's political philosophy that had a particular bearing on 'judging'. Her comments in these relatively brief extracts suggest that Arendt considered judgement to be an indispensable element in enabling us to think politically.

Arendt linked the human capacity for judgement to what – following Kant – she termed 'enlargement of the mind' (LM, II, 257). It is only by comparing our own judgements with other possible judgements that we develop our capacity for discrimination. Unlike thoughts, judgements are therefore *always* public. This distinction between thinking and judging is crucial: whereas thinking involves a necessary element of keeping oneself company, judging invariably presupposes the company of others; while thinking pulls towards 'the duality of the two-in-one' of solitary thought (LM, I, 187), judging is firmly located in what Arendt had earlier termed 'sharing-the-world-with-others' (BPF, 221). Judgements are in effect claims that are seeking assent but that may be challenged. For that reason a judgement – even when couched in terms of an assertion – invariably involves an element of persuasion. 'To judge', as Dana Villa (1999, 98) puts it, 'is to engage in rational public dialogue, deliberating with others with whom I must finally come to an agreement and decision'.

Arendt had already covered some of this conceptual ground in a 1967 essay that she had written in response to the controversy following her coverage of the Eichmann trial. (Entitled 'Truth and politics', the essay was published in *The New Yorker* and reprinted in the second 1968 edition of BPF.) In that essay she wrote: 'Political thought is representative. I form an opinion by considering a given issue from different viewpoints, by making present to my mind the standpoints of those who are absent; that is, I represent them'. She went on to argue that this process of representation 'does not blindly adopt the actual views of those who stand somewhere else'. Rather it 'is a question . . . of being and thinking in my own identity where actually I am not'. Finally, she claimed that 'the more people's standpoints I have present in my mind while I am pondering a given issue, the better I can imagine how I would feel and think if I were in their place, the stronger will be my capacity for representative thinking and the more valid my final conclusions, my opinions' (BPF, 241).

The faculty that allows us to feel and think as if we are in another's place is the imagination. This faculty, argued Arendt, 'makes the others present and thus moves potentially in a space which is public, open to all sides; in other words, it adopts the position of Kant's world citizen' (LM, II. 257). As conceived by Arendt, imagination is diametrically opposed to both fancy and ideology. Both deny the public: in the case of fancy, by turning away from its externality; in the case of ideology, by violating its plurality. The imagination alone – drawing its inspiration from, and finding delight in, the plurality and specificity of the world – affirms the public through its willingness to reach out and accept its hospitality: 'To think with the enlarged mentality – that means you train your imagination to go visiting' (LM, II, 257).

Arendt's own imaginative reach is evident in the range and depth of her response to works of drama, fiction and poetry. She wrote with great insight on authors as diverse as W. H. Auden, Bertolt Brecht, Hermann Broch, Isak Dinesen, Fyodor Dostoyevsky, Randall Jarrell, Rudyard Kipling, Thomas Mann, Herman Melville and Rainer Maria Rilke – and, always, she sought what was distinctive in their work (see RLC). While she related works of literature to her own philosophical and political preoccupations, she never operated according to a critical template but encountered the text in all its particularity. Judgement was, for her, necessarily reflective and consequently not determined by the application of a general rule under which particulars could be categorised. She also, in her imaginative grasp of the work of particular authors, judged the authored work against the author's life and vice versa. The life and the work may have been at odds, but for Arendt they were all of a piece.

Her valedictory piece on Auden is a case in point. She began this piece by quoting one of Auden's lyric poems in full and suggesting that its greatness – its rare 'perfection' as she put it – lies in the untranslatability of its eloquently colloquial idiom. She then recalls the Auden she knew in the last fifteen years of his life: '[H]is face was marked by those famous wrinkles, as though life itself had delineated a kind of face-scape to make manifest "the heart's invisible furies"'. Yet, she continues: 'If you listened to him, nothing could seem more deceptive than his appearance. Time and again, when to all appearances he could not cope any more ... he would begin to more or less intone an utterly idiosyncratic version of "Count your blessings"'. Surely, she suggests, the appearance was deceptive because here was a man who 'never talked nonsense or said something obviously silly' and who had 'the voice of a very great poet'.

But Arendt then performs a double turn by claiming that the appearance was *not* deceptive – that, for whatever reason, Auden did in fact endure misery while at the same time being a life-enhancing poet. Her understanding of Auden is finely attuned to the dishevelled appearance of the man and the authoritative voice of the poet – and her judgement balances each against the other without denying the significance of either (RLC, 294–6).

Nowhere does Arendt develop a detailed exposition of her views on the nature and purpose of critical reading. However, as a serious reviewer of literary texts and as an editor at Schocken Books, she clearly had views on this matter. It was while at Schocken Books that she had helped with the publication of Kafka's *Diaries* and she remained deeply appreciative of Kafka's work throughout her life. It is in an essay on Kafka – the original version of which was published in German in 1946 – that she made one of her clearest statements regarding what is involved in reading. To read Kafka well requires 'at every turn' what she called an 'exertion of the real power of the imagination' (RLC, 105). That is why, as she puts it, 'the purely passive reader ... active only in his identification with one of the characters, does not know what to do with Kafka'. Similarly, 'the curious reader' will be disappointed by Kafka's novels because 'they contain no elements of daydreaming and offer neither advice nor edification nor solace'. Only readers who are themselves on 'a quest for truth' will, she claimed, be able to grasp imaginatively the significance of the work as a whole and as manifest in the minutiae of its 'banal events'.

In its interconnectedness and engagement, reading becomes paradigmatic of 'the enlargement of the mind'. Reading Kafka requires us to connect his life, work and context; to go beyond identification with a single character in order to grasp the underlying structure of the work; and, crucially, to bring our own passion for truth to the act of reading. We judge Kafka – as we would any modernist writer or artist – not only by the demands that his work makes on us as readers, but on our capacity as readers to meet those demands. Any judgement is, therefore, a judgement on the one who is judging as well as on that which is being judged: a judgement, that is, on the imaginative capacity – the capacity for 'enlargement' – of the judging mind.

The world, for Arendt, was an intersubjective reality that both divides us and unites us. What was of paramount importance to her was our own capacity to construct the world in such a way as to ensure that the centre holds – that the complementarities of division and unity hold firm. That was why the conceptual trinity of thinking, willing and judging was of paramount importance to her: thinking is rooted in the inwardness of our being in the world; willing asserts our selfhood within and to the world; and judgement reaches out to engage with the world as it presents itself to us externally and objectively. It is within the world – and only within the world – that we are capable of 'the enlargement of mind' that makes us fully and complicatedly human. What the world 'really is' has to be understood with reference to the dichotomies of sharing and division, separation and linkage, difference and commonality – dichotomies that can only be resolved or held in equilibrium through dialogue and interchange:

> If someone wants to see and experience the world as it 'really is', he can do so only by understanding it as something that is shared by many people, lies between them, separates and links them, showing itself differently to each and comprehensible only to the extent that many people can talk *about* it and exchange their opinions and perspectives with one another, over against one another. Only in the freedom of speaking with one another does the world, as that about which we speak, emerge in its objectivity and visibility from all sides.
>
> PP, 128

Dialogue among equals

At the beginning of *The Life of the Mind* Arendt returns to a consideration of the Eichmann trial. Indeed, she uses her earlier analysis of that trial as the springboard for what were to be her final reflections. A world devoid of thinking, willing and judging would, she argued, be a world devoid of worldliness: a world characterised, that is, by 'thoughtlessness' and inhabited by automatons such as Eichmann, who lacked freedom of will and any capacity for independent judgement. The only notable characteristic she could detect in Eichmann 'was something entirely negative: it was not stupidity but *thoughtlessness*'. He had displayed a complete 'absence of thinking', which, as she disturbingly pointed out, 'is so ordinary an experience in our everyday life, where we have hardly the time, let alone the inclination, to *stop* and think'.

Given the ordinariness of that experience, the question that 'imposed itself' (her phrase) was: 'Could the activity of thinking as such, the habit of examining whatever happens to come to pass or to attract attention, regardless of results and specific content, could this activity be among the conditions that make men abstain from evil-doing or even actually "condition" them against it?' (LM, I, 4–5). This, for Arendt, was not a rhetorical question (a statement masquerading as a question), but a real, pressing question that had been imposed on her by the nightmare that she and so many of her generation had experienced: a nightmare of total domination involving the obliteration of the willing and thinking self and 'the paralysis of the faculty of judgement' (Wessel and Bensmann, 2012).

She was clear from the start that ideology was the enemy of thought. Ideology denies the heterodoxy of thought through its insistence on adherence and complicity. It requires unthinking conformity. She had also become increasingly convinced that the routinisation of the modern world as she experienced it in her adopted country operated ideologically in such a way as to acclimatise us to the unworldly and the thoughtless. In a lecture she had delivered at the University of Chicago in 1964 – a lecture that relied heavily on arguments developed in her earlier *The Human Condition* – she had highlighted the extent to which mechanisation had led to a division of tasks involving a process whereby finished products become wrapped into a ceaseless round of means-end production and consumption: '[I]n a strictly utilitarian world, all ends are bound to be of short duration; they are transformed into means for some further ends. Once the end is attained, it ceases to be an end, it becomes an object among objects which at any moment can be transformed into means to pursue further ends' (PHA, 176). Caught in this endless cycle, the individual can no longer '*express* otherness and individuality'; no longer 'distinguish himself and communicate *himself*' (PHA, 178).

Arendt returned to this theme in *The Life of the Mind*, arguing that this erosion of the powers of human expression and communication not only debases the language but adversely affects our ability to think: 'Clichés, stock phrases, adherence to conventional, standardised codes of expression and conduct have the socially recognised function of protecting us against reality, that is, against the claim on our thinking attention that all events and facts make by virtue of their existence' (LM, I, 4). Writing just ten years later,

Raymond Williams (1983, 18) was to make the same point in relation to what he saw as the cultural crisis of late capitalism:

> There are times, in the depth of the current crisis, when the image materialises of a cluttered room in which somebody is trying to think, while there is a fan-dance going on in one corner and a military band blasting away in the other... It is a systematic cacophony which may indeed not be bright enough to know that it is jamming and drowning the important signals, but which is nevertheless, and so far successfully, doing just that.

For Arendt, friendship was one of the few spaces within which to escape the 'systematic cacophony' and reconnect with at least some of 'the important signals'. As the quotation that heads this chapter suggests, she saw friendship and thinking as inextricably entwined: 'Aristotle, speaking about friendship, remarked: "The friend is another self" – meaning: you can carry on the dialogue of thought with him just as well as with yourself.' The 'two-in-one' of solitary thought spills over into 'the dialogue of thought' that constitutes friendship. But, insisted Arendt, the latter is dependent on the former. This is precisely the proviso that she attributed to Socrates: 'Socrates would have said: The self, too, is a kind of friend' (LM, I, 189). Only those who are capable of being friends to themselves can be friends to others. Friendship – and 'the dialogue of thought' that it sustains – presupposes that each of the friends is in possession of a distinctive self that is valued by both parties.

The emphasis that Arendt places on equality in friendship – and in 'the dialogue of thought' that is sustained through friendship – has to be understood in this context. Arendt was adamant that inequalities exist, but equally adamant that equality can exist in friendship. However, it did not follow that only those of equal status, wealth or education could be friends. Of course, disparities of status, wealth and education may act as a constraint to becoming friends, but that was not Arendt's point. She considered equality in friendship to be based on the assumption that each human being is self-possessed and must therefore take ultimate responsibility for that self. Respect and self-respect are thus two sides of the same coin: we respect our friends insofar as they respect themselves, and they respect us insofar as we respect ourselves. Moreover, this mutuality of respect between friends sustains and strengthens the sense of selfhood enjoyed by each. The equality between friends relies on the recognition by each of what is distinctive and unique in the other.

From this perspective, pity erodes friendship. It was in her critique of the French Revolution – and what she called 'the evil of Robespierre's virtue' – that Arendt was most outspoken in her condemnation of pity: '[W]ithout the presence of misfortune, pity could not exist, and it therefore has just as much vested interest in the existence of the unhappy as thirst for power has a vested interest in the existence of the weak ... Pity, taken as the spring of virtue, has proved to possess a greater capacity for cruelty than cruelty itself.' Its capacity for cruelty – as exemplified in Robespierre – lay in the fact that it 'drowned all specific considerations, the considerations of friendship no less than the consideration of statecraft and principle'. It reduces the 'specific considerations' relating to particular persons to a homogenous mass of suffering humanity whose suffering is then – in a manner that Arendt found perverse – glorified as 'the spring of virtue' (OR, 79–80).

This strong reaction against pity might lead one to believe that Arendt was drawn towards those who were – or at least appeared to be – uniformly tough and resilient. But that is far from the case. She was respectful of fragility in others and was, if anything, drawn to men and women who were both strong *and* vulnerable. McCarthy certainly fell into that category, as did – in their different ways – Walter Benjamin, Heidegger, Randall Jarrell, Jaspers and even Blücher. Her lifelong fascination with Rahel Varnhagen was based on precisely that ambivalence between the woman who survived and the woman who suffered: her survival as pariah and parvenu was at the cost of the indignities and humiliations she endured in that role. In condemning pity, Arendt was not pointing to a particular kind of 'pitiable' person, but to a particular kind of response which sought to categorise others as 'pitiable'. Pity – whether directed towards others or towards oneself – denies the will of the one who is pitied. In so doing it negates thoughtfulness and destroys any possibility of independent judgement.

Through 'the dialogue of thought' friends strengthen one another's will and refine one another's judgements. That is how Arendt responded to the emotional turmoil that McCarthy found herself in during her difficult separation from Bowden Broadwater – not through collusion, but by presenting McCarthy with the reality of the situation and with alternative perspectives of the predicament she found herself in. It is how Blücher responded to Arendt's hurt and anger when she thought he had neglected to write to her – again, not by consoling her, but by confronting her with his own situation and with his own feelings. It is also – and more complicatedly – how Arendt responded to Heidegger. She neither pitied him nor forgave him, but she did find something in him to respect. He was, after all, a great solitary thinker regardless of his colossal failures of judgement and his lack of magnanimity towards colleagues.

Friendship was, for Arendt, a metaphor for a world within which the thinking self communicates with both itself and others. The metaphor highlights the deeply dialogical nature of thinking, whether it be the 'two-in-one' of solitary thinking or thinking as 'sharing-the-world-with-others'. Thinking is conditional upon the human will and makes possible 'the enlargement of mind' that informs human judgement. As such, it reflects the plurality of a shared macrocosm of which friendship is a microcosmic mirror image: friendship as a world within a world. The world constitutes us as thinking agents and we in turn exercise our agency through the constitution of our shared world. Against the implicit individualism of *cogito ergo sum*, friendship provides us with an image of the world as both a collective endeavour and a collective achievement. It is only because we are thinking beings that we are able to achieve a sense of collective purpose beyond the immediate ends and short-term outcomes of individual survival.

But friendship was, for Arendt, more than just a metaphor. It was the reality of actual friendships to which she was deeply and unconditionally committed. Those friendships provided a space within which thinking – through 'the dialogue of thought' – interconnected with what she termed 'the public realm'. Arendt was not in the habit of politicising her friendships in the sense of using them to gain power and influence, but her friendships nevertheless provided a kind of power base in that they realised the potency between people: between Heidegger and herself, Jaspers and herself, McCarthy and herself, Blücher and herself and many others to whom the previous chapters have only briefly alluded.

The 'dialogue of thought' is an actualisation of the power latent *between* human beings. Through its participation in that process of dialogue, friendship is able to reach inward to a validation of the self and the knowable community of which the self is a part and extend outward to a validation of the other and the unknowable community to which the self is nevertheless connected. The boundless conversation with oneself and others that constitutes the 'dialogue of thought' was for Arendt the vital link between the private and the public. It is what makes the world hang together as both intersubjective and objective reality. Without friendship that dialogue would be extremely difficult – if not impossible – to sustain.

The 'dialogue of thought' that constitutes the common ground of friendship continues beyond the lifespan of those who at any particular point in history are sustaining and advancing it. It has an afterlife, but its afterlife is in the world and for the future. It is, Arendt maintained, always subject to the contingency of human affairs and is therefore wholly unpredictable in respect of its outcomes. Arendt could not have known where, if anywhere, her ideas might lead. Her legacy is not, in other words, her responsibility but ours: the debt owed by the living to the dead. The final chapter reflects upon that legacy not with a view to providing prescriptive advice, but in order to highlight the continuing relevance of her thinking to the circumstances we find ourselves in. Although very different from the ones she lived in and through, those circumstances are ones that she largely foresaw and about which she offered her own salutary warnings.

9

The Republic of Friendship

Again, we do not know where these developments will lead us, but we know, or should know, that every decrease in power is an open invitation to violence – if only because those who hold power and feel it slipping from their hands, be they the government or be they the governed, have always found it difficult to resist the temptation to substitute violence for it.

OR, 87

The public realm

Republican thinkers had traditionally opposed hereditary monarchy, been anticlerical in orientation, championed political liberty for their peers and emphasised the collective political obligations of the citizenry. They had also generally subscribed to the conviction that politics was irreducible to other spheres of human life. The political was a discrete realm. It is on that last point that Arendt's singular contribution to the republican tradition can be judged. Politics in Arendt's schema occupies a public space that is both distinguishable – from, for example, the private and the social – and yet common to all humankind. She was, in effect, strengthening the democratic impulse in the republican ideal. To understand what Arendt meant by politics we need therefore to have some understanding of what she meant by the space designated as public, since this is the space of politics: the space termed by the Greeks the *polis* (the city state) and by the Romans the *res publica* (the republic), but which Arendt tended to refer to as 'the public realm'.

In *The Human Condition*, she argued that the public realm has two defining characteristics. First, it is located within the phenomenal world: 'everything that appears in public can be seen and heard by everybody and has the widest possible publicity'. It is the space within which 'the greatest forces of intimate life ... are transformed, deprivatized and deindividualized, as it were, into a shape fit for public appearance'. While it is most evident in the 'artistic transposition of individual experiences', it is manifest '[e]ach time we talk about things that can be experienced only in privacy or intimacy' (HC, 50). Second, it constitutes a common world that relates and separates us:

> To live together in the world means essentially that a world of things is between those who have it in common, as a table is located in between those who sit around it; the world, like every in-between, relates and separates men at the same time. The public realm, as the common world, gathers us together and yet prevents us falling over each other, so to speak.
>
> HC, 52

The public realm – the space of politics – is distinct from the private world of intimate experience but is a space we have in common by virtue of our uniqueness as individual beings.

That emphasis on sameness in diversity is what distinguishes Arendt's reinterpretation of the republican tradition from what she termed 'the main political task of early Christian philosophy', which was to bind the Christian community into the unifying body of Christ as conceived within the Pauline tradition: 'The unpolitical, non-public character of the Christian community was early defined in the demand that it should form a *corpus*, a "body", whose members were to be related to each other like brothers of the same family' (HC, 53). As Brian Patrick McGuire (2010) has shown in his study of the monastic experience of friendship during the medieval period, the Christian tradition during that period placed great emphasis on the friend as 'the guardian of one's soul, *custos animi*'. Moreover, '[t]his bond does not necessarily imply equality or even mutuality. A monk can express friendship to another monk without ever receiving anything in return.' The overriding emphasis was on commonality and community and on fellowship and unity. The ideal type of such friendship was 'the bond of spiritual father and son' (xv).

From Arendt's perspective, this tradition denoted an 'abstention from worldly things'. Given that the world exists in time, it thereby denoted an abdication of responsibility for both past and future: 'Worldlessness as a political phenomenon is possible only on the assumption that the world will not last' (HC, 54). Against the unworldliness – and other-worldliness – of the Christian tradition she claimed that the common world 'transcends our life-span into past and future alike; it was there before we came and will outlast our brief sojourn in it. It is what we have in common not only with those who live with us, but also with those who were here before and with those who will come after us' (HC, 55). Since the world has not only a past and future, but a present, the 'abstention from worldly things' also denies the rich plurality of human life in the here and now: '[T]he reality of the public realm relies on the simultaneous presence of innumerable perspectives and aspects in which the common world presents itself and for which no common measurement or denominator can ever be devised' (HC, 57). To abstain from worldly things is to deny both history and plurality.

That is why public life must, in Arendt's view, be distinguished from the Christian way of life with its emphasis on the unified body of believers, and from family life with its emphasis on privacy within the closed circle of kinship. Only public life allows us to achieve our full human potential: '[E]verybody sees and hears from a different position. This is the meaning of public life, compared to which even the richest and most satisfying family life can offer only the prolongation or multiplication of one's own position with its attending aspects and perspectives' (HC, 57). To grow-up – to present oneself within the common world of plurality – is to take responsibility for what one owes to the past by way of memory and to the future by way of hope. But it is also a matter of taking responsibility for the plurality of the common world we inhabit: a world that is increasingly globalised in its interconnectivity and cosmopolitan in its value orientation, yet deeply entrenched in its territorial protectionism. Arendt's central message was that we must recognise and confront the deep differences that bring us together around the 'in-between' of a world that both binds us and separates us.

Although Arendt frequently drew on the etymological link between 'privacy' and 'privation', she did not deny the necessary interdependence of the public and private realms. Indeed she saw it as one of the major contributions of the Romans – as opposed to the Greeks – that they grasped the political significance of this interdependence: 'The full development of the life of hearth and family into an inner and private space we owe to the extraordinary political sense of the Roman people who, unlike the Greeks, never sacrificed the private to the public, but on the contrary understood that these two realms could exist only in the form of coexistence' (HC, 59). A life spent entirely in public in the presence of others – and conducted without any recourse to the private – would be a diminished life. It would be shallow. The private realm – 'the life of hearth and family' – provides a necessary respite from the rigours of the public realm. But a life spent entirely in private in the presence of one's intimates would be equally diminished and shallow. The public realm provides us with the space necessary to become fully human.

Arendt's point in emphasising the privative character of privacy was to highlight the way in which 'mass society not only destroys the public realm but the private as well'. By reducing human beings to consumers, and human interchange to economic transaction, 'mass society' has produced 'the mass phenomenon of loneliness' (HC, 59). It has atomised human beings by destroying the bonds that hold us together and the differences that make each of us unique. In so doing it has eroded both the public and the private realms: the former by diminishing our potential as active and engaged citizens and the latter through the relentless encroachment of mass culture. Most importantly it has undermined the possibility of politics which can occur only in the common world of shared difference: a world manifest in the public realm but vitally dependent upon the private realm. The diminution of these realms leads to the erosion of the political – and, thereby, to the withering away of friendship as the safe ground between the private and the public.

The erosion of the political

Arendt's analysis of the erosion of the political is, if anything, more apposite now than in her own lifetime. The terms within which she developed that analysis may on occasion seem idiosyncratic, but the thrust of her argument continues to have great relevance.

We do not know what Arendt would have made of the geopolitics of the first quarter of the twenty-first century, but she would undoubtedly have had something to say about the state-sponsored mechanisms of rendition and redaction that have been justified in the supposed interests of security. As Benjamin Barber (2010, 275) points out:

We may not produce extermination camps, but with Abu Ghraib, Guantanamo, and those unnamed venues to which we outsource and redact prisoners whom our codes of law do not quite yet permit us to torture, we seem ready to join the rest of the human race in Purgatory .. Our Arendtian politics of liberty persist, but the economics of social revolution she feared now shadow North/South relations and threaten our own society with deepening inequalities.

What we do know is that representative democracy now faces a widely acknowledged problem of non-participation and disengagement; the public realm has been subject to systematic privatisation; the private sphere has become increasingly vulnerable to the encroachment of consumerist culture and mass society; and friendship has become exposed to social influences and pressures that militate against continuity and sustained dialogue. The idea of politics as collective action – and of power as the collective potential that exists between people – has very little impact on the way in which many democratic governments now operate.

This emphasis on the undemocratic – or even antidemocratic – impulse inherent in representative democracy is a common theme running through the work of a number of social and political commentators. Dan Hind (2010, 46), for example, has analysed the current situation in terms of what he calls 'the paradox of modern power, the fact of a secret public'. That 'secret public' – a public, that is, of private interests – exercises enormous influence and exerts tremendous power. It is, in effect, a privatised public, whose influence is exercised indirectly and whose power is exerted covertly:

> In the current division of labour the views of individuals, in so far as they are freely reasoning beings, are 'private'. They do not trouble the major systems of representation and indeed they are often kept secret by those working within powerful institutions. In what is often, revealingly, called the 'market-place of ideas', no effectual weight inheres in reasoning that is, or attempts to be, stripped of institutional interest, and that is directed towards truth for its own sake.

Hind goes on to argue that '[a]ll private forms of understanding, no matter how grand the institutions from which they derive and which they serve, must give way to the discoveries of a freely reasoning public if we are to inhabit a world safe for truth' (47). Without 'a freely reasoning public', the possibility of collective action is greatly reduced since only individuals acting in a private capacity have any 'effectual weight'. The public realm thereby dissolves into the private interests of atomised individuals, who – precisely because they are atomised – lack the collective resources necessary for political action.

Sheldon S. Wolin (2010) has developed this theme with reference to what he terms 'inverted totalitarianism'. He argues that 'the contemporary phenomenon of privatization by which governmental functions, such as public education, military operations, and intelligence gathering, are shared with or assigned to private entrepreneurs represents more than a switch in suppliers'. It represents, rather, 'an expression of the revolutionary dynamic of capitalism, of its aggrandizing bent' (213). His notion of 'inverted totalitarianism' – with its emphasis on the reshaping of minds though an increasingly privatised system of, for example, educational provision – is in many ways a mirror image of Arendt's notion of totalitarianism as, among other things, total mental domination:

> Services such as public education that had previously been viewed as essential, not only to the literacy of the citizenry but to its empowerment, are now increasingly being ceded to private entrepreneurs ... Privatization of education signifies not an abstract transfer of public to private but a takeover of the means to reshape the minds of coming generations, perhaps to blend popular education and media culture so as to better manage democracy.
>
> Wolin 2010, 213

Wolin concludes with the thought that '[t]his contemporary version of the old struggle between "enclosure" and the "commons," between exploitation and commonality, pretty much sums up the stakes: not what new powers we can bring into the world, but what hard-won practices we can prevent from disappearing' (292). The power that exists in the potential for interaction between people is already in the world. No new powers, as Wolin points out, are required. What are required are the practices necessary to actualise the power that is always latent between people: the practices of civic association, democratic participation, local organisation and community-led education. One of the elements that binds those practices and sustains them is the kind of friendship that Arendt practised and alluded to in her political thinking: friendship based on the recognition of equality in difference and oriented towards the world within and beyond any single friendship.

The theme is further developed by Zygmunt Bauman (2004). In his essay on what he calls Europe's 'unfinished adventure', he argues that in the last sixty years the nations comprising Europe have moved from being 'social states' based on the principles of welfare as generally understood in the immediate aftermath of World War II to 'security states' in which those principles are systematically denied and denigrated. The UK – as the financial hub of neoliberalism – is the European 'security state' *par excellence*: 'In the last account, the policy pursued by the international institutions of free trade prevents the establishment of a public sphere where individual choices could congeal into public choices, citizenship and democratic self-government could take root, and the principles and institutions of collective protection against individually suffered risks could be negotiated into political practice' (105).

Within this new order '[e]xclusion was no longer felt as a momentary stumble, but as a durable, perhaps even permanent condition'. This occasioned in the authorities 'a frightening change in the vocabulary of their programmatic pronouncements: from the elimination and prevention of exclusion to the containment and management of the excluded'. This shift in rhetoric was accompanied by 'the ongoing phasing-out of the collective, institutionalized protection of individual lives' (109). In particular the unpredictability of the labour market led to growing insecurity which in turn fostered widespread anxiety and fear regarding the future. It also exposed '[t]he new vulnerability and frailty of human bonds' as relationships were put under increasing strain. (111). This sense of growing insecurity opened the way to policies that could be presented as an escape from fear and anxiety. 'Nothing sells like anti-fear contraptions', as Bauman puts it, 'and the most salient symptom of the passage of power from the state to the market is the policy of cutting taxes, a policy whose bottom line is the shifting back to the market of the funds previously drawn into state coffers to finance socially provided individual security' (115). The 'security state' does not just overlay the 'social state' in some neat process of historical layering. It seeks to smother it.

One of the strategies the 'security state' employs is to render itself seemingly indispensable. Its mantra is 'there is no alternative': no alternative, that is, to tax cuts, cuts in welfare benefits, curbs on immigration, etc. Since there is no alternative to the policies, then the deleterious consequences of those policies – escalating inequality, an increase in child poverty, a rise in the number of homeless, etc. – are deemed to be inevitable. Alternative policies are dismissed as irresponsible and unrealistic. They would, the 'security state' insists, inevitably lead to the collapse of the market, the rise of skivers and scroungers, the influx of alien and exploitative workers, etc. Fear and anxiety become mechanisms of coercion. The state offers supposed security in return for acquiescence. The message emanating from the 'security state' is carefully modulated but crystal clear: accept the policies on offer or face the ruinous consequences. Trust us – or else!

These variations on the common theme – the theme, that is, of the erosion of democratic politics within the democratic West – highlight the continuing significance of Arendt's critical analysis of 'mass society'. Without an active and engaged citizenry the bonds between humans are weakened, and, without those bonds, the public realm fragments and politics is deprived of the conditions necessary for its collective enactment. What Arendt termed 'the mass phenomenon of loneliness' denies the efficacy of the public realm and erodes the potential for political action (HC, 59). Once the human bonds become frayed the political fabric is at risk of perishing. The bonds that connect people in the spirit of respectful mutuality – a mutuality based on the recognition of individual difference – are therefore of supreme political significance.

'Living in truth'

Because of the widespread deracination of the political, particular instances of collective action tend to be exceptions to the rule. What Chantal Mouffe (1993) termed 'the return of the political' – 'the pluralism of cultures, collective forms of life and regimes ... the pluralism of subjects, individual choices and conceptions of the good' (151) – can only be documented with reference to events and occurrences that are both exceptional and highly vulnerable. Because of their exceptionality and vulnerability they can all too easily be dismissed as noble in their aspirations, but futile in their achievement of tangible outcomes. With the supposed wisdom of hindsight, these often spontaneous outbursts of collective action can be seen as lacking in strategy and organisation. However, in a world in which strategy and organisation are routinely deployed in the interests of depoliticisation, it is difficult to see how collective action can be anything other than spontaneous, tactical and counterintuitive.

Jonathan Schell (2004) has argued that the rebellions against the Soviet empire in Eastern Europe – in East Germany in 1953, in Poland and Hungary in 1956 and in Czechoslovakia in 1968 – fall into this category. They should, he argues, be interpreted not as exercises in noble futility but as ways of living in truth: 'Every step they took was ventured without a chart or clear destination. Yet the revolution they made was peaceful, democratic, and thorough'. That revolution 'initiated the creation of more than a dozen new countries. It was the equivalent of a third world war except in one particular – it was not a war' (189). This 'living in truth' – 'directly doing in your immediate surroundings what you think needs doing, saying what you think is true and needs saying, acting the way you think people should act' – is diametrically opposed to 'living within the lie' (i.e. 'conforming to the system's demands') (196). Living in truth, he argues, requires an 'understanding that action properly begins with a predisposition to truth' (197).

The idea of 'living in truth' was fundamental to the Velvet Revolution – or Gentle Revolution – that took place in 1989 in what was then Czechoslovakia. The Velvet Revolution brought to an end in Czechoslovakia forty-one years of communist rule and led to the establishment of a parliamentary republic which in 1993 was peacefully dissolved into the Czech Republic and Slovakia. Many of the elements Arendt had identified – and admired – in the councils or *soviets* of earlier revolutionary periods were clearly in evidence in the Velvet Revolution: 'the spontaneity of their coming into being'; their desire for 'the direct participation of every citizen in the public affairs of the country'; their 'cross[ing] of all party lines'; their 'refus[al] to regard themselves as temporary organs of revolution' and their insistence on 'establishing themselves as permanent organs of government'; their creation of 'spaces of freedom' (OR, 254–6).

Vaclav Havel is the dissident most closely associated with the Velvet Revolution. With the collapse of the communist state he became the president of the Federal Republic of Czechoslovakia (1989–1992) and, following the dissolution of the Federal Republic, the first president of the Czech Republic

(1993–2003). His political activities resulted in multiple periods of imprisonment and constant government surveillance. In an address he was due to give at the University of Toulouse in 1984, he provided a succinct – and highly Arendtian – summary of what he saw as the nature and purpose of politics:

> I favour 'anti-political politics', that is, politics not as the technology of power and manipulation, of cybernetic rule over humans or as the art of the useful, but politics as one of the ways of seeking and achieving meaningful lives, of protecting them and serving them. I favour politics as practical morality, as service to the truth, as essentially human and humanly measured care for our fellow humans ... I know no better alternative.
>
> Havel, 1989, 155

Ahdaf Soueif (2012) provides us with a more recent example of how under exceptional circumstances collective action remains a possibility. Her diary account of the days preceding the toppling of Hosni Mubarak on 11 February 2011 was written as events in Egypt unfolded. We read her account against our retrospective understanding of the outcomes of the events she is describing, but for her those outcomes were unknowable: '[Y]ou, as you read', she reminds her readers, 'know a great deal more than I can know' (186). In retrospect the events chronicled by Soueif can be interpreted as tragic given the situation currently pertaining in Egypt and across much of the Arab world. But Soueif is concerned primarily with what those events meant at the time for those involved: 'I believe that optimism is a duty; if people had not been optimistic on 25 January, and all the days that followed, they would not have left their homes or put their wonderful, strong, vulnerable human bodies on the streets. Our revolution would not have happened' (186).

Soueif's account places her own – and her fellow citizens' – love of Cairo at the heart of her story: '[A] story about me and my city; the city I so love and have so sorrowed for these twenty years and more ... [H]er memories are our memories, her fate is our fate' (8–9). For Soueif – as for many of her fellow Cairenes – the imminent sale of the public spaces at the centre of Cairo was the crucial catalyst for revolutionary action:

> [W]e found out that the regime had been planning to sell Tahrir. They'd been planning to sell the central public space in our capital to a hotel chain, to a foreign hotel chain ... [W]e knew that everything was up for sale: land

monuments, islands, lakes, beaches, people's homes, antiquities, stretches of the Nile, natural resources, people, sovereignty, national parks, human organs, goldmines, the wealth under the ground, the water in the river, the labour of the people – everything.

Soueif 2012, 113

Midan el-Tahrir – or Tahrir Square – is the central point of Greater Cairo and is not so much a square or circle as a massive curved rectangle covering about 45,000 square metres. Soueif tells us that she prefers to describe the area using the Arabic word, '*Midan*', because 'it does not tie you down to a shape but describes an open urban space in a central position in a city' (10). The Midan has not only geographical significance located as it is at the heart of Cairo, but also emotional and political resonance as the historic meeting place and forum of the city. It was natural, therefore, that when the people of Cairo took to the streets on 28 January they should have gathered in Midan el-Tahrir, since it was 'home to the civic spirit' (11). It was natural, also, that, when the people's delegations came to the Midan from other cities and the provinces to set up their banners, they should join together in chanting: '[L]egitimacy comes from Tahrir' (14).

The Midan provided a public space in which the collective action of the citizenry could present itself to the world. Paradoxically, as one of the young revolutionaries quoted by Soueif pointed out, it was because Tahrir was pure spectacle that it became an undeniable reality as people around the world watched events unfold on their television screens and via YouTube: 'The people know that Tahrir was simply spectacle. They know that the revolution was won in the streets and the factories. But they also know that the spectacle is important in the battle of ideas, and if Tahrir falls, the dream falls. Tahrir is a myth that creates a reality in which we've long believed' (190).

Three words in particular point to what was – and remains – distinctive about that 'myth'. The first word is '*selmeyya*'. Meaning 'peaceful', '*selmeyya*' is the Arabic word that was constantly chanted by the demonstrators as they faced the combined violence of cavalry, Molotovs, snipers and militias. It was not, insists Soueif, fear of violence that held the demonstrators back: 'No, we the people were implementing a doctrine of minimum force, minimum destruction. This was a revolution that respected the law, that had at its heart the desire to reclaim the institutions of the state, not to destroy them' (168).

She provides a vivid illustration of that doctrine in action. One of her friends who had remained off the streets during the violence decided she would venture out. A young man volunteered to accompany her to her car:

> On the steps he told her he was a butcher and had looked at his knives that morning and considered. 'But then,' he said, 'I reckoned we really wanted to keep it selmeyya so I didn't bring any.' He held her arm to run to her car and as they ran he was taken. 'I tried to hold him,' she says, 'but they took him ... He was on the ground and five men were kicking him.' Every few metres, she said, there would be a group gathered around a fallen young man kicking his head in.
>
> Soueif 2012, 139–40

The second word is '*shabab*', which derives from the root 'sh/b', to grow. Soueif tells us that 'it carries the same emotional load as "youth" with an extra dash of vigour ... Unpacked it carries the signification of "people, men and women, who are at the youthful stage of life with all its energy, hope, optimism, vigour, impulsiveness and love of life, and who are acting communally, together"' (196). The *shabab* led the revolution. They were central to its spontaneity, organisation, discipline and persistence. When they were not holding the front line, maintaining the flow of information and provisions, rushing the injured to makeshift field hospitals, they kept up an insistent drumming: 'A loud, energetic, rhythmic drumming, drumming, drumming on the metal shield ... They keep it up all night long. It tells any approaching regime baltagi that the shabab are awake and waiting and it helps to keep everybody going; it says we're here, we're here, we're undefeated' (139). It was the *shabab* – the young people of Egypt, some of whom were not old enough to vote in the elections held the following year – who made the Arab Spring possible, 'because it was they who changed the world, and it now belongs to them' (187). Many of those young people died in and around the Midan and elsewhere in Egypt.

The third word – '*shuhada*' – defines those who died as martyrs. The point about defining a particular death as martyrdom is to highlight its enduring symbolic value. The life of the martyr gains meaning from its afterlife. For the *shuhada*, as evoked in Soueif's account, that afterlife is *now*: not another world, but this world; not eternal, but temporal; not abstracted from history, but integral to it. The *shuhada* help the living to define their ends and purposes in this world and in the here-and-now. That, Soueif seems to suggest, is their supreme legacy. As the people of Egypt gathered in Tahrir Square on the evening of Friday 11 February after Mubarak had stepped aside and the armed forces were in control of Egypt, Soueif wrote in her diary:

> And in the centre of the Midan a stillness. The pictures of the murdered. The shuhada. Sally Zahran, massive blows to the head, glances upwards and smiles. Muhammad Abd el-Menem, shot in the head, his hair carefully gelled. Ali Muhsin, shot, carries a laughing toddler with a big blue sea behind him. Muhammad Bassiouny, shot, lies back with his two kids ... Ihab Muhammadi smiles but his eyes are thoughtful ... and more, 843 more. In the triumph and joy and uncertainty of the moment, they are the still centre ... Our future has been paid for with their lives.'
>
> Soueif 2012, 181

The words '*selmeyya*', '*shabbab*' and '*shuhada*' touch on many of the themes that preoccupied Arendt. '*Selmayya*' reminds us that '[p]ower and violence are opposites; where the one rules absolutely, the other is absent ... Violence can destroy power; it is utterly incapable of creating it' (OV. 58). '*Shabab*' is a reminder of the necessity of new beginnings: '[T]he fact of natality, in which the faculty of action is ontologically rooted ... the birth of new men and the new beginning, the action they are capable of by virtue of being born' (HC, 247). '*Shuhada*' recalls the great emphasis Arendt placed on continuity across generations and how the duties of friendship are owed to both the living and the dead: how the dead are alive in the present and help inform our vision of the future.

Those three words also convey something of the collective experience that brought people together and which relied upon – while at the same time generating – immensely strong bonds of friendship. Survival was dependent on existing friendships and on friendships formed swiftly and sometimes pragmatically in life-threatening situations. It was also dependent on a collective bond of trust between those who had chosen to take the immense risk of being present in the Midan: '[O]nce you're inside, the Midan is amazing ... Everyone is suddenly, miraculously, completely themselves. Everyone understands. We're all very gentle with each other ... Our selves are in our hands, precious, newly recovered, perhaps fragile; we know we must be careful of our own and of each other's' (Soueif, 2012, 159). Friendship is what people brought to the Midan through their existing affiliations and associations and what developed through their sense of common purpose and collective action. It became an indispensable political resource.

Common ground

During those months of occupation the Midan el-Tahrir constituted a common ground that was committed not only to the overthrow of an undemocratic regime but to the establishment of an inclusive and participative democratic government. In an earlier collection of her essays, Soueif had referred to this common ground as 'Mezzaterra'. In what now reads like a prefiguring of the events of 2011, she wrote of the need 'to inhabit and broaden the common ground ... the ground where everybody is welcome, the ground we need to defend and to expand. It is to Mezzaterra that every responsible person on this planet needs to migrate. And it is there that we need to make our stand' (Soueif, 2004, 23). In Arendt's terms the Mezzaterra is the public realm: '[T]he common world [which] gathers us together and yet prevents us falling over each other' (HC, 52).

Friendship sustains that world by acknowledging its plurality. Our friendships provide a private space within which to explore the plurality inherent in the friendship itself and from which to re-enter the public space of plurality. They connect us to the world, while enabling us to cope with its complexity. Sometimes, as in the Midan el-Tahrir, friendship may be a matter of life or death; at other times – more mundanely – it may be a matter of being alone or being with another. We need friendship because it eases the two-way flow between the private and the public, ensuring that we are neither overwhelmed by the world nor in denial regarding its plurality. Friendship makes the world a safer place, while acknowledging its inherent uncertainty. It is precisely because of that uncertainty – and the unpredictability and contingency that gives rise to it – that we need friendship.

But friendship is only able to fulfil that need – only able to inflect towards both the private and the public – insofar as it is inclusive and outward-looking. A friendship that – through its exclusivity – denies the possibility of other friendships becomes inward-looking and self-enclosed within the private realm. Eventually, it becomes a denial of the plurality that sustains and nourishes it. Such friendships become compensatory: an escape from the world rather than a space within which to gather the resources necessary to appear and present ourselves within it. As the public realm becomes increasingly privatised and the state increasingly secretive, friendships are pushed towards isolation within the private realm and dislocation from the public realm. They thereby become disconnected from what Arendt saw as the source of human power – namely, the plurality of the world and the possibility of collective action that is implicit in that plurality. Our everyday friendships provide a vital link to the world which is part of us and of which we are a part. To lose that link is to lose the common ground between us – and to lose that common ground is to lose our potential for collective action.

The consequences of this loss were clear to Arendt: '[E]very decrease in power is an open invitation to violence – if only because those who hold power and feel it slipping from their hands, be they the government or be they the governed, have always found it difficult to resist the temptation to substitute violence for it' (OR, 87). Arendt was writing about the violence advocated by some on the left in the wake of the student demonstrations of the late 1960s. She was reminding the advocates of violence of the clear distinction between violence and power. Violence – undertaken for whatever reasons and justified by whatever principles – violates power. In so doing, it always renders politics inauthentic. For, as Dana Villa (2008, 352) argues, 'authentic politics – and however unfashionable, the phrase is unavoidable with Arendt – is possible only where diverse perspectives on a common world have a durable and institutional space for their free play'. Restrict the free play of power, warns Arendt, and violence in one form or another will be given access.

Violence – as a substitute for power – is played out in many different arenas and takes many different forms: self-harm, alcohol and drug abuse, domestic violence, state-sanctioned torture, etc. Of course, there are important distinctions to be made between these various forms of violence, but they are all substitutes for the loss of power experienced by those who are violating either themselves or others. They are all indicators of the failure of an 'authentic politics', just as the vibrancy of human affiliation – as evidenced, for example, in friendship – is an indicator of its success. Without friendship – or something very like it – the world as Arendt understood it would be both unthinkable and unworkable.

Friendship helps guarantee a world within which – and for which – people together can make things happen rather than have things happen to them. For Arendt, continuity was central to her experience of friendship and to how she saw it contributing to human flourishing. Friendship is not transient, but provides a respite from the impermanence and uncertainty of the world. Duty is also fundamental to friendship. It is what we owe one another by virtue of our friendships and what makes continuity possible. Above all, friendship reaches out to the world. It refuses enclosure and exclusivity. There are in Arendt's world no preconditions of friendship, other than the mutuality of respect, the reciprocity of trust and the shared understanding that the other is always there in the world. These constitute the common ground – the republic – of friendship.

If we were to undertake a thought experiment that involved constructing a friendless world, we would soon find ourselves confronting one or other of Arendt's two dystopias: totalitarianism, in which friendship would be systematically eradicated, and late capitalist 'mass society', in which friendship would be distorted into a commodity. Of course, friendship alone cannot act as a bulwark against either totalitarian domination or mass consumerism, but it does provide us with an indicator of our own and others' wellbeing and of the overall health of the body politic. Whether or not the current state of friendship should give us cause for concern is a moot point. Personal experience suggests to me that young people are remarkably good at friendship and possibly much better than previous generations at forming and maintaining cross-gender friendships. But personal experience also suggests that the continuity of friendship that was so important to Arendt may be more difficult to sustain in a world of instantaneous global communication. So, it is worth reminding ourselves that a world devoid of enduring friendships would be a world lacking in what Arendt termed 'worldliness' – and that humans with no recourse to friendship would become devoid of what she understood to be their humanity.

EPILOGUE

A Woman of the World

The main thing was to have no illusions and to accept no thoughts – no theoretical systems – that would blind you to reality.

RLC, 298

In his 1644 pamphlet *Areopagitica*, John Milton famously declared: 'I cannot praise a fugitive and cloister'd vertue, unexercis'd and unbreath'd, that never sallies out and sees her adversary, but slinks out of the race, where that immortall garland is to be run for, not without dust and heat' (Milton, 1999, 17). Arendt – a fellow republican – would undoubtedly have agreed. She herself had confronted her adversaries – experiencing considerable 'dust and heat' in the course of doing so – and had consistently argued that the virtues could only be acquired through human interaction and cooperation. For her, 'a fugitive and cloister'd vertue' would have been a contradiction in terms: to be 'fugitive and cloister'd' was to deny the ethical, and to deny the ethical was to renounce the political. The 'immortal garland' could only be gained in the mortal world of humankind.

So, Arendt became a woman of the world. But the world was – and is – a tough place. The long trek from Hanover – by way of Königsberg, Berlin, Marburg, Heidelberg, Paris, Prague and Geneva – to New York was not for the faint-hearted. Nor were the years of statelessness in France and the United States – and the long and demanding lecture tours that Arendt undertook throughout her life – for those who preferred to remain 'unexercis'd and unbreath'd'. Being a woman of the world was no easy option, insofar as it was an option. In some ways – and at certain crucial junctures in her life – it was the world that chose Arendt. In fleeing Germany and then France she was – given the extreme vulnerability of her position as a Jewish woman first in fascist Germany and then in Occupied France – responding to necessity rather than exercising her own freedom of choice. However, even in these extreme situations she showed remarkable self-determination: the determination, that is, to survive as a person, to connect with others and to understand the world.

Arendt's friendships were crucial in maintaining that self-determination. They provided both refuge and hospitality in a world characterised by uncertainty and unpredictability. The ethic of hospitality had been developed within the Hebraic tradition in response to the dangers of exilic life as exemplified in the story of Israel's exodus from oppression in Egypt. The right to immunity and to hospitality was clearly defined in the Jewish Torah. In the fourth of its five books – the Book of Numbers – God ordered Moses to institute cities which would be places of refuge or asylum. Although a deeply secular Jew, Arendt carried forward this tradition of hospitality through her friendships and the emphasis she placed within friendship on continuity and duty. In a world of ineluctable uncertainty, friendships were both evidence of having survived the unpredictabilities of the past and an assurance of surviving the inevitable insecurities of the future.

Within the safe space of her many and varied friendships Arendt was able to gather her resources, re-establish a sense of continuity and connectedness and relax into well-known routines. Friendship was a halfway house between the public and the private, incorporating elements of both but in different combinations with different friends: robust argumentation and the sharing of intimacies; working together and holidaying together; cooking for others and being entertained. The point about such activities is that they are mundane, ordinary and commonplace. For those of Arendt's generation who had witnessed totalitarianism at first hand, managed to keep one step ahead of its ruthless advances and/or known those who had fallen victim to its deadly policies, the commonplace would always have a certain pathos – an awakening of the emotions – that those who have not had to bear witness in that way more usually associate with the exceptional. Its sheer ordinariness rendered it extraordinary.

Arendt's friendships also provided an opportunity for friends to move from what she called 'the two-in-one' of solitary thinking into the two-on-two of thinking together. Friendship became a space within which one's opinions can be tested and explored without being subject to public scrutiny and accountability. Arendt was able to work out her ideas in dialogue with friends because she felt able to express her opinions within the circumscribed context of that dialogue. Although thinking begins in very early infancy through social interaction with the prime carer, it becomes internalised into the 'two-in-one' of solitary thinking as the infant gains a sense of personal identity. That process continues throughout our lives and is never straightforward or just one-way. We move between the 'two-in-one' and the two-on-two as we develop our sense of selfhood, thereby gaining on the way the capabilities necessary to operate discursively and thoughtfully within and across a wide range of contexts. Arendt was interested in the movement backward and forward between solitary thinking and thinking together – and the implications of that to-and-fro for what it means to enter the public domain.

She was, to the very end, struggling with a language and a conceptual framework with which to explain the full reach and depth of her intuitions regarding the nature of thinking. She was all too aware of how solitary thinking can lead to misjudgement, but she was also aware of how thinking is necessary for connecting us to a world of common sense through dialogue with both the living and the dead. At the heart of her thinking was the felt need to reach out, enlarge her own mind and the minds of others, and involve herself in the boundlessness of communication. She was, conceptually, playing with a huge jigsaw puzzle of an idea into which the conceptual pieces of the puzzle were never quite arranged into the final closure of a complete theoretical picture. The idea was that of 'plurality', but around that idea notions of 'thinking', 'willing' and 'judging' spinned in their separate and interconnected spheres.

Through her friendships Arendt sustained the virtuous dispositions that were fundamental to her world view. Duty was inseparable from her notion of friendship, as were the virtues of truthfulness, honesty and prudence. The continuity of friendship – particularly the idea of a continuing friendship between the living and the dead – was reliant on a sense of duty. Arendt was assiduous in honouring her dead friends. Without duty, continuity was unsustainable. Similarly, friendship presupposed truthfulness – if not the whole truth and nothing but the truth, then at least the truth regarding matters of mutual interest and concern. So, honesty is both a precondition and outcome of friendship – as is the prudence required to know when and how the truth should be spoken and under what circumstances. Within our friendships we nurture and develop the dispositions necessary for engaging with one another in the here and now and across the boundaries.

Friendship, for Arendt as for most of us, was an exercise in lifelong learning. It was – and is – how we learn to live together. She had few given relationships of kinship in her life, so chosen relationships of friendship played a particularly important part in her development as a person and as a public intellectual. She moved forward into the wider world through friendships that she adhered to tenaciously and with a taken-for-granted sense of duty. Some of those friendships were difficult – and some were fractured – but Arendt held onto them until the point of irreparable rupture. She willed her friendships into continuity and enlargement. Her friendships constituted a diasporic network of friends across her old Europe and her adopted United States.

They were in effect the *sine qua non* of collective action, which she saw as the source of human power and the basis of democratic politics. If the interconnectivity between human beings is the powerhouse of politics, then politics must be grounded in our existing interrelationships. Friendship – as one of the constituents of interrelationship – thereby becomes a necessary condition for the sustainability of a democratic body politic. All other forms of political regimes deny friendship or shape it to their own ends and purposes: theocracies subordinate it to belief in a supreme being; oligarchies twist it into a hierarchy of vested interests; and autocracies distort friendship through their demand for unconditional loyalty to the autocrat. Totalitarianism, as we have seen, is unique in its systematic eradication of all forms of friendship. Only a genuinely participative democracy respects and nourishes friendship as an element that both binds the citizenry and provides a context within which citizens can grow and develop.

Arendt was not only *of* the world, but *for* the world – not only moulded by her experience of the world in one of the most tumultuous periods in human history, but actively engaging with the uncertainty and contingency of the world in all its plurality. Her friendships were an expression of that engagement. She rarely generalised about friendship – hence the focus on the specificity of particular friendships in the central chapters of this book. But the concept of friendship was – as I have tried to show throughout – central to Arendt's view of the world as plural and yet, within the scope of that plurality, providing spaces for both individual freedom and the power implicit in human interchange. She was flawed like the rest of us – difficult and sometimes contrasuggestible, self-willed and occasionally demanding, a little self-dramatising – but she was undoubtedly a woman of the world for whom friendship was of supreme and undeniable importance.

To imagine a politics of friendship is to recall that although none of us has a fixed abode, friendships provide some measure of albeit provisional stability and continuity. It is to remind ourselves, also, that through friendship we become more fully ourselves and thereby embrace one another not as an indistinguishable unity but as the one embracing the other. Friendship thereby becomes one of the ways in which we learn to live together and to acquire the dispositions necessary to do so: dispositions that we carry forward into the world. But to imagine a politics of friendship is also to acknowledge the fragility of what Arendt understood by politics: its vulnerability to the contingency of circumstance and the unpredictability of history. If friendship sustains and strengthens the body politic, then its diminution, distortion or manipulation sounds the death toll of a vibrant and healthy politics – which is no doubt one of the reasons why Arendt valued friendship and sought to maintain and sustain her many and varied friendships throughout her life.

But we must beware of over-systematising Arendt's thought. What she said about Auden might equally well be said of her: 'The main thing was to have no illusions and to accept no thoughts – no theoretical systems – that would blind you to reality' (RLC, 298). Her thinking was constantly evolving in response to world events and in conversation with herself and others. We need to read her work against her life, and her life against the other lives that made up her world. She developed no theory of friendship, but provided important and still highly relevant insights into the significance of friendship and into the dire consequences of losing the human bonds that are forged and sustained through friendship.

Above all, she reminds us of what it means to become *thoughtful*: what is taken, what is given, what is shared.

APPENDIX

Chronology of Arendt's Life and Works

1906   Born 14 October in Linden, Germany (now part of Hanover).
1909   Moves to Königsberg with her parents.
1913   Father dies.
1920   Mother remarries.
1922–23   Studies at the University of Berlin in preparation for the university entrance examination (the *Abitur*).
1924   Enters Marburg University where she studies under Heidegger (born 26 September 1889).
1925   Embarks on a clandestine relationship with Heidegger.
1926   Breaks relationship with Heidegger, but continues intermittent correspondence until 1933. Summer semester: moves to the University of Heidelberg to study under Jaspers (born 23 February 1883). Winter semester: studies with Edmund Husserl at the University of Freiberg.
1927   Heidegger's *Sein und Zeit* (*Being and Time*) published.
1927–28   Studies at the University of Heidelberg. Autumn receives doctorate (under the direction of Jaspers).
1929   Meets Günther Stern (the writer Günther Anders), whom she marries later that year.
1930   Moves with Stern to Berlin. Receives grant from the Notgemeinschaft der Deutschen Wissenschaft for her project 'the problem of German-Jewish assimilation, as seen through the example of the life of Rahel Varnhagen'.
1930–33   Publishes essays in magazines and newspapers.
1933   The Reichstag fire in Berlin. Stern flees to Paris. Arendt and her mother arrested and questioned for over a week. Flees to Paris via Prague and Geneva and begins eighteen years as a 'stateless person'.

1933–42	Member of the World Zionist Organisation.
1934	Becomes friends with Walter Benjamin and Raymond Aron in Paris.
1935–38	General secretary of Youth Aliyah in Paris.
1935	Undertakes three-month trip to Palestine in connection with work for Youth Aliyah.
1936	Meets Blücher (born 29 January 1899).
1936–39	Makes yearly trips to Geneva.
1937	Divorces Günther Stern, 26 August.
1937–38	Completes Rahel Varnhagen project.
1938	Mother flees Königsberg and moves in with Arendt and Blücher in Paris.
1938–39	Works for the Jewish Agency in Paris
1940	War declared between France and Germany. Marries Heinrich Blücher, 16 January. Blücher detained in internment camp in Villernlard and released after two months. Detained with her mother in Gurs internment camp for women in the South of France. France defeated. Escapes with mother to Montaubon, France.
1941	Escapes Vichy France with Blücher via Spain to Lisbon. May: arrives in the United States. After an initial stay in Massachusetts moves with Blücher into furnished rooms at 315 West 95th Street, New York. 26 June: Mother, Marta Arendt, arrives in New York
1941–45	Staff writer for the New York weekly *Aufbau*.
1942	News of the German concentration and extermination camps for Jews begins to filter out.
1944	Meets Mary McCarthy (born 21 June 1912). Initial antipathy, but reconciliation several years later. Arendt begins work on *The Origins of Totalitarianism*.
1945–46	Research director for the Commission on European Jewish Cultural Reconstruction.
1945–47	Lecturer in European history at Brooklyn College.
1946–48	Editor at Schocken Books in New York.
1946	Publishes a paper in *Partisan Review* that is highly critical of Heidegger.

1948	Mother dies.
1949–52	Director of Jewish Cultural Reconstruction.
1949	Moves with Blücher into apartment at 130 Morningside Drive in New York.
1949–50	Makes first post-World War II trip to Europe. Reunited with Jaspers and his wife Gertrud. Has meeting with Heidegger and his wife Elfriede. Renews correspondence with Heidegger.
1950	Becomes senior editor at Schocken Books in New York.
1951	*The Origins of Totalitarianism* published. Becomes US citizen, 11 December.
1952	Begins work on 'Totalitarian elements in Marxism', which is never completed but feeds into her later work.
1955	Visiting professor at the University of California, Berkeley.
1958	*The Human Condition* published. *Rahel Varnhagen: The Life of a Jewess* finally published.
1959	Awarded the Lessing Prize of the City of Hamburg. Moves with Blücher to an apartment at 370 Riverside Drive in New York.
1961	Covers the trial of Adolph Eichmann in Jerusalem for *The New Yorker*. *Between Past and Future: Six Exercises in Political Thought* published.
1963	Publishes a five-part article in *The New Yorker* on the Eichmann trial. A revised version is published in book form as *Eichmann in Jerusalem: A Report on the Banality of Evil*. *On Revolution* published.
1963–67	Professor at the University of Chicago.
1967	Awarded the Sigmund Freud Prize of the Deutsche Akademie für Sprache und Dichtung in Darmstadt.
1967–75	Professor at the New School for Social Research in New York.
1968	*Men in Dark Times* published. Second edition of *Between Past and Future* published with additional material.
1969	Jaspers dies 26 February (aged eighty-six). *On Violence* published.
1970	Blücher dies (aged seventy-one).
1973	Gives the first series of Gifford Lectures on thinking at the University of Aberdeen, Scotland. New edition (with added prefaces) of *The Origins of Totalitarianism* published.

1974	May: suffers heart attack while giving the first lecture in the second series of Gifford Lectures on willing.
1975	Awarded Sonning Prize of the University of Copenhagen. Goes to Germany to put Jaspers' papers in order. Visits Heidegger for the last time. Dies of a second heart attack on 4 December (aged sixty-nine).
1976	Heidegger dies 26 May (aged eighty-six).
1978	*The Life of the Mind* (two volumes) based on the Gifford Lectures of 1973–74 and edited by McCarthy published posthumously.
1989	McCarthy dies 25 October (aged seventy-seven).

Bibliography

Adelman, J. (2013) *Worldly Philosopher: The Odyssey of Albert O. Hirschman*. Princeton, NJ and Oxford: Princeton University Press.

Applebaum, A. (2012) *The Iron Curtain: The Crushing of Eastern Europe 1944–56*. London: Allen Lane.

Arendt, H. ([1951] 1973) *The Origins of Totalitarianism*, new edition with added prefaces. San Diego, New York and London: Harcourt Brace & Company.

—— ([1957] 1997) *Rahel Varnhagen: The Life of a Jewess*, edited by L. Weissberg; translated by R. and C. Winston. Baltimore, MD and London: Johns Hopkins University Press in cooperation with the Leo Black Institute (first published by Leo Black Institute).

—— [1958] (1998) *The Human Condition*, 2nd edition. Chicago and London: The University of Chicago Press.

—— ([1961] 1977) *Between Past and Future: Eight Exercises in Political Thought*. New York: Penguin Books (first published by Faber & Faber, 1961, and with additional material by Viking Press, 1968).

—— ([1963] 2006a) *On Revolution*. London: Penguin (first published in the USA by Viking Press).

—— ([1963] 2006b) *Eichmann in Jerusalem: A Report on the Banality of Evil*. London: Penguin Books (first published in the USA by Viking Press).

—— (1970a) *Men in Dark Times*. London: Jonathan Cape.

—— (1970b) *On Violence*. Orlando, FL, Austin, TX, New York, San Diego, CA, London: A Harvest Book, Harcourt, Inc.

—— (1978) *The Life of the Mind* (one-volume edition). San Diego, CA, New York and London: Harcourt Inc

—— (1994) *Essays in Understanding 1930–1954: Formation, Exile, and Totalitarianism*, edited by J. Kohn. New York: Schocken Books.

—— (1996) *Love and St Augustine*, edited by J. V. Scott and J. C. Stark. Chicago and London: The University of Chicago Press.

—— (2005) *The Promise of Politics*, edited by J. Kohn. New York: Schoken Books.

—— (2007) *Reflections on Literature and Culture*, edited with an introduction by S. Y. Gottlieb. Stanford, CA: Stanford University Press.

Arendt, H. and Blumenfeld, K. (1995) *In keinem Besitz verwurtzelt: Die Korrespondenz*, edited by I. Nordman and I. Philling. Nordlingen: Rotbuch.

Arendt, H. and Scholem, G. (2010) *Der Briefwechsel, 1939–1964*, edited by M. L. Knott. Judischer Verlag/Suhrkamp.

Aristotle (1976) *The Ethics of Aristotle: The Nicomachean Ethics*, translated by J. A. K. Thompson. London: Penguin Books.

Armstrong, K. (2006) *The Great Transformation: The Beginnings of our Religious Traditions*. New York: Knopf.

Bakewell, S. (2010) *How to Live or A Life of Montaigne in One Question and Twenty Attempts at an Answer*. London: Chatto & Windus.

Barber, B. R. (2010) Hannah Arendt between Europe and America: optimism in dark times, in S. Benhabib (ed.) *Politics in Dark Times: Encounters with Hannah Arendt*. Cambridge: Cambridge University Press, pp. 259–76.

Bauman, Z. (2004) *Europe: An Unfinished Adventure*. Cambridge: Polity.

Bellah, R. N. and Joas, H. (eds) (2012) *The Axial Age and its Consequences*. Cambridge, MA and London: Harvard University Press/Belknap Press.

Benhabib, S. (2000) Arendt's 'Eichmann in Jerusalem', in D. Villa (ed.) *The Cambridge Companion to Hannah Arendt*. Cambridge: Cambridge University Press, pp. 65–85.

—— (2003) *The Reluctant Modernism of Hannah Arendt*, new edition. Oxford: Rowman & Littlefield.

—— (2010) International law and human plurality in the shadow of totalitarianism: Hannah Arendt and Raphael Lemkin, in S. Benhabib (ed.) *Politics in Dark Times: Encounters with Hannah Arendt*. Cambridge: Cambridge University Press, pp. 219–43.

Berlin, I. (1953) *The Hedgehog and the Fox: An Essay on Tolstoy's View of History*. London: Weidenfeld & Nicolson.

Bernstein, J. M. (2012) Political modersnism: the new, revolution, and civil disobedience in Arendt and Adorno, in L. Rensmann and S. Gandesha (eds) *Arendt and Adorno: Political and Philosophical Investigations*. Stanford, CA: Stanford University Press, pp. 56–77.

Bilsky, L. (2010) The Eichmann trial and the legacy of jurisdiction, in S. Benhabib (ed.) *Politics in Dark Times: Encounters with Hannah Arendt*. Cambridge: Cambridge University Press, pp. 198–218.

Brightman, C. (1993) *Writing Dangerously: Mary McCarthy and her World*. London: Lime Tree.

—— (ed.) (1995) *The Correspondence of Hannah Arendt and Mary McCarthy 1949–1975*. London: Secker & Warburg.

Burt, S. (2002) *Randall Jarrell and his Age*. New York: Columbia University Press.

Camus, A. (1947) *La Peste*. Paris: Gallimard.

Camus, A. (1979) *Selected Essays and Notebooks*, edited and translated by P. Thody. London: Penguin Books.

Canovan, M. (1992) *Hannah Arendt: A Reinterpretation of her Political Thought.* Cambridge: Cambridge University Press.

Caute, D. (2013) *Isaac and Isaiah: The Covert Punishment of a Cold War Heretic.* New Haven, CT and London: Yale University Press.

Cicero (2012) *Treatises on Friendship and Old Age,* translated by E. S. Shuckburgh. No place of pub. given: Another Leaf Press.

Dalos, G. with Dunai, A. (1998) *The Guest from the Future: Anna Akhmatova and Isaiah Berlin,* translated by A. Wood. London: John Murray.

Derrida, J. (1997) *Politics of Friendship,* translated by G. Collins. London and New York: Verso.

—— (2005) Others are secret because they are other, interview with A. Spire, reprinted in J. Derrida, *Paper Machine,* translated by R. Bowlby. Stanford, CA: Stanford University Press, pp. 136–63.

Duarte, E. (2001) The eclipse of thinking: an Arendtian critique of cooperative learning, in M. Gordon (ed.) *Hannah Arendt and Education: Renewing Our Common World.* Boulder, CO and Oxford: Westview Press, pp. 201–23.

Dunne, J. (1997) *Back to the Rough Ground: Practical Judgment and the Lure of Technique.* Notre Dame, IN: University of Notre Dame Press.

Ettinger, E. (1995) *Hannah Arendt Martin Heidegger.* New Haven, CT and London: Yale University Press.

Feinstein, E. (1984) *The Border.* London Hutchinson.

Fuchs, T., Breyer, T. and Mundt, C. (eds) (2014) *Karl Jaspers: Philosophy and Psychopathology.* New York: Springer.

Hansen, P. (1993) *Hannah Arendt: Politics, History and Citizenship.* Cambridge: Polity Press.

Havel, V. (1989) *Living in Truth: Twenty-two Essays Published on the Occasion of the Award of the Erasmus Prize to Vaclav Havel,* edited by J. Vladislav. London and Boston, MA: Faber & Faber.

Heidegger, M. ([1927] 1962) *Being and Time,* translated by J. Macquarrie and E. Robinson. Oxford and Cambridge, MA: Blackwell.

Hill, M. A. (1979) *Hannah Arendt: The Recovery of the Public World.* New York: St Martin's Press.

Hind, D. (2010) *The Return of the Public* London and New York: Verso.

Hobsbawm, E. (1995) *Age of Extremes: The Short Twentieth Century 1914–1991.* London: Abacus.

Honneth, A. (1995) *The Struggle for Recognition: The Moral Grammar of Social Conflicts,* translated by J. Anderson. Cambridge: Polity Press.

Hudis, P. (2011) Introduction: rediscovering Rosa Luxemburg, in G. Adler, P. Hudis and A. Laschitza (eds) *The Letters of Rosa Luxemburg,* translated by G. Shriver. London and New York: Verso.

Hudis, P. and Anderson, K. B. (2004) Introduction, in P. Hudis and K. B. Anderson (eds) *The Rosa Luxemburg Reader*. New York: Monthly Review Press.

Jaspers, K. (1953) *The Origins and Goal of History*, translated by M. Bullock. London: Routledge & Kegan Paul.

—— ([1947] 1961) *The Question of German Guilt*, translated by E. B. Ashton. New York: Capricorn.

—— (1969–71) *Philosophy*, 3 volumes, translated by E. B. Ashton. Chicago and London: University of Chicago Press.

—— ([1922] 1977) *Strindberg and van Gogh: An Attempt of a Pathographic Analysis with Reference to Parallel Cases of Swedenborgt and Holderlin*, translated by O. Grunow and D. Woloshin. Tucson, AZ: University of Arizona Press.

—— (1994) *Basic Philosophical Writings*, edited by E. Erlich, L. H. Erlich and G. B. Pepper. Atlantic Heights, NJ: Humanities Press.

—— ([1913] 1997) *General Psychopathology*, 2 volumes, translated by J. Hoenig and M. W. Hamilton. Baltimore, MD and London: Johns Hopkins University Press.

Judt, T. (2008) *Reappraisals: Reflections on the Forgotten Twentieth Century*. London: Vintage Books.

Judt, T. with Snyder, T. (2012) *Thinking Twentieth Century*. London: William Heinemann.

Kazin, E. (1982) Woman in dark times, *New York Review of Books*, 24 June, pp. 3–6.

Keynes, J. M. ([1919] 2007) *The Economic Consequences of the Peace*. New York: Skyhorse Publishing.

Kiernan, F. (2000) *Seeing Mary Plain: A Life of Mary McCarthy*. New York and London: W. W. Norton and Company.

Kirkbright, S. (2004) *Karl Jaspers: Navigations in Truth*. New Haven, CT and London: Yale University Press.

Koestler, A. (1940) *Darkness at Noon*. London: Jonathan Cape.

Kohler, L. (ed.) (2000) *Within Four Walls: The Correspondence between Hannah Arendt and Heinrich Blucher 1936–1968*, translated by P. Constantine. New York, San Diego, CA and London: Harcourt, Inc.

Kohler, L. and Saner, H. (eds) (1992) *Hannah Arendt Karl Jaspers Correspondence 1926–1969*, translated by R. and R. Kimber. New York, San Diego, CA and London: Harcourt Jovanovich.

Kohn, J. (1996) Evil and plurality: Hannah Arendt's way to *The Life of the Mind*, I, in L. May and J. Kohn (eds) *Hannah Arendt: Twenty Years Later*. Cambridge, MA and London: MIT Press, pp. 147–78.

Kristeva, J. (2001) *Hannah Arendt*, translated by R. Guberman. New York: Columbia University Press.

Lilla, M. (2013) Arendt and Eichmann: the new truth, *New York Review*, 21 November, pp. 35–45.

Ludz, U. (ed.) (2004) *Letters 1925: Hannah Arendt and Martin Heidegger*, translated by A. Shields. Orlando, FL, Austin, TX, New York, San Diego, CA, Toronto and London: Harcourt, Inc.

Maier-Katkin, D. (2010) *Stranger from Abroad: Hannah Arendt, Martin Heidegger, Friendship and Forgiveness*. London and New York: W. W. Norton and Company.

McCarthy, M. (1942) *The Company She Keeps*. New York: Simon & Schuster.

—— (1956) *Venice Observed*. New York: G & R Bernier.

—— (1957) *Memories of a Catholic Girlhood*. San Diego, CA, New York and London: Harcourt Brace/Harvest Books.

—— (1959) *The Stones of Florence*. New York: Harcourt Brace & World.

—— (1963) *The Group*. New York: Harcourt Brace & World.

—— (1970) *The Writing on the Wall and Other Literary Essays*. New York: Harcourt Brace & World.

—— 1971) *Birds of America*. New York: Harcourt Brace Jovanovich.

—— (1974a) *The Seventh Degree*. New York: Harcourt Brace Jovanovich.

—— (1974b) *The Mask of State: Watergate Portraits Including a Postscript on the Pardons*. San Diego, CA: Harcourt Brace/Harvest Books.

—— (1979) *Cannibals and Missionaries*. New York: Harcourt Brace Jovanovich.

—— (1987) *How I Grew Up*. San Diego, CA, New York and London: Harcourt Brace/Harvest Books.

—— (1992) *Intellectual Memoirs: New York, 1936–1938*, edited by E. Hardwick. New York: Open Road.

McGuire, B. P. (2010) *Friendship and Community: the Monastic Experience, 350–1250*. Ithaca, New York and London: Cornell University Press, 2nd edition with a new introduction.

Milton, J. (1999) *Areopagitica and other Political Writings of John Milton*. Indianapolis, IN: Liberty Fund, Inc.

Montaigne, M. (1958) *Essays*, translated by J. M. Cohen. London: Penguin.

Moorehead, C. (2012) *A Train in Winter: A Story of Resistance, Friendship and Survival in Auschwitz*. London: Vintage.

Mouffe, C. (1993) *The Return of the Political*. London and New York: Verso.

Neiman, S. (2002) *Evil in Modern Thought: An Alternative History of Philosophy*. Princeton, NJ: Princeton University Press.

—— (2010) Banality reconsidered, in S. Benhabib (ed.) *Politics in Dark Times: Encounters with Hannah Arendt*. Cambridge: Cambridge University Press, pp. 305–15.

Nussbaum, M. C. (1997) *Cultivating Humanity: A Classical Defence of Reform in Liberal Education*. Cambridge, MA and London: Harvard University Press.

Orwell, G. (1949) *Nineteen Eighty-Four*. London: Secker & Warburg.

Ott, H. (1993) *Martin Heidegger: A Political Life*, translated by A. Blunden. New York: Basic Books.

Pangle, L. S. (2003) *Aristotle and the Philosophy of Friendship*. Cambridge: Cambridge University Press.

Peeters, B. (2013) *Derrida: A Biography*, translated by A. Brown. Cambridge and Malden, MA: Polity Press, first published in French by Flammarion, 2010.

Plutarch (1992) *Essays*, translated by R. Waterfield. London: Penguin Books.

Popper, K. (1945) *The Open Society and its Enemies*, 2 volumes. London: Routledge.

Rée, J. (2000) *I See a Voice: A Philosophical History*. London: Flamingo.

—— (2003) *Journey in Thought – Hannah Arendt*, BBC Radio 3 programme first broadcast on 23 November 2003, with a repeat on 28 August 2004. Available at: www.bbc.co.uk/radio3/journeys in thought/pip/ashxz/.

Rorty, R. (1990) Diary, *London Review of Books*, 12(3), 8 February. Available at: www.lrb.co.uk/v12/n03/richard-rorty/diary.

Rosenfeld, S. (2011) *Common Sense: A Political History*. Cambridge, MA and London: Harvard University Press.

Scammell, M. (2010) *Koestler: The Indispensable Life*. London: Faber & Faber.

Schell, J. (2004) *The Unconquerable World: Power, Nonviolence, and the Will of the People*. London: Allen lane.

Sherratt, Y. (2013) *Hitler's Philosophers*. New Haven, CT and London: Yale University Press.

Shrenon, P. (2013) *A Cruel and Shocking Act: The Secret History of the Kennedy Assassination*. London: Little, Brown.

Skoller, E. H. (1993) *The In-between of Writing: Experience and Experiment in Drabble, Duras, and Arendt*. Ann Arbor, MI: University of Michigan Press.

Snyder, T. (2011) *Bloodlands: Europe Between Hitler and Stalin*. London: Vintage Books.

Soueif, A. (2004) *Mezzaterra: Fragments from the Common Ground*. London, Berlin, New York and Sydney: Bloomsbury.

—— (2012) *Cairo: My City, Our Revolution*. London, Berlin, New York and Sydney: Bloomsbury.

Stanghellini, G. and Fuchs, T. (eds) (2013) *One Century of Karl Jaspers' General Psychopathology*. Oxford: Oxford University Press.

Stern-Gillet, S. (1995) *Aristotle's Philosophy of Friendship*. Albany, NY: State University of New York Press.

Sznaider, N. (2011) *Jewish Memory and the Cosmopolitan Order: Hannah Arendt and the Jewish Condition*. Cambridge: Polity Press.

Taylor, D. J. (2003) *Orwell: The Life*. London: Chatto.

Tillich, P. (1952) *The Courage To Be*. New Haven, CT: Yale University Press.

Villa, D. (1996) *Arendt and Heidegger: The Fate of the Political*. Princeton, NJ: Princeton University Press.

—— (1999) *Politics, Philosophy, Terror: Essays on the Thought of Hannah Arendt*. Princeton, NJ: Princeton University Press.

—— (2001) *Socratic Citizenship*. Princeton, NJ and Oxford: Princeton University Press.

—— (2008) *Public Freedom*. Princeton, NJ and Oxford: Princeton University Press.

Walter, G. (ed.) (2006) *The Penguin Book of First World War Poetry*. London: Penguin Books.

Wessel, J. S. and Bensmann, L. (2012) The paralysis of judgement: Arendt and Adorno on anti-Semitism and the modern condition, in L. Rensmann and S. Gandesha (eds) *Arendt and Adorno: Political and Philosophical Investigations*. Stanford, CA: Stanford University Press, pp. 197–225.

Williams, R. (1983) *Towards 2000*. London: Chatto & Windus/Hogarth Press.

Wilson, E. (1931) *Axel's Castle: A Study in the Imaginative Literature of 1870–1930*. New York: Charles Scribner's Sons.

—— (1940) *To the Finland Station: A Study in the Writing and Acting of History*. New York: Harcourt Brace & Co.

Withington, P. (2013) Modernity's bodyguard, *London Review of Books*, 35(1), 3 January, pp. 15–16.

Wolin, S. (2001) *Heidegger's Children: Hannah Arendt, Karl Lowith, Hans Jonas, and Herbert Marcuse*. Princeton, NJ and Oxford: Princeton University Press.

—— (2010) *Democracy Incorporated: Managed Democracy and the Specter of Inverted Totalitarianism*. Princeton, NJ and Oxford: Princeton University Press.

Yeats, W. B. (1967) *The Collected Poems*. London, Melbourne and Toronto: Macmillan ('The Second Coming' was originally published in 1921 as part of a volume entitled *Michael Robartes and the Dancer*).

Young-Bruehl, E. (1982) *Hannah Arendt: For Love of the World*. New Haven, CT and London: Yale University Press.

—— E. (2006) *Why Arendt Matters*. New Haven, CT and London: Yale University Press.

Young-Bruehl, E. and Kohn, J. (2001) What and how we learned from Hannah Arendt: an exchange of letters, in M. Gordon (ed.) *Hannah Arendt and Education: Renewing Our Common World*. Boulder, CO and Oxford: Westview Press, pp. 225–56.

Zaretsky, R. (2010) *Albert Camus: Elements of a Life*. Ithaca, NY and London: Cornell University Press.

Index

Abraham, 47, 48
action, 16, 46, 50, 67, 165, 183
action-and-reaction, 47
    collective, 26, 27, 29, 34, 146, 179, 180, 182–5, 188–9, 194
    conditionality of, 88
    and freedom, 44
    irreversibility of, 43
    and natality, 187
    outcomes of, 38
    and philosophy, 144, 156
    political, 29, 34, 35, 141, 146–8, 180, 182
    and relationality, 58
    revolutionary, 184
    and speech, 25, 26
    thinking and, 138, 141, 163
agency, 3, 29, 46, 173
    collective, 44
    and contingency, 88
    and evil, 154
    and freedom, 58
    individual, 46
    moral, 112
    and plurality, 38
anti-Semitism, 3, 13–15, 18–19, 23, 71–2
Arab Spring, 186
Aristotle, 51, 52, 53, 54, 159, 161, 171
assimilation, 28, 94, 97–102
Auden, W. H., 152, 167–8, 195
'Axial age', 106–7

Bard College, 141, 142, 143, 145, 147, 154, 155
Benjamin, Walter, 10–11, 17, 81, 119, 161, 172, 178
Berlin, Isaiah, 15, 115, 116
Between Past and Future, 33, 45
Blumenfeld, Kurt, 17, 18

Camus, Albert, 30, 116–17
Christianity, 63, 73, 165, 176–7
Cicero, 51

Commission for European Jewish Cultural Reconstruction, 12
common sense, 38, 126–8, 129, 193
    and *sensus communis*, 69
Communist Party of Germany, 139
complementarity, 27, 59, 89, 92, 102, 114–18, 169
consumerism, 35, 190
contingency, 6, 11, 38, 99, 174, 188, 194, 195
covenant, 48, 49, 94, 99, 101

democracy, 127, 128
    birth of, 106
    management of, 180
    participative, 194
    representative, 37, 179
    survival of, 37
    Western, 97
de Montaigne, Michel, 52–5, 83
dialogue, 4–6, 85, 90, 93, 131, 141, 145, 148, 163–4, 169, 179, 192–3
    among equals, 169–74
    deliberation and, 146–7
    internal, 126
    meta-, 128
    and philosophy, 156
    public, 166
    Socratic, 153
    of solitude, 86
    of thought, 159, 171–4
    'truthful', 51–5
diaspora, 14, 34–8, 99, 100, 101
duty, 135, 152, 156, 161–2, 184, 190, 192, 193, 194
    beyond death, 128–32
    of care, 125
    of optimism, 184

Eichmann, Adolf, 81, 102, 127, 152, 161, 166, 169
    and evil, 14–19

Eichmann in Jerusalem, 14, 17, 102
equality, 7, 8, 28, 92, 171, 176
   as restrictive, 114
   and difference, 25, 26, 28, 29, 37, 165, 180
   and freedom, 48, 55, 63
   gender, 55
   and mutuality, 49
   within relationships, 37
eros, 155
   and *philia*, 135–8, 160
Europe, 12, 14, 15, 19, 27, 30, 42, 75, 77, 124, 140, 142
   and America, 44
   between the wars, 1–2
   debt to USA, 104
   Eastern, 15, 24, 32–3, 183
   Enlightenment ideal, 43
   Jewish community, 46, 101
   links with, 43, 159
   and Nazism, 11
   news of atrocities, 41
   'old', 32, 45, 93–7, 104, 109, 153, 194
   Renaissance, 51
   'unfinished adventure', 181
   unified, 107
evil, 137, 154
   and Eichmann, 14–19
   and thinking, 170
   of virtue, 172
exile, 9, 38, 42, 43, 50, 54, 104, 192

fascism, 10, 94, 139
   and Marxism, 25
   and Nazism, 58
   'rough beast of', 2
   and Stalinism, 29
force, 28, 30, 176, 185
   versus power, 26, 32, 146
forgiveness, 47, 63, 76
   and irreversibility, 46–7
   and promise, 62
   redemptive, 62
Fränkel, Hilde, 140, 149, 150
freedom, 59, 68, 69, 105, 154, 169
   to act, 47
   of choice, 192
   collective, 150
   desire for, 32
   and duty, 161
   and Eichmann, 169
   equality and, 48, 55, 63
   eradication of, 24, 48
   fusion of, 105–6
   liberty and, 91
   negative and positive, 33
   and philosophy, 93
   and plurality, 38, 58, 194
   political, 34, 36, 147
   public, 36
   and recognition, 50
   revolution and, 44
   spaces of, 3, 183

Germany, 61, 86, 90, 91, 101, 102, 161
   Arendt's country of origin, 42,
   Blücher's attitude towards, 153
   Blücher's country of origin, 138
   Blücher's early life in, 155
   East, 183
   escape from, 9, 14, 21, 38, 139, 140, 149, 191
   Heidegger's reputation in, 78
   Jaspers as conscience of, 105
   national identity, 94–6
   Nazi, 18
   post-World War I, 1–2
   post-World War II, 93, 97, 98
Gifford Lectures, 129, 131, 145
Gurian, Waldemar, 13

Harper's Magazine, 115
hermeneutics, 29, 159–74
Human Condition, The, 25, 33, 45, 46, 80, 126, 170, 175

identity, 56, 116
   assimilation and, 97–102
   German, 94
   intellectual, 23, 104
   Jewish, 55, 62, 94, 109
   personal, 193
   and plurality, 160
   as *principium individuationis*, 165
   public, 15
   thinking and, 166
   and will, 164–5
imperialism, 14, 23
inequality, 48
   economic, 35
   escalating, 182
   in relationships, 37
Israel, 17, 90, 91, 93, 98, 101, 103, 192

Jarrell, Randall, 13, 167, 172
judgement, 2, 104, 124, 125, 132
   of Auden, 168
   Blücher's power of, 137–8, 156
   as 'enlargement of mind', 166–9, 173
   of Heidegger's philosophy, 73
   lack of, 15, 80, 86, 121, 169, 173
   and pity, 172
   and thinking, 156, 170, 172, 193
   and willing, 156, 170

Kafka, Franz, 168
Kennedy, John F., 102–4
Kierkegaard, Søren, 5, 6, 143
kinship, 8, 160, 177, 194
Koestler, Arthur, 30

liberty, 34, 91, 175, 179
Life of the Mind, The, 121, 131, 156, 160, 161, 162, 164, 165, 169, 170
love, 7, 68, 76, 78, 95, 123, 124, 125, 130, 135, 136
   and acceptance, 154
   between men, 53
   of Cairo, 184
   erotic, 8
   and friendship, 148
   inclusive, 117, 155
   of Jewish people, 17
   of life, 186
   lost, 63
   as oasis, 7
   of persons, 1, 17
   romantic, 28
   and St Augustine, 56
   of victims, 116
   without *eros*
Luxemburg, Rosa, 2–3, 139

McCarthyism, 30–1, 43, 103, 143
Mendelssohn, Anne, 3–4, 12, 132
Men in Dark Times, 119
mutuality, 28, 55, 164, 165, 176
   of need, 118, 128
   and promising, 49
   and reciprocity, 6, 47, 118, 128, 150, 160
   and recognition, 182
   of respect, 8, 171, 190

Nation, The, 115
Nazism, 58, 91
   Heidegger's support of, 72–3
   and Stalinism, 24, 25, 26, 29, 30
New Republic, The, 115
New School for Social Research, 142, 143, 145, 155
New Yorker, The, 14, 18, 152, 166
New York Review of Books, The, 115

On Revolution, 33, 34, 35, 43, 44, 45, 91, 120
Origins of Totalitarianism, The, 21, 22, 23, 24, 25, 28, 29, 30, 32, 34, 35, 42, 43, 44, 56, 79, 91, 142

Palestine, 9, 14
Partisan Review, 114, 115
patriarchy, 55
pedagogy, 90, 144, 155, 156
phenomenon, 22, 164–5, 175, 176
   of intimacy, 7
   of loneliness, 178, 182
   of privatization, 180
   of totalitarianism, 19, 23, 29
philia, 135–8, 160
philosophy, 86, 166, 176
   Arendt's critique of Heidegger's, 73–5
   Arendt's repudiation of, 4–7, 23
   Blücher's approach to, 137–8, 142–6, 148, 156
   existential, 73, 83, 92
   of friendship (Aristotle's), 51, 53
   Jaspers' contribution to, 88, 90, 92–3
   'philosopher citizen', 146–7
pity, 152, 172
   self-, 80
plurality, 19, 29–39, 47–9, 54–5, 58–9, 173, 193–4
   boundless, 116, 156, 164
   common ground of, 177, 188–9
   and difference, 160
   human, 18, 74, 177
   violation of, 167
Plutarch, 51
polity, 32, 33, 37, 50, 51, 52, 91, 147
power, 26, 32, 34, 54, 55, 74, 146, 179, 180, 184, 194
   of destiny, 53, 71
   and forgiveness, 47, 62
   of friendship, 133, 166, 173

of the imagination, 168
of judgement, 137
language and, 147–8, 170
of the market, 181
paradox of, 179
and pity, 172
of promising, 39, 46–9, 59
in relationships, 77, 125, 162
technological, 45
and violence, 175, 187, 189
Western, 44, 93
principium individuationis, see under identity
private realm, 177–9, 188, 189
promise, 9, 19, 32, 39, 41–59
public realm, 173, 175–8
and 'the common world', 188
erosion of, 179, 180, 182, 189
and public happiness, 36

Rahel Varnhagen, 12, 56, 58, 90
Rahv, Philip, 114, 116
reciprocity, 6, 47, 118, 128, 150, 160
of trust, 190
recognition, 28, 50, 55, 171, 180, 182
of collective guilt, 97
public, 21, 131
struggle for, 61–84, 85
republicanism, 175–6, 191
of fear, 33
ideals, 161
revolution, 34, 43–4, 131, 147
American, 34–6, 44
and Eastern Europe, 33, 183
French, 34–6, 44, 91, 172
'gentle', 183
German, 138–9
Hungarian, 32, 44
industrial, 45
Russian, 1, 91
social, 179
'velvet', 183

Schocken Books, 12, 13, 27, 42, 168
Scholem, Gershom, 11, 17
sensus communis, see under common sense
sine ira, 22
Socrates, 4, 37, 92, 138, 144, 145, 147, 152, 153, 154, 156, 159, 171
Soueif, Ahdaf, 184–8

Spartacus League, 138–9
Stalinism, 23, 24, 25, 26, 29, 30, 91
statelessness, 9, 21, 31, 38, 42, 43, 93, 102, 135, 160, 161, 191
St Augustine, 56
Stern, Günther, 9, 68, 90
student protest, 104
'Suez crisis', 32

thinking, 93–4, 131, 138 157, 162–6, 169, 170, 193
community, 155
critical, 144
representative, 166
together, 141, 172, 173, 192, 193
'two-in-one', 6, 162, 163, 164, 165, 166, 171, 173, 192, 193
thoughtlessness, 169, 170
Tillich, Paul, 140, 149
totalitarianism, 19, 22, 23, 29, 30, 91, 194
anti-politics of, 25–6
atomisation and massification, 25–9, 190
bureaucratic technicalities of, 25
and charismatic leadership, 73
crimes of, 24
and destruction of privacy, 111
and human mentality, 24
imperialism and, 14
'inverted', 31, 180
invincibility of, 33
and utopian promises, 48
versus plurality, 38
Treaty of Versailles, 1
'two-in-one', *see under* thinking

university, 73
of Aberdeen, 73
of Basel, 129
of Berlin, 139
of California, 27
of Chicago, 31, 170
of Freiberg, 70, 71, 72, 77, 81, 83, 86
of Heidelberg, 86, 87, 90
of Marburg, 64, 72, 73
of Texas, 103
of Toulouse, 184

Varnhargen, Rahel, 56, 98, 115, 172
Vietnam, 104, 129

violence, 2, 111, 131, 175
  mob, 35–6
  and power, 146, 187, 189
  racist, 103
  state, 185–6
  towards Jews, 10

Watergate, 129, 131
will, 53, 58, 129
  free, 39, 169
  and judgement, 156, 157, 165, 169, 172, 193
  loss of, 53, 54, 170
  and pity, 172
  and thinking, 131, 156, 157, 162–5, 169, 172, 173, 193
Wilson, Edmund, 114
worldliness, 55, 96, 151
  and appearance, 164
  and encompassing, 94
  lack of, 169, 190
  un- and other-, 170

Youth Aliyah, 14

www.ingramcontent.com/pod-product-compliance
Lightning Source LLC
Chambersburg PA
CBHW062220300426
44115CB00012BA/2147